THE PEOPLE PUZZLE

THE PEOPLE PUZZLE

UNDERSTANDING YOURSELF AND OTHERS

Morris Massey

Reston Publishing Company, Inc.
A Prentice-Hall Company
Reston, Virginia

Research Coordinator: Kim Woods
Illustrations: Bryan Gough

Library of Congress Cataloging in Publication Data
Massey, Morris E
  The people puzzle.

  1. Values. 2. Developmental psychology.
3. Civilization, Modern—20th century. I. Title.
BF778.M32   301.1   79-15120
ISBN 0-8359-5477-3

© 1979 by Reston Publishing Company, Inc.
A Prentice-Hall Company
Reston, Virginia   22090

10   9   8   7   6   5   4   3   2   1

Printed in the United States of America

With love to

My parents, Roy and Rose, my original programmers

My wife, Judy, a continuing Significant Emotional Event

Our twins, Blake and Ryan, entrusted to us for their initial programming

CONTENTS

Marketing Association, and state and local groups across the country. The applications of the material seemed limitless: business, government, education, religion, media, military, law, medicine, science all seemed to relate because the material dealt with something so basic—human behavior.

The next milestone occurred when Dow Chemical U.S.A. videotaped the program for national use in its employee relations programs. We were all stunned by the demand. Dow employees responded as never before to any in-house program. They brought their families for special night showings and borrowed the tapes for their churches, schools, and civic organizations. Dow soon had to cope with suppliers, contractors, business associates, and even competitors who wanted to "borrow" what became known as "The Massey Tapes."

Dow's orders for more copies caught the attention of Magnetic Video Corporation. Al Eicher of MVC contacted me about shooting a "general" version for sales to other companies and organizations. With a handshake in Denver's Stapleton International Airport, we sealed the agreement to film. Al's faith and untiring efforts have been a continuing source of support and encouragement.

As the sales spiraled upward, I was swamped with requests for "something in writing." This book is in answer to all those letters, calls, and conversations. I sincerely wish I could personally thank those thousands who, in responding to me and "What You Are. . . ," have changed my life. To all those thousands in audiences where I appeared in person and to all those who have viewed the presentation on film, I am truly indebted for your support.

As the demand for personal appearances grew, I expanded and took on one associate, and then another. First, Terry Heineman learned the program and began to deliver "What You Are. . . ." With a background in counseling, journalism, and personnel relations, he is a first-class platform lecturer. I'm sincerely appreciative of his efforts and the insights he has brought back. His contributions, especially to the Postscript of this book, helped round out the material.

After Terry began to reach scheduling limits, Kim Woods became another associate. As an outstanding educator, Kim brought new depth to the application of the material. As a thoroughly professional speaker, she has brought numerous "show me" audiences to their feet in standing ovations. This book would never have been written without Kim's contributions. A year ago she committed herself to helping, and she has made significant contributions since then. To her I am eternally grateful; and to her husband, Pat, I am sincerely appreciative of his understanding of her dedication.

As "What You Are . . ." grew, a lot of people helped and sup-

PREFACE

The substance of this book came about simply enough: the material was originally developed for my classes at the University of Colorado. Faced with teaching a new course in consumer behavior (applied social sciences), I worked closely with my good friend and colleague Phillip Cateora to create a general model of human behavior. Although many academicians had described why and how people behave, none of them really seemed to "put it all together" in a form we could use. Our efforts resulted in the basic model presented in this book.

As I began to expand beyond the classroom professionally, I began to use the material in programs for management development, civic organizations, and continuing education courses. Audiences reacted intensely—a few were threatened by it, but the vast majority found the message challenging, helpful, and relevant to their own lives, both personally and professionally. The word spread, and I was invited to make presentations more and more frequently. My appearance before the Sales and Marketing Executives of Los Angeles, arranged by John Hammond, then president of American Motivation Association, was a milestone. The response of these critical executives was literally overwhelming—I received the second standing ovation in the history of their group. That night in Los Angeles changed my life forever. My basic "classroom material" had much wider appeal.

More companies and organizations began to request presentations. "What You Are Is Where You Were When" was born. Its growth was nurtured in programs for companies like Pepsi, Anheuser-Busch, Motorola, The Royal Bank of Canada, and organizations like the Chamber of Commerce of the United ported me. Betty Fitzner, my secretary at the University, was a super-star. Lana Leonard, my first official schedule coordinator, conquered the rising tide of inquiries. Sue Douglas now coordinates all the associates in a totally professional manner and is also responsible for typing the original manuscript. William Baughn, Dean of the College, has been not only a valued personal friend, but the ideal "boss." Jack Kelso, Professor of Anthropology, has provided continuing support as a close friend and professional critic. Without all of those mentioned above and many others, I couldn't have made it. Of course, my wife and my children have been tolerant beyond reasonable expectations.

There are many other people who have been instrumental in reinforcing my efforts with the message of "What You Are. . . ." I especially wish to acknowledge the following supportive friends and associates:

— Jim Haynes, Dorthie Miller, and Bill Barker, Dow Chemical U.S.A.
— Bud Wurzer, the *Chicago Tribune*
— Charles Blanchard, Midwest Industrial Management Association
— Dick Bailey, Chamber of Commerce of the United States
— James Faltinek, Bank Marketing Association
— Mel Kallet, Dresser Industries
— Wilbur Nickel, Elanco (Eli Lilly)
— Janelle Latshaw, Edison Electric Institute
— Col. Erving Monclova, Commander, Selfridge Air National Guard Base
— George Spaulding, Pontiac Motor Division
— George Schutt, American Bankers Association
— Randy Goldrich, National Association of Electrical Distributors
— Eric Haynes, Royal Bank of Canada
— and all of the rest, including my former students, who have supported me with your affirmations.

Morris Massey

ACKNOWLEDGMENTS

Grateful acknowledgment is made to the following for permission to reprint the materials listed.

Russell Baker, "The Good Life: Dead at 28, But Mourned by All Survivors," © 1974 by The New York Times Company. Reprinted by permission. March 23, 1974.

Newsweek excerpt from "What TV Does to Kids," February 21, 1977, and "TV of Tomorrow," July 3, 1978. Copyright 1977 and 1978 by Newsweek, Inc. All rights reserved. Reprinted by permission.

Saul Pett, "Snap!—The Plastic Life Cracks at the Seams," Associated Press Newsfeatures. Reprinted by permission.

Merton P. Strommen, editor, *Research on Religious Development*. Published by Hawthorn Books. Reprinted by permission of The Religion Education Association.

TIMES BOOKS, a division of Quadrangle/The New York Times Book Co., Inc. for material from *Great Songs of the Sixties*, edited by Milton Okun.

The author researched and developed the presentation "What You Are Is Where You Were When," which became the basis for this book. This copyrighted program has been presented to hundreds of audiences over the past few years.

Professor Massey has been Associate Dean of Undergraduate Studies at the University of Colorado College of Business in Boulder, Colorado. He has been at the University since 1967 and has received three University teaching excellence awards.

Originally from Waco, Texas, Dr. Massey received his undergraduate and M.B.A. degrees in Marketing from the University of Texas, and his Ph.D. in Business from Louisiana State University.

Recently Dr. Massey has served as Academic Dean for the University's ocean-going campus affiliate, Semester-at-Sea.

He is director of his own consulting firm, Morris Massey Associates, located in Boulder, Colorado.

Having adopted the western lifestyle, Dr. Massey is also part owner of the Diamond J Guest Ranch near Meredith, Colorado, where he and his family enjoy the summer months.

Over 1,000,000 people have seen Morris Massey live in his superb program "What You Are Is Where You Were When." The enthusiastic response to the program by the following organizations or their divisions is sincerely appreciated.

Pratt & Whitney Aircraft
Nevada National Bancorporation
General Electric Engine Division
Ft. Carson Executive Development
   Department
Blue Cross of Ohio
WTTV, Indianapolis
Old Kent Bank and Trust
Greeley National Bank
Harding College
Buick (Industrial Executive Club)
Wisconsin Veterinarians Association
Administrative Management
   Society, Grand Rapids
Wells Fargo Bank
Washington Mutual Savings Bank,
   Seattle
Fidelity Bank & Trust Co.,
   Minneapolis
Harris Trust & Savings Bank
The Event—Motivational
   Development Seminars

Midwestern State University
National Association of Printing Ink
   Manufacturers
Northwood Institute
Sandbury Building Corporation
Personnel Association of Toronto
Spring Valley Farms & Foods
Container Corporation of America
Michigan Home Economics
   Association
Metromedia Television
Executive Women International
Midwest College Placement
   Association
Hermann Hospital, Houston
Industrial Bearing & Transmission
   Co.
Electrical Apparatus Service
   Association, Inc.
Canadian Electrical Distributors
   Association
Wickes Lumber

Banquet Foods, Southerland
   Division
International Toastmistress Clubs
Colorado Association of Tobacco
   and Candy Distributors
John Deere & Company
Advertising Age
Garrett-Bromfield and Co.
Quaker Alloy Casting
The University School, Chagrin
   Falls, Ohio
Maynard Steel Castings
Bank of America
American Institute of Banking,
   Dayton Chapter
Missouri Bankers Association
North Dakota Retail Lumber
   Association
Indiana Electric League
National Association of Electrical
   Distributors
Sonny Hancock Pontiac, GMC
Boettcher and Co.
Crown Zellerbach
Petro-Lewis Securities Corp.
Michigan Plumbing and Mechan-
   ical Contractors Association
The Hydril Company
Junior League of Winnipeg
The *Chicago Tribune*
High School Guidance Counselors,
   North Central Technical College
Dresser Industries
Kansas Motor Car Dealers
Airco Welding Products
Michigan Association of Curricu-
   lum and Development
Material Handling Equipment
   Distributors Association
Pepsi-Cola Management Institute
Elanco
Waterloo Board of Education
St. Clair College

United Insurance Co. of America
Colorado Optometric Association
Frederick Atkins Inc.
Associated General Contractors of
   Colorado
Auto Ad Agency
Department of Energy, Hanford
   Reservation
Mason & Hanger—Silas Mason Co.,
   Inc.
Metal Building Dealers Association,
   Rocky Mountain Chapter
Edison Electric Institute
Printing Industry Association
Southwest Placement Association
Automotive Market Research
   Council
Ad Club of Fort Worth
Fannin Bank, Houston
Texas Personnel and Guidance
   Association
General Motors, Photographics
   Division
National Screw Machine Products
   Association
Billings Chamber of Commerce
Panhandle Eastern Pipeline
American Bankers Association
E.I. DuPont de Nemours & Co., Inc.
Credit Union National Association,
   Inc.
American Motivational Association
Home Federal Savings & Loan
   Association
National Installment Banking
   School
Consolidated Natural Gas Company
National Guest Relations
   Association
American Gas Association
Montana-Dakota Utilities Co.
Greeley Public Schools
Charmglow Products

American Collectors Association,
Inc.
Chamber of Commerce of the
United States
Hospital Financial Management
Association
Eastern Gas Conference
LSU Mid-South Executive
Development Program
Bank Marketing Association
National Association of Bank
Women
Colorado Juvenile Council
Anheuser-Busch, Inc.
The National Secretaries
Association
American Society for Engineering
Education
National Electrical Manufacturers
Association
Oklahoma Association of Com-
munity and Junior Colleges
The Royal Bank of Canada
Motorola Executive Institute
Western Electronic Manufacturers
Association
Regional Management Conference,
Aurora, Illinois
Wolf Point, Montana, Chamber of
Commerce and Agriculture
Student American Pharmaceutical
Association
Stonier School of Banking
Southern College Placement
Association
Dallas Public Library
National Society of Sales Training
Executives
National Retail Merchants
Association
Harris Flote-Bote
Union Carbide Corporation
Business Week

Chevrolet Motor Division
Clark Equipment Company
American Institute of Industrial
Engineers
Mercury Marine
Florists Transworld Delivery
Association
Society of Certified Public
Accountants
Kelly & Morey Inc.
Michigan Association of School
Administrators
American Association of
Accountants
Kelly Services
Los Angeles City Unified School
District
American Telephone & Telegraph
Michigan Bell
Wholesale Beer Distributors of
Texas
Public Relations Society of
America
Celanese Corporation
Steel Founders Society of America
Life Office Management
Association
American Women in Radio and
Television
American Newspaper Publishers
Association
Canadian Electrical Association
Sales and Marketing Executives
(Atlanta, Dallas, Flint, Colum-
bus, San Francisco, Los Angeles,
Erie, Minneapolis)
United Church of Christ Ministers
Conference
Management Health and
Development Corporation
TRW Capacitors
Peralta Community College
District

Colorado Conference on Juvenile
Justice
Electric Service League of Manitoba
Canadian Institute of Management
Young Presidents Organization
American Association of University
Women
Bonneville Productions
Michigan State University,
Cooperative Extension Division
International Newspaper Promotion
Association
Ohio Association of School
Librarians
National Association of Service
Managers
Eli Lilly and Company
Dow Corning Corporation
West Texas Consumer Credit
Conference
The Sigman Meat Company
Thoren Consulting Group, Inc.
Arthur Young & Company
Tollycraft
United Banks of Colorado, Inc.
The Northwestern Mutual Life
Insurance Company
Wellcraft Marine Corp.
Photo & Sound Company
Phi Chi Theta
Idaho Automobile Dealers
Association
Arkansas Bankers Association
Administrative Management
Society
Maryland Bankers Association
Chamber of Commerce, Cedar
Falls, Iowa
Ingersoll-Rand Company
National Ski Areas Association
Kansas Bankers Association
Texas Bankers Association
Southern Gas Association

Kansas City Advertising and
Marketing Club
Advertising Club of Cedar Rapids,
Iowa
American Advertising Federation
South Carolina Bankers Association
First National Bank of Denver
Del Calzo & Associates
Denver Public Schools
Mile Hi Church of Religious
Science
Eastman Kodak Company
Colorado State University
Colorado Insurors Association, Inc.
California Business Education
Association
National Association of Accountants
Brookings Area Chamber of
Commerce
Arthur Anderson & Company
Kansas Business Education
Association
Mountain-Plains Business
Education Association
United States Civil Service
Commission
The University of Nebraska,
Lincoln
Society of Mechanical Engineers
State Library of Idaho
University of Denver
Colorado Law Enforcement
Training Academy
KAID TV (complete program
broadcast)
Dixon Paper Company
Juvenile Justice Association of
Michigan
Central Michigan University
Allied Boating Association of
Canada
National Association of College
Admissions Counselors

Ashland Oil, Inc.
National Conference of Governors'
    Highway Safety Representatives
Chrysler Management Institute
Bluewater Management Seminar
Pontiac Motor Division
IBM, General Systems Division
National Alliance of Businessmen
IBM, Application Division Center

IBM, Office Products Division
Wisconsin Electric Power
    Company
Center for Creative Leadership
Credit Union Volunteers
Book Manufacturers Institute
Iowa Daily Press Association
Mountain Bell
American Marketing Association

Magnetic Video Corporation is the producer of the

television and film presentation "What You Are Is Where You Were
When" and "What You Are Isn't Necessarily What You Will Be."
The material in this book is based on these presentations. Purchasers
include:

AMOCO Oil Company
Dow Chemical, U.S.A.
Pepsi-Cola Management Institute
Burroughs
Chevrolet Motor Co.
Rockwell International
Chevron Oil
Eastman Kodak
U.S. Steel
Ford Motor Company
AT&T
Monsanto Chemical
Phillips Petroleum
Chrysler Corp.
Reynolds Metals
Caterpillar Tractor
Packard Instruments, Chicago
Shell Oil Company
Dresser Industries
Union Carbide
E.I. DuPont de Nemours & Co.
Eli Lilly and Company
Western Electric
John Deere & Co.
IBM

Consolidated Natural Gas, Ohio
Gates Rubber Co.
Mobil Oil
General Motors
Fisher Body
Westinghouse Electric
General Electric
Mountain Bell Telephone
Ohio Bell
General Telephone
Northwestern Bell
Southwestern Bell
Warner-Lambert
Exxon
Continental Oil
Fruehauf
Lockheed
The Boeing Co.
Ashland Oil
Marathon Oil
Clark Equipment Co.
Champion Spark Plugs
FTD
Ex-cello Corp.
Royal Canadian Mounted Police

Disneyland
Federal Law Enforcement Training
M&M Mars Co.
Jefforson County Schools
Granite School District
Bay Arenac Schools
Detroit Public Schools
Bettendorf Community Schools
Houston Independent School
   District
Bloomfield Hills Schools
Kent Intermediate Schools
Oakland School District
Newark School District
Purdue University
Michigan State University
University of Texas
University of Michigan
Brigham Young University
University of Minnesota
New Mexico State University
University of Pittsburgh
Mississippi College

Washington State College
Federal Aviation Administration
Office of Personnel Management
U.S. Department of Agriculture
FBI
CIA
Social Security Administration
Bureau of Alcohol, Tobacco, &
   Firearms
U.S. Department of Interior
U.S. Department of Health, Educa-
   tion & Welfare
Dept. of Natural Resources
Internal Revenue Service
USDA, Forest Service
NASA
The Armed Forces, all branches
Walter Reed Army Medical Center
National Naval Medical Center
Henry Ford Hospital
Blue Cross of Southern California
Methodist hospitals
United Methodist Church

Orders for this book and Morris Massey's videocassettes/films may be placed through Reston Publishing Co., Inc., 11480 Sunset Hills Road, Reston, VA 22090.

ACT NOW!! ORDER MORE COPIES OF
THE PEOPLE PUZZLE

Over 1,000,000 people have seen Morris Massey on tape. Now you can buy the book for a fascinating inside look at the way people think, feel, and act!

☐ YES! Please send me _____ more copies of this outstanding new book, THE PEOPLE PUZZLE. I've enclosed my check for $10.95 per copy, plus my state's sales tax. (Publisher pays shipping when you send your check.) OR

☐ I want to charge _____ copies of this book to my VISA/MASTER CHARGE account: ☐☐☐☐☐☐☐☐☐☐☐☐☐☐☐☐☐☐☐☐☐
Expiration date: _____
Master Charge Interbank number: _____

OR

☐ Please SHIP AND BILL _____ copies of *The People Puzzle*. Upon receipt, I'll send a check for $10.95 per copy, plus postage and sales tax.

* * * * *

☐ I'm interested in *quantity purchases*. I'm connected with a business, trade association, school, seminar group, civic group, government agency, etc., and I would like to explore a large purchase of this book in its present form or in a custom format for my organization.

For special sales, contact VICTOR E. ERICKSON, Reston Publishing Company, Inc., 11480 Sunset Hills Rd., Reston, VA 22090 or call toll-free (800) 336-0338.

* * * * *

I've checked off the payment plan I prefer. Send my books to:

NAME _____
FIRM/ORGANIZATION _____
STREET _____
CITY _____ STATE _____ ZIP _____
TELEPHONE ( )_____

TO ORDER: Clip this coupon and mail today to:

Reston Publishing Company, Inc.
A Prentice-Hall Company
Book Distribution Center
Route 59 at Brook Hill Drive
West Nyack, NY 10994

Feel free to reorder now through your local bookseller.

THE PEOPLE PUZZLE IN ACTION
ON VIDEOCASSETTE AND FILM
FOR YOU, YOUR ORGANIZATION, YOUR FIRM

I want to *see* Morris Massey's stimulating, thought-provoking presentations and discover his dynamic "no holds barred" approach for myself! ✳ ✳ ✳ ✳ ✳

☐ Please ship Massey's THE PEOPLE PUZZLE (*WHAT YOU ARE IS WHERE YOU WERE WHEN . . .*) in the following format and in the number of copies indicated below.

Number of programs	Each program is 90 minutes, available in the following formats	Price
_____ 2 ¾ U color videocassettes		$750 for first copy
_____ 2 Betamax color videocassettes		$450 each for 2nd copy
_____ 2 VHS color videocassettes		$295 each for 3 or more
_____ 2 45-minute reels, 16mm color		$975, any quantity

☐ Please ship Massey's THE PEOPLE PUZZLE (*WHAT YOU ARE ISN'T NECESSARILY WHAT YOU WILL BE . . .*)

Number of programs	Each program is 61 minutes, available in the following formats	Price
_____ 1 ¾ U color videocassette		$500 for 1st copy
_____ 1 Betamax color videocassette		$375 for 2nd copy
_____ 1 VHS color videocassette		$275 for 3 or more
_____ 1 61-minute reel, 16mm color		$750, any quantity

NOT SURE? You can examine an 18-minute preview tape, free of charge, right in your own office for 10 days. TELL US THE FORMAT YOU WANT TO PREVIEW.

SEND ORDERS/PREVIEW REQUESTS TO:
Victor E. Erickson, Reston Publishing Co., Inc.
11480 Sunset Hills Rd., Reston, VA 22090
Call toll free (800) 336-0338

☐ This form is my purchase order, or my company's purchase order is attached. Please ship and bill the videocassettes/reels in the format and quantity checked above, including my state's sales tax. If appropriate, list your tax exempt number. _____

Ship to: Firm _____Purchase Order # _____

Attn.: _____Street _____

City _____ State _____ Zip _____

Telephone ( )_____

All video orders FOB Farmington Hills, Michigan. Reston accepts VISA/Master Charge. Keep the 10-day preview tape if you wish and remit the $70 purchase price, or return at the end of the 10-day trial period.

OVERVIEW:RIGHT/WRONG?

What's happening in our world?

Community Has Failed U.S. Schools, Families
(*Denver Post*, 10/26/78)

The First Test-Tube Baby
(*Time*, 7/31/78)

Public Schools Flunk CBS Series
(*Boulder Daily Camera*, 8/22/78)

Do you believe our basic institutions are failing us? Who's to blame? Where are we headed? Is science playing God?

Nixon Approved Break-Ins, Ex-FBI Aide Tells Court
(*Washington Post*, 11/16/78)

Nixon Welcomed to Kentucky by a Cheering Crowd
(*New York Times*, 7/2/78)

Are you now willing to "forgive" Richard Nixon? Do you think all politicians are crooks?

The Big Tax Revolt
(*Newsweek*, 6/19/78)

Welfare Thieves Use New Method to Collect
(*Chicago Sun-Times*, 11/25/78)

Former CIA Man Convicted as Spy for Sale of Secrets
(*Washington Post*, 11/16/78)

Do you trust anyone in government? Whatever happened to loyalty and honesty?

Eight U.S. Nazis Sentenced in Beating of J.D.L. Member
(*Denver Post*, 10/29/78)

Israel to Build on Arab Land
  (*Denver Post*, 10/30/78)
Jersey Hearing on Anti-Homosexual Bill Disrupted
  (*New York Times*, 11/21/78)
Blacks Told Their Lot is Not Improving
  (*Washington Post*, 11/19/78)

What do we really believe about equality for others? Can we ever really learn to live together?

Up to 90% in Some G.I. Units Use Drugs
  (*Denver Post*, 11/21/78)
Couple Separate to Live Austere Hare Krishna Lives
  (*Los Angeles Times*, 11/23/78)
Cult Horror Mounts; 775 Dead are Found
  (*Chicago Sun-Times*, 11/25/78)

Why can't some people cope with reality anymore? Why are people running away from responsibility?

What are your reactions to the headlines and questions listed above? Millions of other people have reactions directly opposite to yours. Who is right?

Why are other people "different" from you? Why are our interactions, understanding, and communication often so very difficult? What makes you behave in certain ways while others behave differently? We each think we're "normal," no matter how dissimilar our behavior may be. What controls and directs these behavioral differences? How can we cope with them in others?

Every psychologist, sociologist, and philosopher has addressed the *how* and *why* of human behavior. Theologists, economists, historians, and bartenders have their theories, too. This book concerns a way of viewing human behavior—a way that gives us all room to be "normal" yet different, a way that has helped literally hundreds of thousands of very "different" people understand themselves and each other.

This approach focuses on a very critical factor that guides the behavior of all humans; that factor is a gut-level *value system*. Your value system has just been at work in the past few seconds. You've been making some *value judgments* about this book—its cover, type style, the words being used. You're using your *value system* to make value judgments about this book just as you use it to make judgments about:

  —the *people* you see (sex, hair color, race, age, clothes, hair length, etc.)

—the *events* in the world (nuclear contamination, Watergate, the Olympics, oil spills, whale kills, SSTs—everything you might know about)

—the *products* available (fast cars, cigarettes, drugs, TV, natural ingredients, laetrile, contraceptives, etc.)

—the *issues* of our times (ERA, pornography, abortion, equality, communism, human rights, inflation, etc.).

Your value system determines how you relate to your family, what products you buy, how you vote, and how you perform your job. It dictates your leisure time activities, what information you absorb, and your religious convictions.

Literally everything is sifted through the gut-level value systems operating in each of us. Values are our subjective reactions to the world around us. While some items are purely functional and can be viewed rationally and objectively (chalkboards, picture hooks, lightbulbs, rulers, etc.), most items involve a subjective reaction, especially when our feelings come into play. Gut-level value systems automatically *filter* the way we view most of the things around us. Your filters operate in degrees and shades of good/bad, right/wrong, normal/not normal, or acceptance/rejection.

As an example of a *stated* value system, you may look at religion. Christianity defines a series of "Thou shalt do these things" and "Thou shalt not do those things." Interestingly, if you check with some non-Christian religions, some of the things that Christians are told "Thou shalt not do," others think are kind of nifty to do, and vice versa. Other examples of stated values are found in laws and institutions.

In *The Nature of Human Values*, Milton Rokeach systematically defines thirty-six operationally-based concepts that are divided into two types of values: instrumental and terminal. Instrumental values are described as a means to an end and include such concepts as honesty, freedom, cleanliness, and responsibility. Terminal values are the "ends actually sought," including salvation, peace of mind, an exciting life, or a world at peace. A legion of educational researchers have come up with yet another whole series of value definitions.

While all of these works are valuable, in this book we will use value systems in a broad "umbrella" sense. We include not only specific values but also feelings, attitudes, beliefs, opinions, interests—all of our underlying subjective reactions. Our approach is to try to understand in a general way the total package of our gut-level value filter systems: *where* they come from and *how* they are used on a day-to-day basis by all of us.

Obviously, human behavior is determined by many factors: biological, chemical, environmental, educational, sociological, situational, technological, and genetic. Each of these influences on behavior not only affects the creation of gut-level values but also is responded to by the value systems themselves. Hence, an understanding of value systems from their creation to their operation provides a good base for us to begin to understand human behavior.

Part I

THE "COMPUTER" ARRIVES: YOUR PROGRAMMING BEGINS

The process of simple value creation may actually begin long before birth, as argued by many sociobiologists and popular authors such as Carl Sagan in *The Dragons of Eden* and Desmond Morris in *The Naked Ape*. Many experts suggest that *some* behavior patterns in our primitive ancestors might have been encoded in the DNA which in turn now guides *our* behavior patterns. Whatever the degree of genetic input, for our purposes it is enough to assume that genetics guide broad patterns of human behavior. Our concern is with behavior patterns that are learned from the moment of birth forward. The birth event itself, studied so thoroughly, may well affect individuals throughout their entire lives. Recent research in both primal therapy and birthing has substantiated the long-term impact on behavior. The programming begins.

Have you asked your parent(s) about *your* birth experience? Do you know whether you were born at home or in a hospital (or even a taxi)? Was your mother drugged? Was it a traumatic labor? Were you put in your mother's arms or an incubator? Did your mother nurse you? Many people were never told or have never asked about these initial programming experiences, yet literally the first hours affect your entire life.

So, you arrive as a human infant. Rapidly shifting, changing, your physical growth continues on through your late teens; then actual physical deterioration begins to occur. Your body itself reacts: some of it turns gray, some of it expands, some of it may fall off. But basically, except for possible medical modification, your physical equipment is set and continues in its basic form. But your mental development in relation to the external world has just started, and with it you begin a series of programming experiences that literally create the very values you will use to relate to the world for the rest of your life. These programming processes that you experienced and interpreted also *commonly* affected and molded others who were "programming" at the same time. It is these *groups of individuals* who experienced *similarity* in programming that are our ultimate concern.

While each of us has developed as a unique individual, slightly different physically and mentally, there is always a great deal of similarity in a generation's programming inputs. Family life styles are amazingly similar at any point in time. School systems consistently "feed" a set of expectations/values to entire generations. Popular religions impose their unique inputs of rights and wrongs. Media bombard the young with consistent and reinforcing messages. For each generation, common forces within the society program millions in highly similar ways.

In this age of computer technology, where human beings are all too often reduced to some appropriate number, the term *programmed,* when applied to human beings, is automatically rejected by many (especially those whose values do not allow them to accept the computer itself, or who feel that such a concept denies individual free will). In our context, the use of the word *programmed* focuses on the impact of outside forces as these inputs shape and mold the individual. In this way, values programmed into us through our experiences will act as filters for other later experiences. Of course, values may change over a period of time. Our behavior is not static, unchanging, or totally predictable. However, many of us obviously do not change readily. In fact, we may change our behavior because of a unique situation. While the cat's away, the mouse may play. When the situation changes back, then the value, perhaps dormant or laid aside, will reassert itself. On the other hand, some people never change in their value reactions to the world and will even go to an extreme of self-destruction to avoid changing their original value. Some martyrs do die in vain.

Dramatic changes in values probably occur only when an individual experiences what might be called a *Significant Emotional Event.* Such events are so *mentally arresting* that they force individuals to closely, critically examine their original values. This examination and incorporation of some new perspectives results in behavior that is radically different from the past. Significant Emotional Events will be explored later. But first, what are those critical programming processes that start at birth?

OUR FIRST "LOOK" AT THE WORLD

Social scientists in psychology, sociology, and anthropology have generated vast amounts of information about what happens to infants during their early years. There is relatively little agreement on the exact phasing of the programming. However, there is general agreement on what happens during the "processing" periods of the first few years. Everyone agrees that a series of events begins that programs developing infants. There are many definitions of periods of time, stages of development, sequences, and influences. For our purposes, we use *imprinting* as a broad term to cover the programming events of the first six or seven years (detailed by Don Fabun). During the imprinting period, the mind accepts and imprints a number of "patterns" for future "filtering" of the world. A child's orientation to the world is created: up/down, inside/outside, external/internal.

Experts also agree that during these early years physical development occurs most rapidly. Simple behavior patterns are quickly adopted. For example, during this period, everyone "learns" the "correct/normal" way to eat. If you watch people eating in the United States, you'll notice that everyone eats in approximately the same way. We stab our food, cut it, transfer it from the left hand to the right, and stick it in our mouths. But if you look at the way people eat in Europe, you'll notice that they don't eat the "right" way—they are not "normal!" They stab their food, cut it, stick it in, and don't bother to transfer it. Orientals are even "stranger": they don't even use knives and forks. They use little sticks to put the food in their mouths. And then, many Arabs and Indians eat with their hands—no forks, knives, or sticks! While we don't get "up tight" about the way people eat—viewing that "different" behavior—we probably think "That's not the *right* way to do it! *Our way* is the right way, the *normal* way to eat." That's value judgment coming into play: value analysis based on the programming that "created" us during our imprinting period.

In addition to *physical* behavior development, a tremendous amount of *mental* development takes place during the imprinting period. Priests and teachers of the Middle Ages are quoted as believing: Give me a child until he is six, and you can have him thereafter (because he is already molded for life). The popular analogy "As the twig is bent, so the tree shall grow" is perhaps so obviously simple that we frequently fail to apply it to our own children. Yet, casual observation clearly reveals the complexity of this early stage in everyone's

programming. Even a two-year-old child "observes" the adult world. They think, in effect, *"That's* what a mother is; *that's* what a father is; *that's* what adults do! If *I* become an adult [and some aren't sure they're going to make it when they're only two feet tall] *that's* what I'm going to do!" A two-year-old child clearly distinguishes differences in sex roles. They are very aware of differences in the way males and females express emotion, dress, look, what they can do, and how they act. Unfortunately, in our society, we don't pay very much attention to small children. Two-year-olds are frequently treated like pets and confined to "crib-cages"—they rattle their bars and observe the adult world. Even though two- and three-year-old children don't have a lot of words to think with, we know that they're paying a fantastic amount of attention to everything. They're absorbing value patterns that will be used again and again as they move through life.

What were your early years like? When did you learn to walk, talk, use the toilet, and dress yourself? Were you free to explore or were you restrained? Was your life a constant "no-no"? Was your mother home all day, or were you left with babysitters? Did your father help change your diapers and bathe, dress, and feed you? Was your home sterile or stimulating, calm or chaotic? Were you pushed to learn or allowed to develop at your own pace?

In *What Do You Say*, Eric Berne labels the period between two and six years as the "plastic" years. The parental programming that occurs is vital in a child's development. According to Berne, "The comedy or tragedy of each human life is that it is planned by an urchin of pre-school age who has a very limited knowledge of the world and its ways and whose heart is mainly filled with stuff put there by his parents. Yet this wonder child is precisely who determines in the long run what will happen to kings and peasants, and whores and queens." Berne's work in developing Transactional Analysis clearly elaborates on this critical portion of the programming sequence. In *Games People Play,* he notes: "Parents, deliberately or unaware, teach their children from birth how to behave, think, feel and perceive. Liberation from these influences is no easy matter. . . ." At this stage, a systematic "script" is being imposed on developing children, as Claude Steiner discusses in *Scripts People Live.* That script is creating a foundation for a value system and the behavior patterns for future lives. Lying deep within the subconscious, at a gut level, the script is accepted and acted out by most people without really ever questioning its validity. For those who cringe at the idea that we are all *programmed* and exercise little real choice, transactional and script analysis must create real panic! Not only are we programmed, but events in our lives become totally predictable as we follow the *same* scripts again and again.

The early years of childhood may be compared to the foundation and frame of a building. The foundation determines the quality and strength of the structure that goes on top. The completed structure depends on its base, even if additions are built. The foundation of a person is the child as formed in his early years. And even though real "formal" learning does not start in the preschool period, there are many important stages that determine how, how much, how well, and what the child will learn as he develops.

"AND WHAT DO YOU WANT TO BE WHEN YOU GROW UP?"

As the child enters the formal learning process of a school system, the imprinting foundation is put to use: filtering, categorizing, and shaping the new information from teachers and books. His world expands in an application sense. However, some mental development actually slows while the applications are absorbed and tested. As the developing child moves toward ages seven, eight, nine, and ten, another process, begun in the early years, becomes more refined. The process of identification—initially with the mother, then the father and important "others" around the child—expands. The child shifts into intense *modeling*—relating to family, friends, and external "heroes" in the world around him. People the child would "like to be like" are carefully observed. Who were *your* heroes when you were about ten years old? Stop and think about it. What kind of people were they? Why did you like them? What did you admire about them? Can you still look back at them with admiration?

Identification, or modeling, is one of the important factors in establishing our personality, standards, and goals. The process starts with rote imitation of our parents. Considering them superior beings, we try to gain some of their qualities and abilities for ourselves, taking on their attitudes and behavior as our own. Somewhat blind acceptance gives way to selectivity, and we absorb parental characteristics which seem most appropriate to us. Our emerging conscience (moral standards) and sex role begin to develop in this process. Boys absorb initial masculine traits through identification with their fathers, while girls develop femininity related to their mothers. Older brothers or sisters may also contribute significantly.

Our initial close models give way to more expanded contacts. Soon, group membership begins to exert its influence. We identify not only with play groups or gangs as a whole, but also with certain "important" individuals within them. New values and behavior

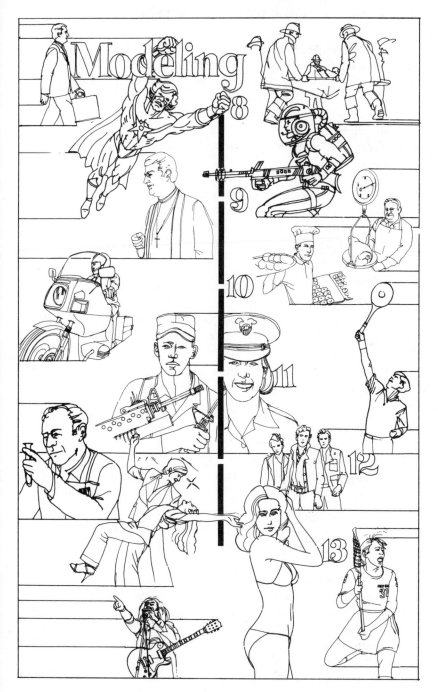

patterns are combined with the ones we absorbed from our family. Once in school, the process of identifying extends to the heroes of history and fictional stories. Further, our increasing involvement with media during this period will bring in characters from movies and television as additional heroes. We use these models to construct our internal "ego ideal," the person we would like to become. We are now a complex composite of absorbed inputs. The programming accelerates.

For all of us, the scope of our hero models shifts from those very close (parents, other children, teacher, ministers) to those distant and remote whom we may never see personally or individually (historical figures, sports champions, television personalities, movie stars, rock singers, etc.). Identification with any of these heroes may be either good or bad:

• One U.S. President "never told a lie," another resigned in disgrace after blatantly lying to the nation;

• Fifteen years of daily practice produced an Olympic gold-medal skater, while a pro football star made headlines for indecent exposure (hero one day, pervert the next);

• Some television figures are little more than flashing smiles and shiny hair, while others range easily from Shakespeare to commercials;

• From the silver screen, an international comedian dedicates thousands of hours to charity in contrast to a well-known actress whose overinflated salary supports revolutionary violence;

• Some music superstars focus their talents on environmental concerns as others burn themselves out on drugs and alcohol.

Who were *your* heroes?

Parents themselves may leave much to be desired: some have alcohol problems, others are prone to child abuse, and others are workaholics who provide only token weekend family relationships. Outside of the family, peer groups or gangs may create distorted values and promote undesirable behavior. In many cases, the child may never have had an adequate opportunity to identify with constructive models. During the past few years a number of social-scene commentators have noted the lack of effective models for ethnic minorities and women. Without such models, it is difficult for these groups to develop expectations comparable to those of the white male in our society (the dominant model figures).

As a child continues toward adolescence and young adulthood, new models emerge. During this period adolescents are searching for security and approval and seem particularly prone to hero worship. Again, this may be good or bad. One of the most important problems relates to the selection of models. Are they positive and inspiring or negative and demeaning? If identification is carried to an extreme, either type may be destructive. Individuals who reach too high and identify themselves with unrealistic or unattainable models set themselves up for an emotional crash: they inevitably fail.

A model whose behavior is antisocial is also destructive. Consider the hit movie *Saturday Night Fever*. A major character portrayed is demeaning of females, profane in the extreme, dependent only upon his youth and hips for success—generally an uninspiring character. Yet, this character stereotype was common in both movies and television appealing to young people throughout the late 1970s. During this period, the heroes for our young have tended to extremes in aggressiveness, sexual behavior, language, permissiveness, and self-indulgence. The impact of this recent hero group, coupled with a lack of heroes in many areas of our society (especially politics), may have a dramatic impact on the future behavior of millions.

Do you remember your own modeling activities? When you were ten years old, whom did you want to grow up to be like? Whom did you secretly look up to, try to imitate in the way you talked, the way you walked, the way you dressed, the way you wanted to be? The hero models in our lives are very critical people. They are the people we try to behave like, the people that we want to be like when we become adults. The modeling period is a critical period during which we absorb values from a diverse selection of models.

EVERYONE . . . EVERYONE . . . EVERYONE

Beginning around seven years of age, we develop an increasing dependence upon "groups"—those we associate with, belong to, or admire. Within a few years, our social life will be structured primarily in terms of our friends. This intense *socialization* with one's peers is easy to measure. Talk to a fourteen-year-old and ask him questions such as: Why are you doing that? Why do you want to go there? and Why do you dress like that? He will most likely respond: Because *everyone* does it, *everyone's* going there, and everyone dresses like this.

It's "everyone, everyone, everyone"—our "significant others," friends and close associates. It's trite but true that "birds of a feather" *do* "flock together," especially during this period in our development.

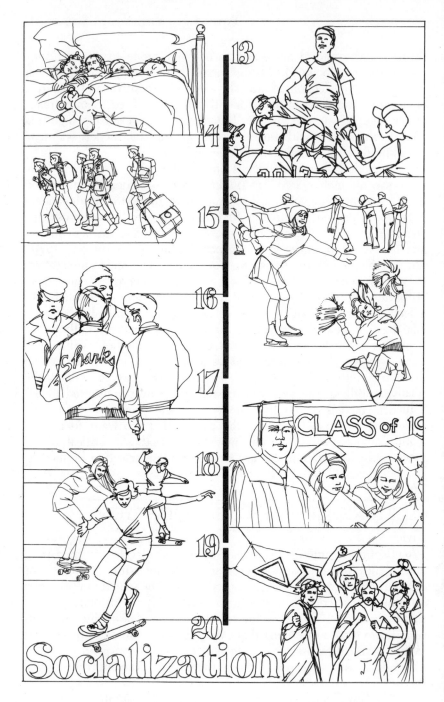

People of *like* interests, behavior, and developing value systems associate intensely with one another and reinforce each other in their development. Who were your friends? What was your "best friend" like? What did you talk about? What about sex? Were you a leader or follower, a joiner or loner? Did your friends have a nickname for you? What did you do together? How long have your friendships lasted?

During the teen-age years, the period of adolescence, we are in the process of defining and integrating values, beliefs, and standards of our particular culture into our own personalities. It is during this period when we achieve full physical maturity *and* a "dominant value direction." This direction complements our basic personality. During this period of socialization, we engage in experimentation, verification, and validation of our basic life plan and script. Several authorities have pointed out that adolescents tend to form an entire subculture of their own. They depend on one another (instead of parents, teachers, or adult society) for rewards and recognition. Several studies conclude that adolescent groups not only create their own language, customs, and value systems but in reality maintain only a few "threads of connection" with adult society.

The main linkage with adults during the late teens is probably financial support. As young adults approach their late teens, final value system lock-in begins. Sometime around twenty years old, perhaps from seventeen to twenty-two, actual entry into the adult world is completed. A totally independent adult materializes only when the financial umbilical cord to the family is cut. From then on, value systems will change *only* when challenged by *Significant Emotional Events*.

In *The Seasons of a Man's Life*, Daniel Levinson defines this period of "around twenty" as the "early adult transition." In behavioral terms, we begin questioning the world and our place in it. We often change existing relationships with important people, groups, and institutions, and we evaluate our "self" that formed during our programming. During this transition, our value system programmed during childhood and adolescence locks in, and we then "test" it against the reality of the world. For many of us, this is a time of real experimentation and validation. College students seem particularly prone to a great deal of experimentation. Many of them are still under the protective umbrella of their parents. Nevertheless, some try out life styles, living arrangements, political philosophies, and modes of behavior that may, on the surface, be in direct conflict with the values programmed during their early development. However, at the end of the transition period, around twenty to twenty-two, they generally seem to revert back to the original programmed values.

In recent years our higher education system has shown a tendency to prolong this period of transition as long as possible, postponing actual entry into the "responsible" adult world. Whatever the length of the transition period, our values are well established and basic programming has ended. This value set is our operating filter for "viewing" the world for the rest of our lives. This system dominates as the individual moves through a relatively orderly sequence during the adult years. Levinson's remarkable discovery of consistency in these patterns shows how predictable our phases of life are. He defines a series of alternating *stable* (structure building) periods and *transitional* (structure changing) periods. For each structure (life style behavior pattern) and for each transitional period (change, experimentation, frustration, alienation), our value system guides and molds our options and behavior.

SEEs, "OLD DOGS," AND LOCKED-IN VALUES

Dramatic change in the gut-level value system may occur at any time during our life. If something significantly affects us and forces a reassessment of our gut-level values, then we may change. Such change may occur in a slow buildup (continued exposure to media messages, behavior pattern changes, job variations, etc.) or through dramatic events (involvement in a war, a *real* energy crisis, divorce, being fired, etc.). The closer such events occur to our early programming periods, the more likely significant change will occur. The less dramatic the event, the longer we hold our programmed values, and any change in values will occur more slowly, if at all. It is possible to "teach an old dog new tricks," but the learning is much more difficult than for the younger animal.

The common denominator of *Significant Emotional Events* (SEEs) is a challenge and a disruption to our present behavior patterns and beliefs. In job situations or family relationships, such challenges might be "artificially" created, but more likely, SEEs occur in an unplanned, undirected manner. We must be careful to distinguish between SEEs, which actually change our gut-level value system, and external events, which simply modify our behavior. For example, a law externally imposed on us may demand that we hire people who were formerly "unacceptable." Our behavior may change to conform to the law because of the consequences of violating it.

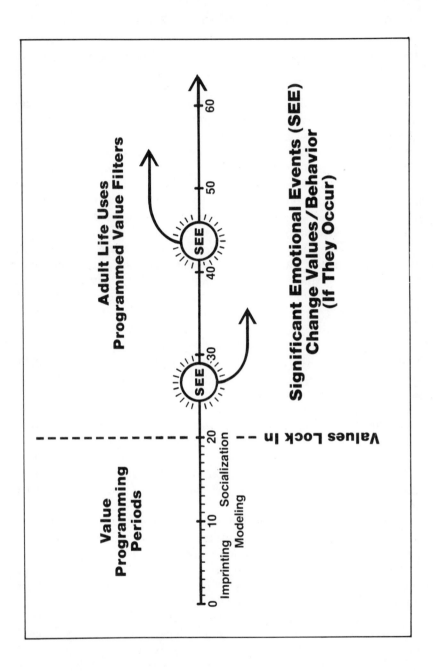

Value Programming Periods

Adult Life Uses Programmed Value Filters

Significant Emotional Events (SEE) Change Values/Behavior (If They Occur)

0   10   20   30   40   50   60

Imprinting
Socialization
Modeling

Values Lock In

SEE

SEE

However, our gut-level values are still *basically* the same. If the law were repealed, we would revert to our original behavior. Another variation is possible. The existence of the law may cause us to change our behavior because of the consequences. Then, the behavior change (actual contact and interaction with people formerly avoided or ignored) may shift our values. Such value changes fall into the category of a slower, cumulative SEE sequence.

It is important to remember that we carry with us a "package" of extremely complex values. Some of these values may in fact be in direct contradiction with one another as they are expressed in behavior. Because we choose how we are going to operate, this contradiction is not usually apparent to us. Further, if an SEE or a series of events is going to create change, the change itself is not in our *total* value system, but only in a specific *part* of our system. For example, in a divorce case (if it's *really* an SEE), parties may exit the marriage with changed values about security, self-image, sexual aggressiveness, and/or sense of worth. However, most of their other values are not changed.

In a historical view, most people probably were not exposed to many SEEs; therefore, they did not change many—if any—of their basic values. In today's world of rapid change, "future-shock" technology, and radical social behavior patterns, SEEs are affecting our total society at a more rapid rate. Such patterns are particularly characteristic in Western industrialized, technological societies. More primitive, less technologically developed societies are not experiencing such dramatic SEE impacts. But as the jets land in more remote places and television invades primitive dwellings, Westernization encroaches and the potential grows for these societies to experience the same value changes.

When SEEs challenge our value systems, the likely reactions are rejection, frustration, or hostility. For most of us, it is much easier to maintain the status quo: what we believe and have always believed, how we behave and have generally always behaved. To accept the possibility that a completely "different" way is equally as correct and as right as ours is very threatening.

Throughout history each new generation has probably challenged, to some extent, the older generations' "ways of doing things." However, in the past, generations were more likely to be consistent in their basic beliefs. The values of sons were very similar to their fathers', whose in turn were very similar to their grandfathers'. The programming events for each of these generations were relatively stable throughout the decades. Parental values remained valid for children because the context in which they were used remained unchanged.

In recent decades, the acceleration in the rate of change of technology, legal dimensions, social behavior, education, and economic systems has created vastly diverse programming experiences between generations. The differences in these experiences have created a spectrum of widely varying value systems within our society. Recently a popular label was "the generation gap"—but it is much more! In volumes of material, people have attempted to reconcile differences between generations which, in reality, are irreconcilable—perhaps *understandable,* but *non-negotiable.* The gut-level value systems are, in fact, dramatically different between the generations that presently exist simultaneously in our society. The focus *should not be* so much on how to change other people to conform to *our standards, our values.* Rather, we must learn how to *accept and understand other people in their own right,* acknowledging the validity of *their values, their behavior.* American Indians believed that "to know another man you must walk a mile in his moccasins." This is a classic challenge for understanding others. If we can understand and respect other people and their values, then we can interact with them in a more effective manner.

All—or most—of our problems in communication, motivation, and interaction will diminish through such simple respect and understanding. But if another person or group is extremely incompatible with our own behavior or values or our organization's direction and goals, then we may want to consider the creation of an SEE. Such an undertaking may be accomplished only by understanding why people are as they are. What were the major influences that created their value systems during their programming periods?

Value programming is not simply a process of indoctrination. Nor is the behavior of people the result of a series of processes that simply overlay a particular culture upon the biological core of individuals. Rather, society shapes a person's inherited temperament, but it does not transform that person into a complete opposite of his own basic nature. We each emerge with somewhat distinctive ways of behaving, despite the common factors in our generation's programming. Our basic physical and mental abilities are influenced by a wide range of inputs. In broad categories, the major sources of programming experiences for all of us were: (1) family, (2) educational experiences of a formal nature, (3) religious inputs, (4) the media, (5) our friends, (6) where we grew up geographically, (7) the amount of money that provided a base for these other factors,

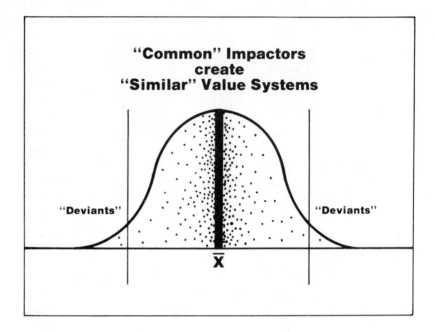

and (8) other formal and "informal" teachers. The commonality of these factors will create highly similar patterns within large groups. The more similar the programming influences, the more similar the behavior of individuals within the group will be.

For example, one frequently hears of the "Depression generation"—those people who were raised and programmed during the 1930s. A common value among these people is financial security. Their resulting behavior is seen in their reaction to the use of cash versus credit cards. While not all of the people in the Depression generation reject the use of credit cards, a major portion prefers a cash basis in their financial dealings. In a similar vein, members of the "rebellious generation" that were programmed during the 1960s are not *all* against war, but a majority of these people hold an antiwar value that results in behavior viewed as unpatriotic by older generations.

Whatever the programming influences, and however the intensity of the factors may vary among individuals, there is still a high degree of similarity in what actually affects each given generation. Furthermore, there is frequently a great degree of overlap and reinforcement *among* the factors. The net result is a programming sequence that creates highly similar gut-level values within each generation. It may well be that today's young people are becoming even more similar within their generations in their gut-level values because today's programming processes are highly simultaneous—they all "get it" at the same time. The impact of the media alone has been omnipresent on virtually all members of recent generations.

Major Value Sources

Part II

VALUE INPUTS: A KALEIDOSCOPE OF SOURCES

Having looked at the basic socialization processes of the programming period, we may now turn to the major elements that are at work during these periods: the critical programming influences. The primary programming unit is the family. Historically, the family was probably far more important in the development of children than it is in today's world. However, since the family, in some form, exists for all people, it is universal in its importance and concern. Because the family is such a critical factor, no society is without it, even though customs concerning marriage and family differ greatly around the world.

FAMILY: FRIEND OR FOE IN PROGRAMMING?

The severing of the umbilical cord physically separates a child from his mother, but the cord is symbolically reconnected in a new context and structure. Immediately, family members replace the cord as a conduit that "feeds" the developing child with ideas and views about the society he has entered. They program him to become part of their world. As Peter Farb discusses in *Humankind*, the family, or its substitute, impacts as the *primary critical influence* on the developing child.

Families are the basic source of social behavior (good little boys do . . .) and social attitudes (nice little girls are . . .). As such, the family is the first and historically most critical of the value factors. Families guide—even dictate—such future behavior as sex

25

roles and how people will relate to others. While the size of the family and the relationships between the children may have some impact on values, the parental attitudes and child-rearing practices have a greater effect. If the climate of the home is warm and nurturing and if democratic relationships exist between the parents and their children, the children will probably adjust to others without sacrificing their own individuality. However, if the child is rejected or treated harshly, he may develop aggressive attitudes that will later interfere in his relationships with others. If discipline is rigid and authoritarian but not necessarily harsh, the child may become reserved and well-behaved but not venture into relationships with more outgoing children. If the child is overindulged, he is likely to be apprehensive, inactive, spoiled, and too egocentric to be easily accepted by his peers, as Goldenson points out.

For each of us, the family was a major source of our value programming. From our family we "absorbed" how it took vacations, paid taxes, interrelated, fought, enjoyed, played, solved problems, cooperated, laughed, cried, and survived. Our family was most critical during our early imprinting period; later it decreased in importance as other value elements began to exert themselves. As we went off to school and came in contact with media and other sources of values, the impact of our family diminished. Unfortunately, many parents seem to be very naive about the real effect they have on their children, especially after the children are of school age and are interacting with a broader environment. It's not uncommon to hear a father talking about "communicating" with his teen-age son: "I've really got him under control, really understand him. I know this is true because each year, for at least a week, we go fishing together." It's difficult to know what the father *thinks* the kid is doing the other fifty-one weeks of the year! Obviously, he's *not* just thinking about going fishing! Instead, he's being bombarded by sources of values and programming experiences from a multitude of areas of which the father is completely unaware. But the father goes on believing that he's in control.

It's tragic that there is so little training or education in how to be an effective parent. "Doing what comes naturally" may create a child but many parents don't seem to know what on earth to do with their creations after they have them. However, an explosion of material in the post-Spock period from the late 1940s has exposed millions to information, knowledge, and understanding that was previously unavailable. Parents have been flooded with materials ranging from an "updated" Spock book, to Parent Effectiveness Training, to Dodson's *Dare to Discipline*. While no one approach appears to be foolproof, the information in some currently popular publications does help parents who are truly concerned. The parenting task is complex and challenging and no simple formula exists. In actual practice the best way to be "good" parents is to have had some good parents yourself. Furthermore, observing parents of well-developing children (and picking up techniques) is probably more useful than "going by the book."

Until relatively recent times, the family's role, relationships, and processes simply were automatically passed on from one generation to the next. Although writers have lamented the decline of the family as an institution for literally thousands of years, the current status, especially of the American family unit, seems particularly precarious. Dynamic trends are well established that show *real changes* in the basic family unit as we "expect" it to be. Our expectation has been that the so-called *nuclear family unit* (father, mother, and children living together) is the ideal norm. Realistically, this unit is an American invention, characteristic of only the past few decades in our society. Examination of European patterns and families in other parts of the world reveals a multitude of different variations from our nuclear family concept. Historically, the *extended family* included not only the parents and their children but also other relatives, especially elders. The American nuclear family was created by mobility, education, and economic independence. As these forces change in our society, it is inevitable that the nuclear family concept also will change. Some of the current trends include:

1. The rising divorce rate (doubled over the past ten years)

2. Estimates that two out of every five children born in the 1970s will live in a single parent home for at least part of their youth

3. The number of households headed by women will increase by more than one-third during the 1970s, thus more than doubling in one generation

4. More than one-half of all mothers with school-age children are now working outside the home, as are one-third of the mothers with children under the age of three

5. One out of every three children now lives in a home headed by only one parent or relative

6. Day care of irregular quality has replaced the parental role in many working families; similarly, there has been an extraordinary growth in the classification that sociologists call "latch-key children" (unsupervised for portions of the day, usually between the end of school and when the working parents return home)

7. The average number of children per family has dropped from a record high of 3.8 in 1957 to 2.04 in 1977, signaling a further *constriction* of the nuclear family, but an *expansion* of legal kinships through divorces and remarriage.

Whatever the family structure—nuclear or extended—family interactions exert powerful programming influences on the developing young. During the first few years, the family's influence focuses on behavior and conduct rather than on abstract concepts. Social behavior is developed in two particular ways. First, through direct training and teaching, parents show children what to do and what not to do in specific situations. They reinforce the child's behavior with discipline and/or rewards. Generally, studies conclude that punishment and criticism are less effective motivators than praise and reward. Behavior is also developed through identification with parents and other people the child admires. In this process the child patterns and models his behavior after those "significant others" in his environment. Through voluntary or unconscious imitation, values are being accepted and become part of the developing individual.

As the child grows, he gradually learns more specific behavior and generalizes to abstract principles of right and wrong. A child of six or seven may say "It is bad to steal," but by eight or nine the child may use the general concept "Stealing is wrong." Within three or four more years he can relate this concept to the broader issue of social justice.

A child's acquisition of values is no simple, clear-cut affair. Some children lack the intelligence or attention span to understand moral reasoning. In some cases, they are confused by their parents' inconsistent behavior. For example, some parents may tell their children to respect the law. These same parents are observed by the children using a CB radio to avoid "Smokey" on the highway, talking about cheating on income taxes, and smoking marijuana socially. "Do as *I say*, not as *I do.*" *Hypocrisy* is the message.

Conflicts between the moral codes and pressures exist both inside and outside of the home. Children are told by parents and others not to have premarital sex. But 40 percent of their teen-age friends are engaging in sex. What's a teen-ager to do? Further, parents tend to emphasize what is wrong *without* showing or explaining *what* is right and *why* it is right. Such confusion hampers the learning process and makes it difficult for a child to create his own moral codes. He may then take the simpler path of following his social group—his friends for good or bad—because such following wins him approval. One frequently hears about a lot of "good children" going wrong. "I just don't understand—they came from such a good home. Their parents did *everything* for them"—except, perhaps, give guidance, responsibility, structure, and emotional support.

FRIENDS: BIRDS OF A FEATHER FLOCKING TOGETHER

As children move into their teens, their friends take on an increasingly important role in their programming. One of the key features of adolescence is a keen social interest. Childhood playmates give way to more intimate friendships. In our society, this social interest tends to focus around the individual's own age group, and the schools with their grade-level stratification reinforce "age-group isolation." Relationships with adults, especially parents, drop to a low ebb, and many teen-agers go to great lengths to win acceptance and approval from their immediate peers. Teen-agers quickly adopt the prevailing fashions in dress, language, and behavior. They do this for several reasons: partly because they lack the courage to defy the "in" customs, partly because they grope for the "right" way to behave, and partly because group approval provides the security they need in facing a confusing world. The need for group conformity during this transitional period is probably intensified by the *real gap* that exists in our society between the world of children of adults. Teen-agers band together to bridge the two extremes. Peer-group relations enable teen-agers to develop a clear self-identity in their relationships with other people and also to fulfill many of their physical, social, and psychological needs.

Increase in peer influence does not necessarily mean that the parent programming is rejected. In fact, if the parental influences were *strong* and *consistent*, those influences may override the peers' pressures. However, in a study of children from the fourth to tenth grades (ten to sixteen years old) documented by Goldenson in his *Encyclopedia of Human Behavior*, there was an increasing tendency to associate with the peer group and, to a lesser degree, actually accept its values as norms. This tendency increased the older the children became. But again, it is not inevitable that the parental influence of the early years will decline. The key is probably the *amount of time* that the teen-ager is spending with the two different sources of information. Parents who are "too busy" to be with their children force them to seek other companions.

The actual role that the adolescent plays in his peer group molds, to a great extent, his conception of himself as a member of society. If he sees himself as a leader, follower, a fringer, or an isolate, then this self-image tends to last for the rest of his life. If he is fully accepted by the group of his choice, he gains confidence and self-assurance. If the individual is only partially accepted, he may experience intense anxiety and self-doubts. If the child is actually rejected by a group, he may experience a genuine trauma. He may react by becoming hostile, retreating into apathy, or escaping into his own fantasy world, as Goldenson explains. Children and teenagers can be innocently cruel to one another. If anyone called you "egghead," "four-eyes," "piggy," or "Dumbo" you might be adversely affected; similarly, such nicknames as "Rocky," "Muscles," or "Angel" might enhance your self-image. Differences in programming influence between parents and peers can also be affected by the youngster's sex. As Dorvan and Adelson explain in *The Adolescent Experience,* peer groups seem to be much more important to boys and wield more influence over their behavior; girls tend to view peer groups primarily as a source of friendship and intimate relationships. Perhaps there has been more caring and sharing "bred" into girls and less "jockeying for position" in the pecking order.

If you want to see the impact of the teen-ager's social group, just watch them as they "herd" together in public places. They're all standing around trying to imitate each other. Their dress, language, posture, disposition, loudness, etc., are amazingly the same. Within their group, members are receiving a tremendous amount of reinforcement for their immediate behavior *and* also for their developing value systems now approaching a locked-in state. The social norms or standards of behavior "appropriate" for your group determined to a large extent whether you *now* feel that your attitudes are sound and your actions appropriate, i.e., whether you are behaving correctly/incorrectly, right/wrong, normal/not normal.

Formal groups we "join" may exert even more specific influence than our informal associations. The Boy Scouts, Brownies, little league, pep clubs, letterman's clubs, etc., of youth give way to the Jaycees, Rotary, country clubs, Junior League, labor unions, etc., for adults. The clubs and groups one belongs to during childhood and adolescence probably program "acceptance" to groups with "complementary" values to join as an adult. The adult "birds of a feather" *continue* to "flock together" for mutual reinforcement and validation of their values. Formal groups often demand rigid conformity. One study of the Greek fraternity system found a set of standards, which included: making moderately good grades, loyalty to the fraternity, congeniality with fraternity brothers, dating girls from certain sororities and not others, helping on fraternity projects, and believing that one's own fraternity was the best on campus. At the other extreme, some fraternities select members for grossness, drunkenness, lewdness, and "nonconformity" (except for *being* nonconformist!).

Of course, norms or standards of behavior and values are not always ready-made affairs. Sometimes values are established by experience itself. If a group of teen-agers on an expedition in a shopping center suddenly finds that some member—especially a "leader type" —is shoplifting, then the entire group may shoplift. It is the "in" thing to do. Reinforcement comes from group members. There are also positive aspects of acceptance and conformity in doing "what everyone else is doing" in that many groups actually set high standards for their members.

Peers/friends also provide other programming inputs through their family's life-style and interactions.

The leaders in reference groups may serve as models for lesser involved members of the group. In fact, there is some indication that leader models among groups of teen-agers and young adults of college age actually associate with one another in *their own peer context* (a group of leaders). Within this context, they establish the patterns of behavior that they then carry back to their own groups.

As an intense programming factor, the relationships with friends/peers are probably most critical during the socialization process of adolescence. But remember, friendship associations of youth sometimes continue into adulthood because of their positive value, particularly as they reinforce values and norms they originally created.

RELIGION: THOU SHALT . . .
THOU SHALT NOT . . .
THOU SHALT MAYBE (IF YOU DON'T GET CAUGHT)

One important source of value information is our religious affiliation. Religion usually supports the norms and values within a society; indeed, it frequently makes some of them sacred and unquestionable. In the United States there are about 250 different religions sharing certain values in common with our society. One value, according to Milton Yinger in *Sociology Looks at Religion,* is a general acceptance of the "American way of life," including characteristics of work, the desirability of material rewards, and other features of the familiar Protestant ethic. Another value is the belief that a religion is appealing and provides us with satisfaction and reinforcement in our lives.

Until recently, there was relatively little information on the attitudes, concerns, interests, beliefs, and values of young people who are members of religious institutions. While working on *Research on Religious Development,* Merton Strommen searched materials published over four decades and found little solid research on youth where religion was included as a variable. Effects of church attendance and religious training are difficult to assess. It is reasonable to suppose that contact with moral concepts, spiritual values, and religious dogma would have a positive effect on a child's character. However, the few psychological studies that exist do not give direct and conclusive proof. Even though many youths are indoctrinated or exposed to religious training, Sunday school attendance, or parochial schooling, Goldenson has pointed out that "studies do not show on the whole that youngsters who regularly receive religious instruction are significantly more honest or humane than those who do not. [Yet another] study showed that children who regularly attended Sunday school cheated only slightly less than children who did not." Even though the effects are not apparent, religious influences are a major programming element for millions of people in our society.

Typically, children are programmed by their parents' religious institutions. Although there are some variations, the basic approach is to create within a child a series of "thou shalts" and "thou shalt nots." The child may "learn" his lessons well; however, there is not necessarily a relationship between religious *knowledge* and personal *values.* This reaffirms the obvious fact that "indoctrination is not tantamount to communicating values," as Strommen states. A child can learn his prayers precisely. When the parent's friends are visiting, the four-year-old is trotted out to the living room where the parents say: "Johnny, say your prayers!" His immediate "Now I lay me down to sleep. I pray the Lord my soul to keep . . . ." makes for proud parents, but may *or may not* have any implications for his future behavior. A child's rote knowledge of certain prayers and/or his ability to recite standard definitions of religious terms are simply instances of "acquired" religion.

In addition to these acquired pieces of knowledge, Strommen discusses other sources of values that arise out of interaction with the religious world. Children begin to recognize very early if a church's congregation has *factions* instead of *fellowship.* They sense if its leadership is corrupted by self-seekers struggling for power. They hear derogatory remarks about the minister, the church treasurer, the choir director, or the "hussy" on the third row. Sermons are dissected as if they were part of a performance for which admission has been paid rather than a service of worship in which the worshiper should give as well as receive. Children note official discussions to cut the missionary budget to redecorate the sanctuary. As a child hears of and sees such actions, he probably concludes that the biblical quotations and pious statements about love, sacrifice, and brotherly concern may just be words—words that few really take seriously.

Certainly, these illustrations are negative, and fortunately in many churches their opposites are found. Concern and sacrifice, support in times of crisis, and understanding of others also come through to children. Spiritual values are internalized *only* if a child actually experiences them in his church *and* home. Of course, some parents may implant these values without the aid of formal church experiences. As Dorothy Fritz states in *The Child and the Christian Faith*, adults who know the joy of religion are constantly teaching children around them by what they *are* as well as by what they *say* and *do*. A major dimension affecting religious factors is the actual experiences of the developing child. Johnny, who so precociously recited his prayers at four, becomes ten, eleven, or twelve years old. Suddenly his environment provides him opportunities to experiment with some of those "thou shalt nots." When he experiments and finds that he *likes* a "thou shalt not," he begins to question the entire religious "package." On his own, he will ultimately decide what he is going to accept or reject from his earlier religious programming.

During the period of passage between childhood and adolescence, many doubts are expressed and questions raised. Changes in an individual's beliefs and understanding of such a religious concept as God are expressed in the developmental growth theory as outlined by Baker and Koppe and detailed in Strommen's book:

• Ages 2–3—God described in terms of experiences of the child, anthropomorphically. God lived in heaven or in church, made trees, flowers, and babies grow, etc. Children asked to see God.

• Ages 4–5—Children still sought to locate God. Some believed God was in the sky or inside children. God strongly associated with nature, birds, flowers, snow, and rain. A few children believed God protected them at night, watched over them, and punished them when they were bad.

• Ages 6–7—God was the planner for the universe, plants, animals, stars, and man. He was pictured anthropomorphistically. He was Father of all. A few understood God as love or Spirit. God was everywhere to most children. Some still looked for God and asked to talk to Him.

• Ages 8–9—God was described by such attributes as all-powerful, all-knowing, creator, power, law, loving Father who knew everything. Belief that "God was Spirit" was gaining popularity.

• Ages 11–12—The most important new note was a sense of personal relationship between children and God. He was a lawgiver in society and nature. Why does God let people do wrong? More doubts expressed.

• Ages 13–14—God was invisible and everywhere. Traces of anthropomorphisms fade. Less emphasis on nature. More emphasis on the attributes of God: creator, all-powerful, forgiving, loving.

The religious factor varies considerably among individuals. Researchers conclude that there is a great diversity in religious commitment. Some young people have a deep religious commitment and act upon it, while others show almost no religious tendency. The most pressing problems and concerns of adolescence tend to be those of their own personal social relationships. Whatever adolescent concerns may be, even if the seeds of the religious factor were planted, "growth" depends on many other elements.

An interesting series of studies about how value systems operate focuses on prejudice and bias in "religious" adults. These studies have indicated that (1) churchgoers, on the average, harbor more ethnic prejudice than nonchurch goers; and (2) churchgoers who are "intrinsically" motivated are significantly less prejudiced than the "extrinsically" motivated. For the intrinsically-oriented churchgoer, religion is not blind conformity, a security crutch, a tranquilizer, nor a bid for status (as is true with the extrinsically motivated). The intrinsic churchgoer's needs are subordinated to a massive religious commitment. In internalizing their religion, intrinsically religious people necessarily accept the values of humility, compassion, and love of neighbor. There is no place in their lives for rejection, contempt, or condescension toward their fellow man.

In contrast, religion is not a value in its own right for the extrinsically religious person. Rather, it serves other needs and performs purely utilitarian functions. For these people, prejudice is also useful since it provides them with security, comfort, status, and social support. Interestingly, in terms of attendance, the intrinsic churchgoer is much more likely to attend religious services regularly than is the extrinsic churchgoer, who does it on a lip-service basis, showing up at the "correct" high holiday events.

Obviously, children from an intrinsically-motivated family are more likely to be affected by religious values in their overall programming. Extrinsic families, regardless of their verbalizations, will program "lip-service religion" children, children who are apathetic toward religion, and/or children who reject parental religion as hypocrisy.

As value factors, religious institutions seem to be diminishing in importance in the United States. In recent years, if church membership is accepted as an indicator, there has been a dramatic decrease in the influence of churches on individuals and their values. Church *membership* hit a peak of 64 percent of adults in 1960, but has been declining since then. Church membership is one thing, attendance is quite another. Gallup polls indicate that the proportion of the nation's adults *attending* services has declined from about 49 percent in 1958 to 42 percent in 1969, and 40 percent in the 1970s. This may indicate an increase in extrinsic churchgoers; less faith and more show.

The role of religion has been further diminished by the "secularization" of religious institutions, i.e., they have lost their function in directing other aspects of our society. Historically, religion provided the values by which many aspects of our society operated—justice, science, the arts, and all other relative cultural dimensions were evaluated in religious terms. In contemporary society, this view has been replaced with a system in which religion is, at most, only relevant to a limited portion of life and, at least, irrelevant to any of life. Herberg believes that traditional religion has lost its impact on the "American Way of Life" and states: "Religiousness in America has become a 'religiousness without religion,' lacking real inner commitment and stressing social adjustment and legitimization of secular value orientation. Religion becomes a reactive system; it is shaped by secular [worldly] values rather than shaping them. It no longer exerts creative leverage for judging and influencing secular life."

Considerable evidence shows that the declining importance of religion is being recognized by church members themselves. In a nationwide Gallup sample in 1957, 76 percent of the population felt the influence of religion was increasing in daily life. But by 1969, only 14 percent thought religion was an important, influential factor. Nearly every socioeconomic group changed to some extent, but young people have changed even more. In a comprehensive study of college students from 1931 to 1968, Vernon Jones, in *Genetic Psychology Monographs,* concluded: "It would seem that whatever weakening in students' favorable attitudes toward religion that occurred in the last 37 years has not been so much a decrease in belief in the Deity—although there has been some of that—as a disillusionment with the church establishment and the use of its beliefs and preachments in the solution of current social, civic, and economic problems." Although religion as an institution has been generally waning in influence in America and other cultures, it is still very important for many individuals.

The type of religious training, or lack of it, that a person receives during his programming will affect his adult behavior in various ways. Religious practice may determine the use of certain products and services or prevent consumption of others—Orthodox Jews buy kosher products and Mormons are not supposed to drink liquor or smoke cigarettes. Because some religions are more traditional than others in forming attitudes concerning what is good and what is immoral, the individuals' behavior may be affected in the types of entertainment they select, their use of credit cards, or even something as basic as driving a car in our highly motorized society. Whatever their impact—good, bad, strong, or weak—the religious programming inputs have many long-range behavioral, attitudinal implications in the creation of our value systems.

In the late 1970s there appeared to be a new sense of religious commitment and understanding in the United States and many other countries. With the popularity of current Eastern and nontraditional religious movements and the "born again" phenomenon, the net effect may be a rapidly changing role for religious institutions in the 1980s.

The result of such changes may be to create values in the 1980s that will be more personal, more diversified, and less traditional. These values may be different from older generations because they will be based upon such new "religions" in the United States as Transcendental Meditation (which does not define itself as a religion), other Eastern religions, and new forms of Judeo-Christian beliefs. The interest in some of these diverse and nontraditional religious movements appears in the results of a nationwide study of *Psychology Today* readers. Some new religions surfacing included Hare Krishna, Scientology, Zen, Jews for Jesus, Yoga, and Satanism. The impact of religious values may be increasing in younger people because some religious groups have been willing to cater to their newly developing value systems. Today's young people may seek out religions whose values are more compatible with their own.

Once strongly held moral doctrines of churches have been buffeted severely on many issues. No *new* dogma has emerged. Some modern religious leaders are more concerned with creating morally autonomous people, who take a few principles then make up their own minds, than with the traditional consumers of moral absolutes. But, no means have been developed to mold this religiously and morally autonomous person. Many people now feel caught in a no-man's-land between old and new forms of religious guidance.

In the past, religion played a dominant role in the early educational systems in the United States. Church and state supported one another in a great defense of their fundamental principles. The concept of the three Rs was really inadequate, it was actually the four Rs—reading, 'riting, 'rithmetic, and religion. Honesty was the very best policy, thrift was always a virtue, hard work naturally a duty, and material achievement a desirable and righteous goal in life. The puritan ethic, which regards pleasure as sinful, had a significant influence on our values. This ethic, in turn, had a strong impact on how children were raised and educated. In fact, a number of subjects were made a part of school curricula in the past simply because they were tedious and learning them was thought to build character. As a result, the attitude toward pleasure-oriented activities in our culture was negative. Children's play was viewed as irrelevant, frivolous, and nonproductive, having no value in the learning processes. The view of "pleasure as sinful" and drudgery as valuable has disappeared almost as totally as the high school Latin class.

EDUCATION: "PRACTICE MAKES PERFECT"

Everything about the educational system has an impact on the developing values of the young. In our society, schools are particularly critical as the first organized agency outside of the family responsible for socializing and programming individuals. Within schools, children learn behavior patterns and the intellectual heritage of their culture. In theory, each new generation is supposed to benefit from its fore-bearers' experiences and discoveries. All of the components of the educational system communicate values—the structure, the teaching techniques, the content of the materials, and the teachers and administrators.

Before World War II, teachers and professors usually came from a middle-class background. Upper-class parents sent their children to college, but *not* to become teachers. Most lower-class families couldn't afford to send their children to college. Historically, most teachers had middle- or upper-class backgrounds and in their teaching reflected what came to be known as "traditional American values." During the 1950s, a new breed of teachers emerged as college enrollment from *all* social classes mushroomed. The GI Bill from World War II allowed many people to attend college who would have never been able to attend before. To ensure a stable, secure future, many majored in Education. While the middle classes still dominated teaching, teachers and professors now came from the entire spectrum of society.

As we moved into the 1960s and 1970s, students encountered

"new" teachers with values different from their own—in some cases *radically* different. Stern *"Miss* Pringles" ruled classes without question into the 1950s. When they retired, their replacements were *"Ms.* Moderns" and *"Mr.* With-Its" (who team-taught in jeans and preferred to be called Susie and Bill by their students). By the late 1960s, it was not uncommon for Susie and Bill to be "roommates." We had come a long way from "never-even-considering-that-*Miss* Pringle-had-a-sex-life" to third-graders openly wondering whether Susie Modern was on "the Pill" or used an IUD.

Another trend involved the emergence and proliferation of dramatic new teaching techniques. Historically, children experienced grade school as a "robot parade ground" for the mind. Virtually everything was drilled into their little heads through endless repetition. One "approved" method for teaching arithmetic required pupils to spend the entire first year working only on the numbers one through ten—counting, adding, and multiplying. Only in their second year were they permitted to advance to the challenging heights of numbers eleven through twenty. Reading and spelling were the same. Handwriting was a repetitive mechanical process with instructions on precisely how to sit, tilt the paper, and where to place your fingers (even your feet!) before you were permitted to start. The reigning theory was "practice makes perfect."

The teaching techniques typically emphasized description and memorization. The approach to learning was, "This is the way things are; just learn it." There was no latitude for questioning. Then, during the 1960s and 1970s there was a gradual but steady trend away from description and memorization in favor of more analytical approaches. There was an emphasis on *questioning* the "old" and forming "new" approaches and solutions. In many cases, this approach concluded that there was no *one* correct answer. Suddenly, the world could no longer be "tested" in terms of absolute "white right" answers and absolute "black wrong" ones. Reality "grayed" in the classroom as it was graying in the outside world.

The spillover from the educational system caused questioning and rejection of rigid definitions of *right* and *wrong*. This questioning crept into the basic values of people's personal lives. To paraphrase a statement that Engel attributes to Archibald MacLeish, "The central reality of our time is that individuals, particularly younger people, are no longer willing to lead unexamined lives."

More and more people are asking *why* and *why not* in every aspect of their lives. The historical "These are the absolute right answers, all the others are wrong" is no longer an acceptable approach to contemporary problems in any area. Yet millions of older people who were programmed through the "traditional" school systems still search in vain for *absolute* rights and wrongs in the world around them.

The "content" of educational materials strongly but subtly programs values. One of the major ways to explore the values of a society is to look at its school books for the young. The contents are rigidly standardized to *mirror* adult prejudices. The lessons are carefully selected to mold children into the kinds of citizens they "ought" to be.

Within the past few years, many of these biases were questioned, yet real change has come slowly in the traditional "Dick and Jane" approach. Remember the textbooks you used in those early years—Dick and Jane and Spot chasing one another up and down the hills? Those little books were quietly giving us a major value view of part of the world, and we didn't even realize that we were being programmed. Recently a number of lawsuits concerning textbooks have been filed against school systems. Typically, groups of women charged that the texts in use were "sexist" in their orientation. Also typically, when such lawsuits were filed, many people rose up against "pushy women"—the newspapers, radio stations, and Rotary clubs. Their basic reaction was "Ah, it's a bunch of damn women libbers. What the hell do they know? Get 'em back in the kitchen, let 'em bake a cake. They don't know what's going on in the school system!"

Well, they *do* know. And you will too if you look objectively at those texts. You'll notice an amazing thing—Jane never does a damn thing! All she does is look sweet, twiddle her thumbs, and occasionally cook or clean. Dick, on the other hand, the "male chauvinist pig," gets to do *everything*—makes the decisions, carries the ball, and orders Jane around. Literally millions of people in the United States have been programmed to believe that women only do certain things, while men do others. Never the two should meet in a professional, occupational world as equals. Dick is the "assumed" leader for the adult world. The "male chauvinist pigs" in today's world—and there are millions of them—*were programmed to believe* in sex discrimination very intensely through the textbooks' orientation. Those simple little words were prophetic for all of our futures.

From the sexism of Dick and Jane to the subtle "rewriting" of American history—that painted the world in a rose-colored hue ("our" point of view)—content is a major factor in value creation. It now seems incredible that millions "bought" the textbook ideas that "Negroes *appreciated* the way their masters took care of them" and "slaves were basically happy because they laughed, sang, and danced a lot." In another distortion of reality, our history books never described the shabby treatment and atrocious crimes committed against the native American Indian.

As with all value programming, content subtly *combined* with the structure of the schools to reinforce values. The orientation toward "those who are different from us" was significant. This difference was stressed not only in the content of educational materials (which for decades conveniently ignored ethnic minorities and women for their roles in American history) but also in the actual organization of the system itself. Blatant segregation existed sometimes between sexes, but predominately and profoundly between ethnic groups within our society.

Did *you* go to a school that was integrated or segregated? That determines *right now,* to a large extent, how *you* relate to people in the world who are "different" from you. Millions of *real bigots* exist in our society today. Having values programmed through educational systems in communities of the past, it was inevitable that bigots would be created. People were taught to *dislike, distrust,* and *not to relate* to people who were "different" from themselves. They were physically separated within the school systems and influenced by the bias of their textbooks and teachers. This segregation and prejudice was reinforced by "pure white" churches and an "all-white" world. Millions of us never questioned whether certain people might not "like" to ride in the backs of buses, didn't "prefer" separate drinking fountains, or wouldn't "want" to attend churches and schools with white people. We neatly and conveniently stereotyped minorities to justify our prejudices.

Today, many of us can't afford to be bigots, nor do some of us want to, because we *have* to deal with many people who are very "different" from the way we are. But the old values are still very real and lie deep within millions of us. Sometimes, in handling problems with someone who is "different," we find ourselves thinking: "I know what's wrong with you, you SOB . . . (ethnic slur)."

In today's world, if we *truly* don't want to be biased and prejudiced against people who are "different," we must confront the *reality* of our own past value programming. Only by bringing values to the surface and *understanding* those values can we honestly deal with them. Only through such confrontation, examining our own gut-level reactions, can we create our own internal Significant Emotional Events and change ourselves. Unfortunately, it appears that millions of people still *refuse to admit* and *to accept the validity* of their own past programming. Consequently, such people don't understand the basis for their own biases, their own value programming. They are the *real* "Archie Bunkers" of the world. Sadly, prejudice is a two-way street. Some minority children are taught to dislike and distrust all "honkies" and "peckerwoods."

Another dimension of the influence of education in changing people's values has been noted by pollster Louis Harris. In the regular surveys conducted by his organization, the level of formal education in forming attitudes has proved to be decisive. On the key issues of the day, those people with the least education tend to hold the harder line on U.S. foreign policies, favoring a "fortress America," "love it or leave it" point of view. They are keenly suspicious of "too much involvement" in foreign countries. The college educated, on the other hand, are more in favor of limiting the use of American military power abroad and are much more inclined to commit the nation's current resources to international organizations and hope for better relations with the Communist world. On racial matters, well-educated whites are far more receptive to integration than are the less educated. Also, the college educated are far more open-minded about young people and their taste in styles than are those with less formal education. Our educational experiences and exposure have an ultimate impact on our ability to accept change and to modify our value filters.

There is no question that every aspect of the school system affects the participants. Schools cannot avoid being involved in the value programming of their students. It is inconceivable for the schools to take a child for six or seven hours a day for 180 days a year, from the time he is six through the time he is eighteen, and not affect his behavior and how he views value issues.

You can suppress discussion about moral issues and values, but you cannot suppress their formation and development. It is not a question of *whether* schools program values into children, but *how* and *what* values are being programmed. Even to program *no* values gives a definite value orientation to the world around us. Educational systems, then, are a major force for growth or retardation, for good or for evil in the value development of individuals. Because education itself has become such an important value in American society, more and more individuals are being exposed to a greater intensity of programming from this critical source. Until recently, educational inputs did not differ greatly from generation to generation. They were primarily intended to make young people conform to whatever society they happened to have been born into. During our lifetime, rapid change has eliminated such an automatic value "pass-on" system.

The educational systems seldom truly teach people to feel or think. When children enter school, the entire system rewards them for meeting *other's* expectations. Grades, approval from teachers, and competition with other students are all are external reinforcers. Studies show that even when children are naturally motivated from within, the strength of the external rewards acts to make them conform to *other people's standards* instead of acting on the basis of their own feelings. These approvals from "important others" are sufficient to make children absorb values. The educational system, by virtue of its length of contact with children, creates a powerful programming influence on each generation.

Perhaps more important as inputs into value systems are the many things that go on *outside* of the classrooms. The introduction of automobiles, radio, telephone, and television probably *now* has more to do with the education of young people than anything learned from teachers or textbooks. Media have assumed an increasing role in programming values in modern societies.

MEDIA: HIGH-INTENSITY VALUE BOMBARDMENTS

The role of media as a significant programming factor has shifted dramatically, especially during the past few decades. Until this century, media were of relatively little influence because they simply did not exist for the masses. Before the invention of printing presses, there was no form of mass communication. However, printing developed through the years and began to effect changes as printed materials became more widely available. Newspapers, originally sources of advertising, became an important source of programming information during and after the American Civil War. In the late 1800s nationally circulated magazines also became influential. With the advent of the electronic media, inaugurated by radio in the 1920s, media came into homes and significantly affected young people.

The growing importance of radio during the 1920s, 1930s, and 1940s only hinted at the tremendous effect that television would have on value programming for entire generations after the 1940s. The electronic media, especially television, began to invade the "old" world and the "traditional." History became irrelevant, or at least as it was *taught* it became irrelevant. A new "instant," "now" world began to emerge, and this "nowness" became an important programming influence. Electronic media create "strangely" distorted views of the world around us. Besides the electronic media, the development of movies on a mass scale during the 1920s and the creation of sophisticated recording equipment and records added to the developing impact of media on the young.

A very important consideration of media as a value-programming force relates to the *control* of information. Before the advent of mass media, the family, churches, and schools censored and controlled the *type* and *content* of information that was given to young people. But with electronic media, young people began to come in contact with information that was not censored by the traditional value programming forces of family, religion, and education. Further, the *amount of time* spent with media increased significantly, so that in today's world young people are probably in more direct contact with media than they are with any other programming force.

The family has become "controlled" to some degree by the presence of media. For example, a family may sit together as a group to view a television program. But each member experiences on an individual basis, oblivious to one another. This is a subtle but important change from the 1920s and 1930s, when the entire family sat around the radio at night to listen to their favorite programs. Television "demands" that each family member interact with it on an *individual* basis. A modern TV program like "M.A.S.H." irritates the hell out of "patriotic" Dad who actually *fought* and doesn't think war is "funny." Mom "loves" the hero doctors. Junior thinks the transvestite character is a riot (and Mom and Dad won't even comment!). Sis thinks it's great social commentary on the stupidity of war (reinforcing the "ideas" of her liberal political science professor). Since they each interpret the program differently, they don't share a common value reaction—and if they tried, they probably couldn't agree. Of course, with several TV sets in more and more homes, family members probably watch different programs anyway.

Educational systems depend increasingly on media input to supplement information being provided by the more traditional educational sources. Modern educators really have no choice but to incorporate media into schools, although many of them fight it like Don Quixote against the windmills. The young spend so much time with television and popular music that they cannot be ignored as sources. Children are "assigned" some TV programs for homework, since they'll probably watch it anyway and wouldn't do "traditional" assignments. Since the 1950s, the young have grown with and been programmed by the media; they "expect" classes to at *least* be entertaining and exciting. Millions of dollars have been spent on audiovisual equipment that *potentially* stimulates in the classroom with as much intensity as "prime time." Unfortunately, most teachers aren't professional actors, and even audio-visual props won't bring their classes high ratings from their "sophisticated" audiences.

Certainly television, more than any other medium, continues to create controversy. While program content ranges from excellent to useless to harmful, the *process* of watching and the amount of *time* spent viewing are also critical. Television's influence on the young may be one of our least understood modern phenomena.

Today's young people are surrounded by media. They are bombarded by and immersed in a world that really isn't there. But increasing numbers of people are value programming through the "filters" of the media. All types are important, but from a value programming point of view, the most significant are the electronic forms. *Listen* and *watch* the values being programmed into today's young. Most adults haven't bothered to "tune in" over the past few years. Perhaps we should pay more attention to the music of teenagers—the lyrics, the beat, and, of course, the themes of contemporary society. Popular music is the subject of a whole series of hot debates on content, orientation, pervasiveness, and function for the young.

From a value programming perspective, media should be viewed in terms of *content* and *impact*. Each is unique in its characteristics. The emotional involvement with electronic media is intense. Remember Orson Welles' classic Halloween broadcast in 1938, "The War of the Worlds"? Thousands of people across the United States panicked hysterically at the impending "invasion" from Mars. The dramatic events of the 1960s and 1970s (including space flights, assassinations, and war) triggered strong emotions simultaneously in millions of people. Recent concerns have focused on the content of media, especially television and the more extreme movies of our times. But it is perhaps not so much the content as the emotional involvement *coupled with* the content that should be of primary concern.

Later, as we look at the role of these critical forces on developing generations, we will explore the changing importance of media as influences on recently programmed generations. Unlike the educational factors that dryly present information, media not only present information but also actually *create feelings* and *thoughts*. This single element of intense emotional involvement probably programs stronger values than many other impactors.

Because of media's limited nature in detailing information, content is squeezed and condensed. Major problems are "solved" on TV in an hour, with several commercial breaks for the "good life." News is "collapsed" into a few brief comments. The complexity of a sporting event is summarized by a score. The values people absorb from this perspective may be distorted by this brevity. Such major events as the death of a loved one or a divorce are "experienced" and "forgotten" within an hour on TV. In real life, when the hurt lingers on for months, people begin to believe, "Something's wrong with me." Their reality and their television-created expectations are emotional light years apart.

Whatever their content and emotional impact, all types of media have become a major force in our value programming. For most of us presently alive and functioning on this planet, the media have influenced our values—from triggering conflicts for older generations to actually creating the values for those generations molded by media during their programming periods. To understand the changing influence of media is to understand, in a major part, the diverse values in our current society and to preview the future's inevitable value conflicts.

Like all of the major influences on values, media change with time. They have moved from relatively insignificant impact before the 1900s to a *growing dominance* over individuals. Other influences are also changing. Families have shifted in their importance from extended family, to the nuclear family, to the more modern disintegrated family. Working mothers, house-husbands, single parents, and communes have definite impacts on the value programming influences of contemporary families. Educational systems have swung from the basic regimented three *R*s through the 1950s and the 1960s (free-swinging, free-form, anything goes, permissive approach) to a 1970s yearning for a return to those basics. Religion, which waned in the 1960s to a low of "God is dead," is now resurfacing with Eastern variations of Zen Buddhism, TM, assorted gurus, and "born-again" Christians. Another values factor that has seen significant shift in importance over the past century is geography.

GEOGRAPHICAL ROOTS: TAKING THE "BOY" OUT OF THE COUNTRY

Where we grow up may be extremely important in the formation of our values. Before the 1900s, geography was a major determinant of an individual's gut-level values. Each geographic location reflected definite subcultures. As mobility increased and the media erased geographic barriers, geography decreased as a major influence.

Recently, there seems to be a resurgence of geography's importance, along with some other factors that are geographically based.

Kevin Phillips and other social observers now believe that the direction of our nation is locally focused, not federally. The trend of the 1960s has reversed. Thirty years ago, the late Hubert Humphrey urged the Democratic party to "leave the shadow of states' rights and step into the sun of human rights." Now it appears that human rights has become a cliché and states' rights (representing everything from water policy to urban development to sex preference) is a battle cry heard with increasing frequency and attention. Colorado's Democratic Governor Richard Lamm said: "The day of the state has come and gone—and come back again." The United States has been fragmented and divided before, but except for the Civil War, the underlying trend pointed toward unity and increasing federal authority. Now American society seems to be pursuing smaller loyalties—regional, economic, political, ethnic, and even sexual—rather than larger ones.

Stereotypes of geographical values and life styles don't really apply to all individuals. But, how would you match the following?

_____A. Blonde, tanned, athletic,   1. New Yorker
       bathing suit

_____B. Dark, loud, pushy, Brooks   2. Californian
       Brothers three-piece suit

_____C. Loud, drawls, brags, boots   3. Texan

A majority of the American population would probably answer the following match test as A-2, B-1, C-3.

Geography imparts certain "constants" which inevitably influence nearly everyone within that area. It's probably true that people growing up in the Northeast/New England area are more tenacious and industrious, have drier wits, and look on life in a more solemn way. Such would be the natural result of growing up in a physical, geographical environment that was extremely demanding and literally difficult to survive physically. It may also be true that people from the southern states and the South are "slower" in their behavior, simply because one learns to move less rapidly in hot, sweltering climates. Geography also has an impact on programming because certain nationalities settled in certain areas and continued their unique customs and values.

Before the last half of the century, geography had a much greater insulating influence. People simply didn't travel very much. But with the advent of mass travel (cars, trains, planes, vacations, jobs), exposure to several areas came to millions of people, and geography's impact diminished. Physical mobility was coupled with the advent of the mass electronic media, further eroding geographic isolation. It became possible for *everyone* to attend a national political convention "electronically," wherever he might live. Compare this electronic interaction and physical mobility with the time of the American Revolution when it took months for England to realize that the war had started. Sailing ships simply couldn't compete with the 3½-hour Concorde time from New York to London and the millisecond transmission of electronic data by hovering satellites. People remained insulated, uninformed, and uninvolved emotionally.

In *The American Idea of Success*, Richard M. Huber elaborates on the variations in value approaches between the North and the South. He notes that the Civil War marks the contrast between the South and the rest of the nation. Up North and out West the idea of success had long taken hold. It was a goal pursued in the cities, not on the farms. The idea of success developed in a mercantile/commercial world. Later, it embraced manufacturing and finance. In values, actions, heritage, and economy, the North was ready for quick expansion during the last half of the nineteenth century. The South, on the other hand, was shattered by economic destruction and wounded pride. Its crumbling plantation economy and predominantly agrarian values were in no condition to compete with applied science and technology.

Social factors made the South "different." Where the goals were slave ownership and possession of a landed estate, attitudes were different. With its romantic enchantment for the past and reverence for family background, the South refused to acknowledge the self-made man. As someone in the early 1900s noted: "Blood counts far more down here than it does in many other places. . . ." Huber adds, "In the decades following World War I, southern literature and drama swung from the poles of sentimentality over fair maidens, chivalrous gentlemen, magnolias, mint juleps, and Rastus, to a violence based on an authoritarian relationship to the Negro, or the psychological disasters inherent in a pride of caste and the decadence of ancestor worship. These moods reflected the agonies endured by a society at war with itself."

Certainly by the 1960s and 1970s the relative isolationism of certain sections of the country had collapsed considerably. In California it became difficult to find a *native* Californian. The same seemed true in Phoenix, Houston, Denver, Atlanta, or any area that experienced tremendous surges of growth characteristic of developing economic centers. However, even today some old values still cling in certain geographic pockets. Those who have "moved in" are attempting to create legal barriers to prevent further immigration.

Growing geographic isolationism and its ability to protect the values of those already there is an interesting phenomenon in contemporary America. When the governor of Oregon publically states, "It's okay to visit us, but don't try to move here," one can sense the mood of many areas. Hawaii is attempting to stem the flow of new immigrants, following in the footsteps of such cities as Boca Raton, Florida; Boulder, Colorado; and Petaluma, California. The governor of Hawaii is urging an amendment to the U.S. Constitution to permit a state to limit the number of new residents it accepts. Such thinking is reminiscent of the cattlemen versus the sheep herders: "It's our land [our values], don't mess with it, don't invade it."

Modern technology has carried mobility to an extreme. It is now no longer necessary to even live and work in the same geographic area. There are college professors who live in Colorado and commute to New York to teach in the state universities. Airline personnel live in one part of the country and work out of another part thousands of miles away, commuting a portion of their work week at a greatly reduced cost. While such extremes are not characteristic of the majority, they still serve as an indicator of how geography has less control over what one is exposed to in life styles and other programming influences.

Some people seem to be returning to geographic orientations, with *less* mobility becoming a noticeable pattern. A news service report notes that after World War II, American workers seemed restless and on the lookout for better opportunities. As a result, we were a population on the move, with more than one-fifth of us moving each year. That trend has been quietly reversed in recent years—from 21.2 percent of Americans moving in 1951 to 17.7 percent twenty-five years later, according to Census Bureau figures.

Sociologists, struck by the reversal, have presented a number of reasons for the change: (1) worries about moving—so much has been said about the disruptions moving brings, particularly to young children, that most of us look upon such radical change with hesitation; (2) increasing concern about family—which is translated into reluctance to move to places where family contacts are difficult, if not impossible, to maintain; (3) second-income families—years ago when a transfer was suggested, only one person's career was taken into account; today a wife's career may be more important than her husband's, which may present difficulties in compromising; (4) longer unemployment benefits—with unemployment compensation lasting as long as sixty-five weeks, the person who loses a job is less likely to feel impelled to look for work in another location; being able to manage financially during the interim permits the job-seeker time to hope that something will show up in the same community and make a move unnecessary.

The trend to less mobility and stronger geographic roots does not necessarily mean geography will return as a major programming factor. Isolation is impossible when electronic media "take" us everywhere, and jets offer contact with the rest of the world at will.

TECHNOLOGY AND OTHER INFLUENCES

Unlike geography, which has tended to decline in importance, technology is an expanding force on all our programming sources. Technology creates changes in values in every aspect of our lives. At any point in time, the existing technology is operating *within* our major programming institutions, restructuring work, play, home, schools, knowledge, and life.

The family as a major input of programming information is technologically affected by (1) entertainment available (the various media, games, parks, recreation centers, sports, hobbies, etc.); (2) mobility potential (cars, planes, public transportation, highways, commuter services, etc.), (3) appliances and convenience items (anything that frees people from the traditional time-consuming, ongoing activities of cooking, cleaning, washing, and maintaining the family life style); (4) drugs (birth control pills, and mood modifiers that "help" us through various ups and downs; and (5) living structures (suburbia, high rises, cooperatives, condominiums, etc.). Think about how much of your present life style depends directly on cars, electricity, telephones, and thousands of inventions that didn't even exist brief decades ago. It's staggering. There are now people who would panic without their microwave ovens! Furthermore, for each of the other major value influences (religion, education, friends, and media), technology expands their potentials and creates expectations for the future.

In addition to technology, other major forces affect value programming. The state of the economy, standards of living, and laws all influence values. Changes in these areas may occur rapidly, as in a case of technology, but the legal and economic areas generally shift slowly over longer periods of time.

More personal factors, such as income, age, nationality, ethnic background, and sex, also affect individual programming. But our basic model focuses on *groups of individuals* born during a given period of time. These groups move through their value programming period to approximately twenty years old, lock in, and continue on through the rest of their lives using those basic values as filters. For each generation, there is a relatively consistent set of major value forces that operate during the group's actual programming period: shared experiences = shared values.

Part III

PUTTING IT TOGETHER: "WHERE WERE YOU WHEN YOU WERE TEN?"

So what does it all mean? How do we put together a very complicated system of theories, models, and studies to create a general model of "value programming analysis"? We can bring the entire structure into focus by looking at *groups of individuals* who acquired their values during the same general period of time—programmed through the same series of common experiences. In so doing, we'll have a new approach to looking at our differences and understanding how we're all "normal."

It really isn't fair to use value programming analysis to observe an individual. We are each unique, slightly different physically and mentally. But because groups of people were influenced in the same general way, programmed through the same activities, events, and experiences, we may look at a group and understand *why* particular clusters within our society react to today's world as they do. Certainly, any given group or generation is going to have variations within that group. If we can determine the *basic core values* held by the majority of the group because of their similarities in programming experiences, then we can gain a better understanding of contemporary American society. We can understand why *real differences* exist in the way people behave and think in the world today.

We're going to take a "snapshot" of present-day Americans. In our examination we'll go back and examine the period when each generation was approximately ten years old—when they locked in on *their* basic gut-level values. For example, if we are observing people who are now in their fifties, that entire generation was ten years old sometime during the 1930s.

CALCULATION OF THE DEPRESSION
GENERATION'S VALUES LOCK-IN

1979 Age	Year Born	*Time of Lock-In (Around 10 Years of Age)*		
59	1920	1928	1930	1932
58	1921	1929	1931	1933
57	1922	1930	1932	1934
56	1923	1931	1933	1935
55	1924	1932	1934	1936
54	1925	1933	1935	1937
53	1926	1934	1936	1938
52	1927	1935	1937	1939
51	1928	1936	1938	1940
50	1929	1937	1939	1941

This focus of "approximately ten years old" seems to be realistic. It is the *middle* of the "approximate" twenty-year value-programming period. Also, a number of studies indicate lock-in of values around this age. Ten years old is not an absolute. It is *around* ten—earlier for some, later for others. But ten years old seems to be an excellent reference point for looking at other people and asking, What was happening *when . . . when* at about ten *they* looked around and began to use their values that had been programmed in from the earlier strong forces of imprinting and modeling? They said in effect, *"This is it. This is the way the world is and should be.* These are the rights, the wrongs, the goods, the bads, the normals, the not normals." Perhaps 90 percent of each generation's gut-level value reactions "freeze" during this period in their development. Beyond this point, adolescent socialization will prompt experiments, changes, modifications, and validations. But the basic value foundation has been created. Using ten years old as a focus point, one may begin to understand the influence of intragenerational motivating factors in analyzing people's behavior.

"Every person is a product of his or her environment" is a familiar truism. A less familiar one is: "People strive to achieve as adults what they feel they were deprived of in their early stages of life." Thus, *what we grow-up without is what is likely to become important to us. What we grow up with, we can accept, reject, not pay any attention to, or take for granted.* It is particularly those things which we were deprived of that may become very important for us in later life. These generalizations suggest a major reason *why values are changing*—namely, that the programming experiences of young people are *fundamentally and qualitatively different* from those of previous generations. They were programmed differently; therefore, *they are different!*

An individual's personality may differ from others significantly, but each individual fits more or less into his own generational cluster. These generational clusters, viewed as a whole, respond in common patterns to life. The way people live, spend their money, use their time, function on their jobs, raise their children, respond to religion, enjoy themselves—*all* aspects of life reflect the basic gut-level systems.

Consider the broad differences between generational groups in our society. Over 70 percent of contemporary Americans were not yet born during the Great Depression of the 1930s. For most Americans, even World War II predates their own personal history. Yet, the severity of these two events had a profound and indelible impact on the lives of the people who experienced them, especially if they were *programmed* by them. The fact that the effects of these events were so pervasive made their impact a *national* experience, as well as a *private* one. There is a marked tendency for people who experienced the Depression and World War II to hold values that emphasize job security, stability, and the acquisition of wealth and material goods (to note only some of the obvious). These were the *things they were deprived of as children*. What have come to be known as traditional values are reflected in many older people and are a logical consequence of the experiences that programmed them. Many people who lived through these experiences are presently "managers" of our organizations and major institutions. Acting on their own value systems often leads them to communication problems with others, especially younger and "different" people.

After World War II, the life style of our nation unfolded in an age of affluence and materialism. During the 1950s the economy nearly doubled, and nearly doubled again in the 1960s. It was not until the mid-1970s that this expansion lost its momentum. Even though a substantial amount of this growth was represented by inflation, there remained a tremendous proliferation of affluence, over-indulgence, and materialism. The critical lifetime experiences for the young being programmed during this period were further influenced by the nuclear age, the civil rights movement, pockets of poverty amidst mass affluence, questionable space exploration (tempered by the drama of reaching the moon), the Vietnam War, ecological concern, pervasive university experiences, campus disorder and protest, continuing inflation, Watergate, and revolution in communication technology. *The 1960s/1970s were an overload!*

By looking at intergenerational influences, we can predict that we will have an even more diverse population in the future than at present. The "future-shock" phenomenon described by Alvin Toffler is creating an even more diverse value orientation within recent young generations as the rate of change accelerates. Quickly we begin to see broad patterns emerge. In general, older Depression-oriented people place greater emphasis on material things, financial security, and economic criteria. In contrast, younger people place greater emphasis on interpersonal relationships, noneconomic criteria, and pleasure *now*.

A SNAPSHOT OF "NOW" AMERICANS

Now let's shift to an analysis of the *current* American age spectrum, looking at each generational cluster in terms of some major value-affecting experiences, using the "approximately ten" programming period. We'll concentrate on those people who are actively participating in society at the present time. These generations are directly involved in the processes that define "where we are" right now.

Focusing on those who are *active* within the total society right now means that we must ignore the "retired" segment of the population. Unfortunately, this is often what happens to retired people in our society. They *are* left out. While it is not a very nice thing to admit, the reality of behavior in the United States is that we live our lives, have our families, hold our jobs, reach our early or mid-sixties, retire, and are then shuffled off to "Sun City." Many retirees just sit around waiting to "check out." The retired age segment is potentially one of our most important national human resource groups. However, within the United States, the tendency is to ignore this group. All too often, it's "convenient" to abandon the elderly to "warehouse" rest homes, curtailing their usefulness and shifting responsibility for them to custodial institutions. This "modern" American practice is a radical departure from the honored participation of elders in families of the past.

However, our attitudes may be shifting with growing "gray power." As the average age of our population rises, there will be more and more retired people. Those who will retire in the 1980s, 1990s, and beyond will *demand* (because of *their values*) more active participation. Programs in continuing education will become more important than ever before. Such programs as GAP (Generations Alliance Program) will grow to provide activities, interactions, and information *between* the generations. By numbers alone, the older segment of our society will demand increased attention in the future. Exactly *what* they will demand is now rooted in their value systems.

THE 1920s:
ROOTS FOR TODAY'S "POWER ELITE"

The *oldest* generation that is of critical importance in our present *functioning* society is composed of people who are now in their sixties. If any group deserves the label "The Establishment," this is the generation that should wear it. These are the people "at the top," the people who make the decisions and control our nation from an economic, political, religious, military, and, to some degree, social perspective. Even with the emphasis on "youth" over the past two decades, the real control still rests with the oldest generation managing our major institutions. Anyone doubting the importance of this generation should check the average age of military leaders, religious leaders, college presidents, presidents and boards of directors of our major corporations, and school administrators—all of those people who are leading their respective institutions. The average age of the people at the top across the United States is very close to sixty. They are the "power elite"—making policy decisions daily that ultimately filter down and affect all of us. In part—often a *large* part—these people base their decisions on values that were programmed into them during *their* processing period—when they were "about ten" back in the 1920s. If we observe this period of history and the major influencing factors that programmed this generation, perhaps we can begin to understand *why* and *how* they relate as they do to today's world and the people in it.

The 1920s unfolded as an *extension* of earlier generations' values (the people who were "older" in the 1920s). Times became more complicated with the development of major technological advances, especially the automobile, radio, and a greatly improved standard of living. Relatively speaking, the 1920s were a pretty good decade. Those were the "good ol' days" that many people continue to idealize and hope will return.

The Flag Waved On

Riding on the aftermath of World War I, it was a *patriotic* period. For *that* war, Johnny was sent marching off to fight, perhaps die, with bands playing at the railroad station. That's a dramatic difference from the late 1960s, when young people lay down in

front of troop trains to protest men being sent to Vietnam. The stark contrast between World War I dedication and the late 1960s, when across our nation hundreds of thousands of people protested against the Vietnam War, was tremendous. What was the difference? It was a different war, we had different knowledge. But the *values* of war and patriotism changed significantly from the early 1920s to the late 1960s. World War I recruiting posters showed an old Uncle Sam intoning "I Want *You*"—and *they* went. Contrast this to the "Hell no, we won't go" rallying cry against Vietnam. During the 1920s people did what they were *told* to do because that's what they were *supposed* to do, because that was *basic operating value* across our nation. People now in their sixties are genuinely patriotic—rightly, normally so. That's the way they were programmed to be, that's the way they have continued to be. Anyone doubting this should check recent Veterans of Foreign Wars conventions where extreme patriotism was dominant. Many will remember when a campaigning Jimmy Carter announced in 1976 that he would "pardon" all deserters, a VFW convention broke into a chorus of boos and catcalls. Their patriotism is real. President Ford experienced the same extreme negative reaction in announcing amnesty to a 1974 VFW convention in Chicago. Those boos and hisses reflected a *real value* of gut-level patriotism.

Mom and Apple Pie

"Generally-held-truths" that influenced the family, the churches, the schools, the government and other institutions during the 1920s were "holdovers" from earlier times. Operating values were expressed in such maxims as:

- Cleanliness is next to godliness.
- Man earns his bread by the sweat of his brow.
- God is in His heaven, all is right with the world.
- Man was born in sin, but can achieve heaven by good works.
- God created the world and all that is in it, and this has continued from the beginning of time.
- Man through his rationality can solve all of his problems; it is only emotion and feeling that get in the way.
- The important thing is to find answers; not to ask questions. We already know the questions.
- Truth has already been established; it is simply a matter of transmitting it to the young.

• We have a mission in the world, and it is to make other people believe and act as we do.

These "truths" were held to be generally self-evident. No one really questioned who held the authority—*parents* did! Old folks knew what was going on, and they indoctrinated the youth. The family was *the* most critical programming influence, and from its foundation people related to all other areas of their lives. As the young looked around, they saw a very close-knit family, the classic nuclear/extended relationships. Perhaps this was best portrayed by a famous Norman Rockwell cover for *The Saturday Evening Post* which showed the whole family gathered at Granny's for Sunday dinner. They had all "putt-putted" over. Look at today! How can today's average American family join Granny for Sunday dinner? Mobility has scattered family members across the country. Part of them live in Florida, part of them on the West Coast, and part have just moved to Chicago. And Granny? She's not even home. Granny's on a three-week jet tour of the Orient! She's *not* available to cook those giant feasts. If she *were* available, she might be confused by microwave ovens and frozen foods; besides, the whole family can't squeeze into her new condo.

The family unit *is* the basic social and economic unit. When its structure shifts, the value structure of the entire society is altered. The family unit of today is radically different from the family unit of the 1920s. In the 1920s, women were first of all mothers and housewives. They raised their children directly and influentially through the early value programming periods. Compare that to current U.S. Department of Labor statistics which indicate that now nearly half of the mothers of young children in this country are employed. Some projections for the mid-1980s foresee perhaps 85 percent of all mothers actively employed. Yet another study, by the American Restaurant Association, indicates that in today's world an average middle-class American family sits down *as a complete family* to share the experience of a meal together on the average of only *three* times per week. For all other meals, some member is somewhere doing something else. All around us we see dramatic changes in the basic interrelationships of this critical programming unit.

In the 1920s, men were essentially breadwinners. They were willing to work long, hard, sometimes boring, routine, even dangerous jobs just *to have* the job, *to get* the money, *to buy* the new goods spewing forth. They had a sense of *commitment* and a sense of *responsibility* to their employers. Employer/employee relationships were based on *vastly different work-force values* than those in today's world. These values were transmitted to the young early on within the family structure.

$ucce$$

What one actually does for work has always been extremely important in the United States. In America, historically, the most important activity has been "making a living." This has been true not only because making a living was valued for its own sake, but also because it was surrounded with a cluster of values that increased work's symbolic significance. People are satisfied when they are rewarded for work (money or the inner satisfaction of achievement), but they can be far more industrious when work *itself* has a high value. Americans increased their standard of living by pursuing what they believed was actually "saintly." Other societies have remained in relative poverty. The fatalism and mysticism of many non-Christian religions *downplays* rather than *encourages* ambition and self-assertion in the world. A nation's religions can be counterproductive to economic growth. In the America of the 1920s, puritan Protestantism continued to encourage men to be productive. Piling up money was a sure way of worshipping God and direct proof of His favor. As Erich Fromm pointed out, this view "supported the feeling of security and tended to give life meaning and a religious sense of fulfillment. This combination of a stable world, stable possessions, and a stable ethic gave the members of the middle class a feeling of belonging, self-confidence, and pride." Today's establishment group continues to cling to this view of the importance of work and its rewards, both *now* on earth and *later* in heaven.

Another major influence shaping this generation was its school system. People believed that democracy could function only on the foundation of an educated citizenry capable of making decisions in the light of "great American traditions." Many had "faith" that education, like an escalator, could lift their children to higher economic and social positions.

According to Richard Huber in *The American Idea of Success*, free education for all became a meal ticket. One of the school's functions was to program the children of foreign-born parents with the basic values of American culture. In many societies, children are programmed to believe that they have a fixed place in that society's social order. In America, the child was taught that his place could be higher than his parents. In fact, this was the parents' expectation. In encouraging children to be a success, school teachers pushed the values of their own middle-class background. The system was designed to trigger competition. A system of marks, prizes, and degrees from the first grade through high school tracked how a student stacked up against his schoolmates. Competitive grading in academics, athletics, social, and extracurricular activities was designed to teach a student that if he were willing to fight it out in a world where vigorous competition was okay, he would be rewarded. After graduation, rewards were measured by money. The basis for worship of the dollar was well established and prevalent. An overriding value programmed throughout the system was that success could be written $ucce$$.

As the nation struggled for normalcy in the 1920s, there were still many unsettling elements. The "promised" world of peace and democracy (World War I had been "the war to end all wars," "the war to make the world safe for democracy") still had not arrived. After all the death and sacrifices of the war, many people felt that their efforts had not really been worth it. A lot of "absolute certainties" from earlier times were also under attack. Such disturbing notions as the sexual theories of Sigmund Freud and the barely comprehensible discoveries of Albert Einstein began to fuel the growing uncertainties.

With some of its old values going sour, the nation became self-conscious and unsure. Americans were torn between the innocence and security of the past and the wisdom and poise demanded by a maturing world power. Many Americans reacted to the 1920s by adopting a kind of romantic cynicism. As a spokesman for the youth, F. Scott Fitzgerald noted that they professed "to find all Gods dead, all wars fought, all faiths in man shaken." Others simply refused to worry about anything but their own pleasure. Almost everybody agreed that the world was going to hell in a handbasket and they might as well ignore it. Americans turned inward.

Twenty-Three Skidoo and Racoon Coats Too

Instead of solving problems, Americans in the 1920s searched for excitement. What you do for kicks (what turns you on) is a very critical part of a society's value programming inputs. In the 1920s, almost anything—no matter how trivial or preposterous—gave thrills to the public: gory murders in the tabloids, a world championship boxing match, a royal visit from Britain's young Prince of Wales—all such events swept excitement across the nation. The world crowned a new international *hero* when Charles Lindbergh soloed the *Spirit of St. Louis* nonstop from New York to Paris in 1927.

America pulled out the stops. As he rode up Broadway, jubilant crowds showered the returning hero with eighteen hundred tons of shredded paper.

A spirit of frivolity and fun was sweeping puritanical America. Women began bobbing their hair and raising the hems of their dresses to the knees. "Respectable" citizens danced the Charleston, carried hip flasks, and visited speakeasies. The flappers of the 1920s were forerunners of the hippies of our recent times. They were the youth of that period. They were rebelling against the "establishment" of that time and the values of the adults who told them "don't rock the boat," "don't throw out the baby with the bath water" (whatever *that* meant). The basic approach of the older generations was *"no change!"* But the flappers themselves said, "No, we're going to change the world and live life differently." Change it they did, but the world has changed on them a thousand times since that point in history, and sadly, millions of today's older generations simply don't understand what's happened. The flappers of the 1920s were treated virtually the same by adults and the media as so-called hippies were treated in the late 1960s in the United States.

What *did* they do for kicks in the 1920s? What turned them on, got them excited? Compared to today's world, it was a relatively simple time. In a Model T they drove "40 miles-an-hour" down a dusty country road drinking bathtub gin. Do you think *that's* going to turn on a kid today? You've got to be kidding!

Look at today's kids. They are value programmed with their *own* tricycle, bicycle, motorcycle, access to a car by the time they are in high school. "Forty miles-an-hour" *physical speed* is simply not going to turn them on. They've been looking for something stronger, something "kickier." Recently in the United States drugs and alcohol have been very *real*, very *alarming* answers. The *relative simplicity* of kicks and excitement of just a few decades ago has given way to a strobe-lighted, eardrum-shattering, overexposed, drug-numbed, frantic search for fulfillment. By the millions, today's youth ignore drug laws and drinking restrictions (just as millions of their elders also ignored Prohibition).

Prohibition became law in 1920 and turned the simple pleasure of sipping whiskey into a federal offense. Violation of this federal law became a daily routine for millions. While some escaped in bathtub gin, others flocked to the movies. As a new film world emerged, fantasy and flamboyance galloped unchecked, settings became more extravagant, costumes more exotic, sex more direct. By the time Hollywood had supplemented sex with the additional impact of sound, movies had become a way of life for most of America. A major new source of values emerged because of technology. The first "talkie" in 1927, *The Jazz Singer*, starred Al Jolson in "blackface" (reinforcing a stereotype from the past). By the end of the 1920s, the talkies were pulling in ninety million viewers every week.

Perhaps the relative hedonism of this decade, with its widespread disrespect for the law, planted seeds in the young who were being programmed of "Don't not do it, just don't get caught if you do it." The youth of the 1920s are some of the corporate presidents of today, who may be reflecting this programming through corporate payoffs and other acts of social irresponsibility. Many present-day government officials (at *all* levels) also were programmed during this period. In 1978 a convicted felon was reelected to the U.S. Congress.

Complementing the pleasures and frivolities of the 1920s was the most spectacular economic boom the country had ever experienced. Although some felt disillusionment with politics or religion, they found new support in a faith based on the omnipotence of the American dollar. The cult of materialism grew like a new religion. Americans began to "worship" automobiles, washing machines, refrigerators, whatever defined the emerging "good life." If not everyone was in fact rich, many people did believe that the chances for getting rich were getting better every day. The foundation was being laid for "My kid's going to have it better than I had it"—which would explode in the late 1940s and early 1950s. Beneath the push for pleasure in the 1920s, serious problems lurked. Life and its problems did not go away just because people refused to pay attention. The prosperity and excitement of the good life that began to touch millions of Americans left millions of others in the cold. Many people, especially in rural areas, never drank bathtub gin, played mah-jongg, heard of Freud, knew a jazz baby or a flapper. They read their Bible faithfully and believed every word the gospel dictated. In America's rural areas, life went on as usual, as it had through the past decades.

Warning: Troubled Road Ahead

Serious matters continued to intrude on the fun of the 1920s. Even among the most frivolous, there was an air of desperation. "What most distinguishes the generation who have approached maturity since the debacle of idealism at the end of the War," said Walter Lippmann, "is not their rebellion against the religion and the moral code of their parents, but their disillusionment with their own rebellion. It is common for young men and women to rebel, but that they should rebel sadly and without faith in their rebellion, that they should distrust the new freedom no less than the old certainties—that is something of a novelty."

Behind the bright flashes of the 1920s, its carnival of public events, the glitter of its life style, and its dedication to enjoyment lay a foreboding sense of futility. The theme of the 1920s was "Eat, drink, and be merry," but they also added "for tomorrow we may die." Death came not for real, but economically. The event that brought the 1920s to a shattering close occurred on October 24, 1929. The stock market, faltering for weeks, suddenly plunged. October 29th—Black Tuesday: the beginning of the end reared its ugly head. *The Great Depression had begun.* The value programming of those now in their fifties, who processed through the 1930s, was dramatically different from what any preceding generation had experienced.

The 1920s had been a relatively good time—a buoyant time, an improving time, a time when the nation began to taste the possibilities of the "good life." For various reasons, however, that time came to an end. The decade's relative absolutes—rights/wrongs, goods/bads, normals/not normals, this is the way things should be, this is the way life should be lived—all began to collapse. Those who were programmed during the 1920s (now in their sixties) and those who were programmed with the events of the 1930s (now in their fifties) carry values created by the Great Depression.

THE 1930s:
"BROTHER, CAN YOU SPARE A DIME?"

The collapse of the U.S. stock market sent economic shock waves around the world. Those now in their sixties were just getting ready to become part of the adult world, when suddenly, CRASH— everything collapsed economically. The Great Depression must have been an absolutely fascinating event. It must have been traumatic, because people now in their fifties and sixties haven't stopped *talking about it!* When these people talk to anyone who didn't *experience* the Great Depression, they speak in *zero valueless terms. Without the experience, there is no meaning.* People who didn't live it simply can't relate to it.

Oldsters say such things as: "I used to walk to school five miles through the snow." Younger generations think, "How dumb!" They won't even *drive* five blocks if it's a bad storm. But those people *DID* walk because there was *no other way* to get there.

Wear old clothes! Do without? Cardboard in shoes? You've got to be kidding! Today's young people have always had the niftiest, color-coordinated, perma-pressed outfits they wanted to wear—*if* they wanted to wear them. Those in the 1930s wore old clothes because there was *no other choice.*

Miss a meal? Go to bed hungry? Absurd! About the only reason today's college-age people miss a meal is if they *pass out!* But, if they pass out, that's *their choice;* they decide to do it. In the 1930s people missed meals because literally there was no food to eat!

For those who *lived* it, *felt* it, were *value programmed* by it, the Great Depression created a whole series of *indelible* value orientations, and they're *still* operating. Listen to older generations as they say, "You better put away a little for a rainy day." "It could happen again you know." "We're really not sure about the future." Younger generations? Younger generations believe at a gut level: "If it feels good, do it!" "Live!" "Enjoy!" "Get it now!" "To hell with the future!"

Generations now in their fifties and sixties are massively security-oriented in an *economic* sense. Remember: *What we grow up without can become vitally critical for us. What we grow up with, we can accept, reject, take for granted, or ignore.* The generations programmed in the 1930s grew up *without* economic security. Whatever their station in life, whatever their status level in the social system, the Great Depression *did* have an impact on everyone. For these older generations, money *is* motivation. It turns them on—it always has, it always will. For younger generations, they'll take money, expect money, demand money. But does money *alone* really motivate today's young workers? Right now, thousands of managers and supervisors across the United States swear that in today's work world, money alone is *not* a good basic motivator for younger employees. But then, the young have been value programmed *differently.*

Sinking Lower and Lower

In 1930, before the full effect of the Depression was felt, most Americans knew poverty only by reputation. During the next few years, a large percentage of the richest nation on earth learned what it *meant* to be poor—for forty million people, poverty became an unavoidable way of life. Misery swept through every geographic region, social class, and occupation. Black workers, historically the last to be hired if at all, became the first to be fired as the economy slowed to a crawl. Farmers, struggling to survive plummeting crop prices, were battered by a series of natural disasters—floods, droughts, insect plagues, and horrifying dust storms that choked the earth. Former home owners became room renters, and thousands wandered

the streets seeking work. Experience was programming many children as they moved their dolls in a game they called "Eviction."

Herbert Hoover seemed honestly to try, but the Depression proved too much for him and his advisors. The nation plunged deeper into economic chaos. In a little over three years after the stock market crash, the United States and most of the world was in the worst economic crisis in anyone's memory. Industrial output dropped to less than one-half of the 1929 figures. The number of unemployed ranged between thirteen and fifteen million—25 percent of the work force. Those unemployed had thirty million mouths to feed besides their own. Blue-collar wages dropped 60 percent from 1929, and white-collar salaries were down 40 percent. Farmers got five cents a pound for cotton and less than fifty cents a bushel for wheat.

But cold statistics give no real picture of the Depression's human impact. The real story was etched in lines on the faces of the pitiful men who sold pencils on city street corners, the long lines of depressed and silent individuals waiting for dry bread or thin soup, those who foraged in garbage for food, the bloated bellies of starving children, and distraught farmers blocking roads to dump cans of milk in desperate efforts to force prices up. Millions felt that the man (Hoover) in the White House was more interested in the bank accounts of the rich than in the hunger of the poor.

So bitter was the nation against Hoover that his name became an adjective for many of the signs of the times. Hoover "blankets" were old newspapers used for warmth, Hoover "flags" were empty pocket linings turned inside out, Hoover "hogs" were the rabbits that farmers caught for food, and Hoover "wagons" were broken-down cars now powered by mules. All over the country "Hoovervilles" sprang up—filthy shantytowns where the homeless found shelter in sheds made of cardboard and scrap metal. Such conditions are virtually incomprehensible for anyone who didn't experience them.

The New Deal

Franklin Delano Roosevelt emerged as a real messiah with a shrewd combination of politics and instinct for the common man. The new administration left its mark on the nation as it brought it out of bad times. In only one hundred days, the new administration with Roosevelt's charismatic leadership jolted the nation from its apathy and into effective action. The road to recovery was long, but the first steps were finally taken.

The situation in mid-Depression America was summed up by

President Rooesevelt in his second inaugural address in 1937: "I see one-third of the nation ill-housed, ill-clad, ill-nourished." But for the nation's other two-thirds, hard times were not quite so disastrous. Those who were luckier were able to go about the business of living just about as always. Although the Depression acted as a direct physical and economic sledgehammer on millions of lives, millions of others were only psychologically affected. Thus, the Great Depression influenced everyone's values subjectively, even if they were fortunate enough to escape physical deprivation.

In thousands of small towns all over America, the Depression really didn't drastically alter the deep-grained life styles. Even in the toughest years, main-street America kept its traditional optimism: "What Depression?" asked some businessmen. "We haven't had a Depression here." There was a brief reverse migration as Americans, for the first time in decades, moved *out* of the cities and *back* to the small towns from which they originally came. The *root values* and life styles of rural America beckoned with remembrances of stability and strength.

During the 1930s the world of children welcomed a new set of heroes and heroines whose extravagant and extreme lives unfolded in new types of media. Kids pawed through funny papers for the latest adventures of Flash Gordon or Little Orphan Annie. Annie's faith in "good old capitalism" comforted many Depression-ridden parents. From radios, comics, and movies, new heroes and heroines streamed forth for the young. The kingdoms of these new heroes were as varied as the media that brought them to the kids. Heroes ranged across America's playing fields, crept through steamy Oriental jungles, rode the Old West, battled in the slums of gangster-ridden cities, visited Buckingham Palace, and traveled in times long ago and galaxies far away. The idols themselves were just as diverse. Some were real—Joe Lewis; some wholly fabricated—Buck Rogers; while others were physically real but fictitious in their exploits—Gene Autry and Shirley Temple.

The common ground for these heroes was the *traditional value* of virtue. These heroes proved repeatedly that "good clean living" led to unlimited rewards. A major contribution by media heroes during the 1930s was an inexpensive and wonderful world of make-believe. During the hard times when the real world was no fun at all, fantasy worlds led young minds down "yellow-brick roads." Since these worlds and roads were "built" by 1930s adults, their foundations were *traditional values.*

In the late 1930s, big bands broke loose with a new sound of "swing." Actually, swing was basically jazz under a new name, but it simply hadn't been discovered by the masses. Soon all of America was swept by "swing fever." Teens plugged nickles into jukeboxes and set ice cream parlors rocking with complicated jitterbug steps. Radio audiences tuned to favorite bands on weekly programs. Millions followed the changes in "Your Hit Parade" to learn the "top ten hits of the week." This musical revolution was greeted with hostility by some, and the *New York Times* wondered whether the craze was getting out of hand. The newspaper quoted a psychologist on the "dangerously hypnotic influence of swing, cunningly devised to a faster tempo than seventy-two bars to the minute—faster than the human pulse." Those who were being programmed in the 1930s would be the parents of the 1950s, when Elvis Presley "shocked" them in a rock-and-roll explosion.

As the 1930s drew to an end, so did the wrapup of the value programming for those now in their fifties. Massive changes had been wrought in the structure of the American system. The business community was climbing back. New products developed during the late 1920s which had never become really popular suddenly began to move into the marketplace. Every aspect of the system had been affected: family, media, religion, education—none of them would ever be the same because of the results of the Depression. But with a better life on the horizon, most Americans would have to wait for new inventions and life styles for yet another decade. Why? The decade that had opened with the reverberations of a financial crash closed with the distant rumble of war. By 1939, German tanks rolled into Poland. England and France were at war with Germany, and before the decade was out, the United States was beginning to gear up for its own defense. Americans ended the decade by reassessing old habits and values that had helped to lead them to the brink of economic disaster.

THE 1940s:
A COMMITTED NATION

By the late 1930s things were looking up. The Depression was fading as America climbed out of its economic depths. We moved into the 1940s, when the value programming of those now in their forties took place. Little did the nation realize what was in store. On January 1, 1940, Germany controlled central Europe and Japan was wreaking havoc in China. But most Americans concentrated on their own internal affairs. They lined up to see the film version of *Gone*

With The Wind. Teens danced to jukebox music. Coming up was the nation's four-year "circus," the presidential conventions, where the biggest question would be whether *that man* in the White House would shatter yet another tradition and run for a third term.

Of course, everyone knew there was trouble overseas, but most U.S. citizens comforted themselves with the knowledge that "two broad oceans" separated them from "foreigners." Japan couldn't be a real threat, since they wanted China, and China was on the "other side" of the globe. The European war was deadlocked, leading one U.S. senator (a devout isolationist) to refer to the "phony" war. A Roper poll in December 1939 showed that 67.4 percent of the American people were opposed to taking sides.

But the foreign conflicts did not go away; they occupied more and more media space as spring blossomed. Even though the conflicts were heating up by the summer of 1940, some seven hundred citizens' committees sprang up to debate the wisdom of what seemed to be a drift toward war. Many felt FDR was leading the drift. Although the "America Firsters" rallied against the draft, it passed. By mid-August, a Gallup poll indicated 71 percent of the nation was behind the controversial draft bill. Once the presidential election "crowned" FDR for a third term, the president moved boldly, especially with the Lend Lease Act proposals to help our Allies.

As many an "America Firster" had feared, lend-lease resulted in a major step toward a much greater American commitment, but not in a way that anyone was able to guess. The growing military power of the United States and our strengthening bonds with Europe loomed as a threat to one aggressor that America was not watching carefully. On the morning of December 7, 1941, all hopes for peace exploded at Pearl Harbor. So did the last remains of isolationism. "The only thing to do now," said a senator as he joined with the rest of Congress to declare war on Tokyo, Berlin, and Rome, "is to lick the hell out of them."

Getting Involved

As a nation we were angry, irritated! We *thought* that World War I had been "the war to end all wars," "the war to make the world safe for democracy." Suddenly, here we were at war again! As a nation, as a *whole,* we said, "If we're going to be at war, by damn, we're *really* going to be at war." The nation galvanized for the war effort. *If you lived it, you can remember it—when Lucky Strike Green went to war!*

No other event in the twentieth century has matched Pearl

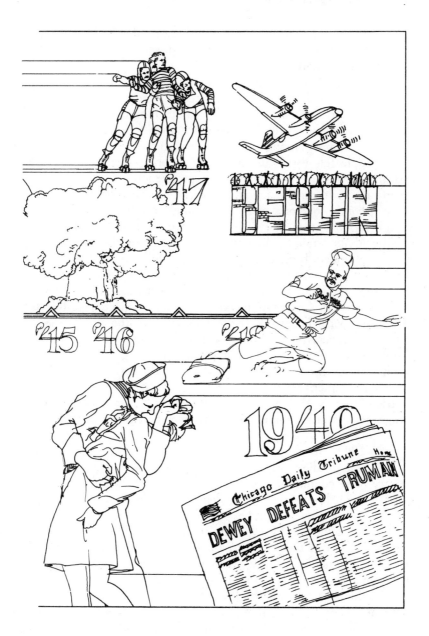

73

Harbor in uniting American citizens. On December 8, 1941, Congress voted 470 to 1 to declare war (the one dissenter, a pacifist, did not *believe* Hawaii had been bombed).

Go back. Look at the newspapers, the magazines. Listen to radio tapes. Watch the movie newsreels. America plunged into its commitment to the war. Across the nation *everyone* knew what the fighting was about. Hitler became a synonym for "mindless tyranny" and "Jap" became, among teen-agers, a verb meaning "to betray." Yet many people felt very frustrated: the shooting was really far away, and there were only so many war production jobs to go around. Trying to get in on the action, American citizens bought $49 billion in war bonds. Victory gardens sprouted across the nation, even though farmers were already producing enough to feed half of the world and its armies. Thousands of miles from the real bombing, citizen volunteers formed an enormous Civil Defense Corps. While the world's greatest industrial complex was fueled by a vast reservoir of natural resources, children across the nation saved their empty toothpaste tubes for scrap metal drives and collected tinfoil from candy wrappers. Today's kids don't even know that candy *came* in tinfoil, much less that it could be saved to help with a war! Such efforts made Americans feel they were "in the game" and actually helped shorten the conflict. To supplement the raw materials needed for defense, Americans went on the biggest scavenger hunt in history. "Patriots" across the nation combed their attics, basements, and garages for discarded materials——any item that could be turned into weapons.

By 1943 "Sunday farmers" in 20.5 million plots were producing at least one-third of all of the fresh vegetables consumed in the country. The commitment of the nation's scrap scavengers was even more overwhelming. Piles of debris sometimes accumulated for months before they could be put to use. Boy Scouts collected so much wastepaper that by 1942 the country's paper mills were glutted and the drive was temporarily halted. Eventually, the mess of scrap was cleared, and by 1945 it was supplying much of the steel, half of the tin and half of the paper that was needed to win.

Compared to the apathy toward Korea and the divisiveness over Vietnam, there was an intense and total *commitment to win*—to win and win alone. That was virtually the *only* issue, the *only* value. No other questions were seriously raised, and with the intensity of that commitment everything began to shift in value programming. Amazingly, only in the past few years has anyone bothered to go back, observe, and analyze the massive impact on value programming of this nation's commitment to *win World War II*. Some of the most significant changes occurred in America's work force.

Rosie the Riveter

A vital part of America's wartime strength became "woman power." In the first five months after Pearl Harbor 750,000 women volunteered for duty at armament plants. Not surprisingly, traditional managers were leery of using female workers. Only 80,000 of the early volunteers got prompt assignments. But by 1944, nearly 3.5 million women stood side by side with 6 million men on America's war assembly lines. They turned out entire cargo ships in seventeen days and reduced the time needed to build a bomber from 200,000 work hours to 13,000. "Rosie the Riveter" became a national heroine! Our work force would never be the same again.

Every major war creates social changes. The very dimensions of World War II were bound to change America greatly. However, very few realized what was happening at the time. Millions seemed to honestly believe that GIs were fighting "to get back to ball games and full tanks of gas." GIs themselves seemed to think that they were battling for "Mom and apple pie." But history does not let those who create it get off so easily. No country could have survived America's gut-wrenching changes from 1941 to 1945 without changing, not only itself, but its view of itself and its values. The homefront was in reality a battleground of customs, ideas, economic theories, foreign policies, and relationships between the sexes and the social classes.

Everything was changing, and at the heart of the change was the American family. As the men went away to fight and women began to work, the family structure changed. From the beginning of the historical American "experiment" in the late 1700s, the family had been a close, cohesive unit. Suddenly, given the demands created by the massive war efforts, the family was torn apart.

Kindergartens "Replace" Mama

With the family disrupted, kindergartens mushroomed and took over the raising *and* the value programming of the young at earlier and earlier ages. With mothers needed in the defense plants, the federal government moved to provide funds to establish day-care centers for children. The government's initial efforts in direct subsidy of early childhood education appeared in the late 1930s in WPA programs. But, it was the programs connected with the war effort that really began to affect children. Even though the end of the war brought the withdrawal of federal dollars, the establishment of these programs and the number of young people enrolled created a value— an expectation that would resurface as these children became parents in the 1960s.

Although our nation's legislators had no great concern for the children's welfare, they established these programs for political and economic reasons. When the war ended, congressmen undoubtedly believed that women should return to their homes and the primary task of child-rearing. However, a major shift had taken place. The very existence of the programs influenced the children who went through them and established a precedent for shifting the programming sequence of young people.

A New Breed: Teen-agers

During the 1940s, young people emerged with a brand new and far more respectable label, they were now "teen-agers." Adolescence had evolved into a cult. It was a period to be prolonged and enjoyed and was commercially catered to as never before. No one really knows why or how this change took place. Clearly, the war played a major role. With everyone over eighteen years old in the service, younger boys were often the "biggest men" in town. For the first time since the Depression, they frequently had money in their pockets, picking up a lot of the jobs available in the scarce labor market. Girls, too, earned money in a new "profession"—babysitting for parents on night shifts at war plants.

By the late 1940s, the teen-age movement was a full-blown revolution. During its early stages, the kids themselves remained responsive to traditional parental guidance. They also became almost compulsively conformist within their own age group. The war effort whirled around them, but they seemed massively unconcerned with world problems. A survey carried out by Purdue University to define the major concerns of teen-agers in the 1940s found that 33 percent believed there was nothing they personally could or should do to prevent war. Of all girls, 50 percent recorded their own figures as *their* number one problem, while 37 percent of all boys were primarily concerned with having a good build. One-third of the two thousand questioned agreed that the most serious problem facing the American teen-ager was acne.

The Front: At Home and Away

Between the two fronts—home and battle—the contrasts were enormous. Aside from sending men off to fight and producing large quantities of materials, the home front war effort was mainly frustrating: watching for enemy planes that never came; rationing meat, sugar, and gas; and trying to make do with a scarcity of tires and nylons.

Realistically, the war actually benefited the nation in economic terms. In 1943, the U.S. living standard was one-sixth higher than in 1939. A bombardier home on furlough in 1944 said, "Their way of life hasn't really changed a damn bit. One day I was riding on a subway and I heard one bastard say to another one, 'If this war lasts for two more years I'll be on easy street!' "

Business prospered, especially big business, which grew larger as it created the giant industrial-military complex. At the height of the effort, $8 billion a month was being spent to "preserve liberty." This further changed the basic programming unit of the family. Families packed up their possessions and left the South and the East to work in the new factories of the North and the West. There was an immense migration. Not only was there mobility on the home front, but as men were catapulted halfway around the world in either direction, Significant Emotional Events affected the lives of those who otherwise might never have changed. They may have seen Paris under war conditions, but once they *saw* Paris, Peoria didn't look *nearly* as good as it had before. They saw *new* ways to do things —new ways to live, to love, to eat—new ways to experience life. *Mobility/change* was programmed in and continues today.

The Media Pitch In

On entertainment stages, popular songs reflected the need for music that would remind the public of its patriotism and the emotionalism of parting lovers. Songs such as "I'll Be Seeing You," "The Last Time I Saw Paris," "When You Wish upon a Star," "The White Cliffs of Dover," and "Praise the Lord and Pass the Ammunition" still evoke sentiment in those who "lived" World War II. The motion picture industry boomed, although nearly a quarter of its personnel were involved in the war effort. The big box office draws were the

escapist comedies of Bob Hope and the musicals of pinup favorite
Betty Grable and "Brazilian Bombshell" Carmen Miranda. Hollywood pitched in with movie scripts directed to the war effort. Such
titles as *Above Suspicion, Keep Your Powder Dry, Five Graves to
Cairo, The Purple Heart,* and *Air Force* fanned the public's emotionalism.

Even the comics got into the patriotic act. When American
men went to war, so did American funny-paper characters. Smiling
Jack joined the Army/Air Force. Terry fought Japs instead of pirates.
While Daddy Warbucks served as a General, his adopted waif Little
Orphan Annie urged real kids to collect scrap metal. Although Super-
man failed his eye test because of his X-ray vision and had to be
content with pushing victory bonds and the Red Cross, there *were*
real flesh-and-blood heroes.

The most honored war hero of all had risen from hard times
as an orphan boy of sharecroppers to become the most decorated
military figure of the war. Audie Murphy's return to Farmersville,
Texas, on June 15, 1945, was a symbolic end to the war's blinding
flash conclusion—August 6 and August 9 of that year. We had
done what we had set out to do. We built a war machine so effective,
so powerful, that on those days of horror, Hiroshima and Nagasaki
virtually disappeared. With the press of a button, 160,000 human
beings died in those two flashes. But the war was *over*. America
rejoiced. However, all future generations would program in the
shadow of "the mushroom cloud." Their expectations for the "future"
were altered dramatically and irrevocably. From then on, everyone
"knew" the world *could* end in a moment. The seeds of a new
hedonism were sown—why bother about "tomorrow" when a turned
key or a pushed button could end it all?

Then came 1946—
1947—
1948—
1949—
America was moving toward "normalcy"—*many changes had
taken place.*

Hints of New Horizons

A major new hero for young people emerged in 1947 in
Tennessee Williams' prize-winning play, *A Streetcar Named Desire.*
The angry young man was Marlon Brando. He wasn't the typical
hero of the past, for he appeared as Stanley Kolwolski in torn T-shirt

and faded worker's trousers, standing at the doorstep of a fading South. Something about Brando told America that youth was about to change—that there was an animalism beneath the happy veneer. Another voice of the times, Norman Mailer in *The Naked and the Dead*, led critics to predict that we would hear from this caustic, realistic voice in the future. But America ignored the storm warnings and preferred at this point that homespun folksiness of Dale Carnegie's *How To Stop Worrying and Start Living* and/or the religiousness of Lloyd C. Douglas' *The Big Fisherman*.

Sports were also changing and gave a hint of the social unrest to come. America was startled in 1947 when Jackie Robinson, a young black rookie from the Brooklyn Dodgers, was named Player of the Year. The Dodger president was ecstatic. He had masterminded what was to be called "the noble experiment" by bringing a black into major-league baseball. The gamble paid off. Robinson said in an interview in 1948, "At the beginning of the World Series of 1947, I experienced a completely new emotion when the National Anthem was played. This time, I thought, it is being played for me as much as for anyone else. This is organized league baseball; and I am standing here with all the others; and everything that takes place includes me." Other super-successful black personalities were emerging. Across the country record players spun out lyrics from the husky-voiced Nat King Cole.

Barriers were crashing all around, but Americans were enjoying themselves too much to notice. Some people now look back on this time as a "lullaby period"—causes weren't championed, people weren't protesting. Much more preferable was the national craze of canasta. When the new game appeared, thousands of eager beginning players bought the manual *How to Win at Canasta*.

When Actress Jane Russell "blossomed" across the silver screen, women rushed to look for extra padding, while Esther Williams' technicolor splashes in the pool sent people diving with new zest. Saturday matinees at the movies were westerns. Familiar heroes rode in and out of the sunsets: Roy Rogers, Dale Evans, Gabby Hayes, and Gene Autry. America began to enjoy itself. *It was a time for material things and pleasure-seeking.* Five million autos yearly were being produced by the end of 1948 as America went on a driving binge. Homes absorbed 6.2 million new refrigerators, 14.6 million modern radios, and by 1950, a staggering 7.4 million television sets. Having won "the big one," America's giant industrial complex, which was created to win the *war, shifted to the consumers.* The "good life" loomed.

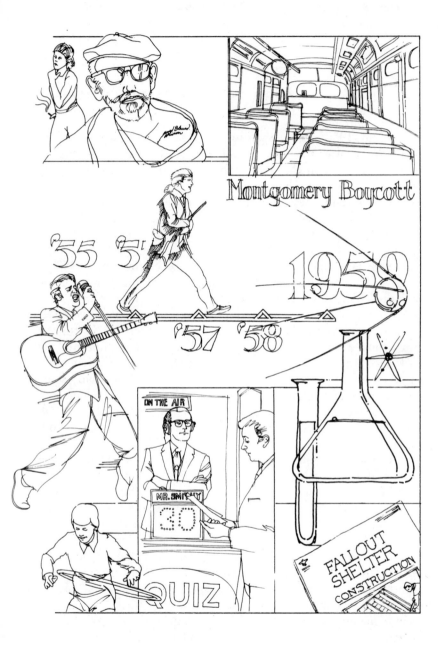

THE 1950s:
THE GOOD LIFE ARRIVES . . . WITH DILEMMAS

From 1950 on, *everything changed.* Those who were value programmed after this time would have substantially different values than any generation that had been programmed previously. As never before, the rate of change accelerated in knowledge, technology, experiences, and the economy. As the decade opened, there was minor disruption with the Korean War. That "conflict," as many preferred to call it, coupled with the fear of atomic warfare from an increasingly powerful Soviet Union, hung over the nation. But essentially, the "conflict" was ignored. In the early 1950s, you could walk into a downtown metropolitan area and hardly be aware that this country was at war. In contrast, had you gone into such an area during the 1940s or during World War I, you would have known *immediately* that this nation was at war. But in the 1950s Americans wanted to *live,* to *enjoy.* They were significantly aided with the "wave" of affluence that swept the nation. Evidence of the surge toward abundance was everywhere. It came from many sources: natural resources, global politics after World War II, demography, the altered economy of Western Europe, Americans' love of work, and the tremendous economic system that had expanded "to win the war."

Consequently, Americans now enjoyed a standard of living beyond the comprehension of the rest of the world. Everyone was so busy *enjoying, living,* and *consuming* the emerging "good life," that only in retrospect can we begin to appreciate the magnitude of the changes. William Manchester's *The Glory and the Dream* provides a brilliant, insightful interpretation in a narrative history of the United States from 1932 to 1972. His work should be required reading for every American. Through his delightful coverage, the adults who "lived it" can relive it, and the young who "missed it" can begin to appreciate, even "experience it" themselves. The following material draws heavily from Manchester's superb coverage, especially chapter 23, "The Pursuit of Happiness."

By the early 1950s, nearly 60 percent of all American families were moving into the middle-class income brackets. Even with growing inflation, there had been a rise in income of 48 percent since the late 1940s. Adults who had survived the Depression and World War II no sooner comprehended their new prosperity than it became obsolete in light of further advances. Economic prosperity and security had been the "impossible dream" of their youth (the 1920s, 1930s, and 1940s). They were timid and defensive. If they could get one hundred dollars together, they stashed it away. But thrift was becoming old-fashioned. Americans who had become adults since World War II had no memory of the lean years. They were spending every cent they could lay their hands on, together with other income they would not earn for a long time. They were living on credit and buying on margins for the future like the speculators before the 1929 crash. The main difference was that they were acquiring consumer goods, not stocks and bonds.

Life for the young became life on the installment plan. Americans hocked themselves to the future and openly enjoyed it. Young couples seemed indifferent to the real rates of interest. Installment buyers asked not the size of the total bill but the size of their monthly payments. Some actually seemed to find security in the entrapment of bank loans and the obligations of coupon books with specified payments. Banks, of course, were delighted to oblige them. Their parents were horrified, but the young were beginning to "live." Over and over during this period, couples in their forties were heard to say of those in their twenties, "When we were that age we wouldn't have dreamed of going into debt." But with the "protection" of hospital insurance and expanded social security, there were fewer reasons to build a nest egg. Besides, the world could blow up any minute, so why not enjoy things *now*?

The old economic values were collapsing. Spending was not only more fun, it also seemed sensible to buy before prices went up. It could even be argued that spending was patriotic: it kept the production lines going. Even if you didn't need what you bought, you were fueling the economic boom. The entire process became known as "the good life." The good life arrived, but the ultimate question became: "What do you do with it after you've got it?" *We still haven't answered that basic question.*

By the early 1950s, the good life focused on the gratification of all of one's desires. Many new American values were defined in specific terms: the split-level home, two cars in the two-car garage, a boat, a place at the beach, more new possessions as old ones wore out or became unfashionable (which was often engineered by the now psychologically-oriented advertising industry), college educations for the children. All of these led to the good life. Everyone was included because everyone needed to be. Mass production assumed mass consumption. Those with lower economic status could not move to the suburbs (which really became the "ultimate" place for the good life).

They participated by buying other products, particularly those pushed by television commercials—beers, toothpastes, pain-killers, hair rinses, frozen foods, laxatives, detergents, records, razor blades, after-shave lotions, cigarettes, and new cars. All purchases fueled the continuing boom.

It was in the early 1950s when the General Electric Corporation announced a "radically" new management philosophy. It was called "The Marketing Concept," and in general said that from now on if a company was to survive it must focus *first* upon the *needs* of their consumers, then provide products that would satisfy these needs. Thus, a company could ensure itself continuing profits. This attitude in American business, developed *first* in the early 1950s, was in direct contrast to the attitude expressed by Henry Ford when he said *and meant* in the 1920s, "You can have any color car you want as long as it's black." This haughty attitude of American industrialists was now being challenged by the newly affluent consumers. The problem was now consumption, not production.

The Grass Was Greener . . . In the Suburbs

An understanding of the social revolts that later rocked the nation in the 1960s is impossible without some grasp of the 1950s life style, which arose from the good life. Nowhere was the mood of the times more evident than in the new suburbs that were ringing America's cities. They were not representative of all of America, but they did represent the direction in which we were heading. It was to suburbia where the climbing executives fled after work. Their wives developed what would be called the "feminine mystique," and *future* hippies and straights mingled at school and on playgrounds.

The mobility surge of the 1940s continued at a somewhat lesser pace. Throughout the 1950s more than one million farmers were leaving their farms each year. At the same time, inner cities, once so dynamic, were being abandoned to become ghettos of the poor and fortresses of the rich. The middle class fled to the suburbs. The standard that became accepted as the "norm to achieve" was that of the suburban life. This was generally true across the entire country in the 1950s.

In the suburbs, one of the most obvious new values was the tremendous emphasis on social skills. In contrast, rural and small American towns had been strongholds of what David Riesman in *The Lonely Crowd* called "inner-directed" people. The *source* of their values and direction in life (he compared it to a gyroscope) was programmed early by their parents and never wavered afterwards. The classic example of such "inner directedness" is the Englishman who dresses for dinner in the jungle—maintaining his "programmed" behavior on the "proper and right" way to have dinner. In the suburbs, an entirely different approach was developing: these new "*other*-directed Americans" had an insatiable *need to be liked*. Riesman compared their behavior to radar picking up impulses. Their response was an "adjustment" to what the *group* expected. The ultimate goal was to be "well adjusted." Although Americans had always related to one another, this new concern became epidemic. There was tremendous stress on an individual's behavior being acceptable to the "team," thus inhibiting the individual. Future generations (the 1960s and 1970s) would react violently to such pressures for conformity. The "team" value had been created in winning the wars, getting out of the Depression, and creating our giant economic complexes. Now, the same "team" orientation, which had been so productive in the past, seemed to be creating a new breed of "yes" men who had lost a sense of inner direction.

William Whyte in his classic, *The Organization Man*, dissected the new work environment. The new worker was best symbolized as a "part" of a corporate structure. In the mid-1950s, the country passed a milestone, as important in its own way as the closing of the great frontiers in the late 1800s. In 1956, the number of blue-collar workers (people *producing* things) was surpassed by that of white-collar workers (people in "service" occupations, frequently government bureaucracies). Increasingly, the typical "worker" was a "pencil pusher" working for a large impersonal organization.

Mobility increased. IBM employees joked that the company initials stood for "I'm Being Moved." According to Atlas Van Lines, during the 1950s the average corporation manager could be expected to move fourteen times in his lifetime, or once every 2½ years. For him and his family, the ability to adjust to new circumstances was important to his acceptance in the corporation. All of this was beyond the comprehension of those generations who had lived their lives in one area. The "swing generation" of the 1940s had become a generation of technicians—interchangeable parts. If people knew it, they still seemed to like the rewards it offered. Even if they felt imprisoned, their prison was the most comfortable one in history and they quickly pointed this out. *Like any change, the change was not necessarily bad. It just was.*

Casual, Cool, and Collective

The new suburbanites were relaxed and informal to the extreme. Dress became casual. Mothers who would not have *dreamed* of going downtown without "dressing up" now saw their daughters going out in hair curlers. These same young people who "discovered" casualness and informality in the 1950s became the "older" adults of the 1960s and 1970s who raised Cain over the way kids looked. They *programmed* their children during the 1950s to *accept* sloppiness. When the young people went to "extremes" (blue jeans, cutoffs, sandals, work shirts, no baths or grooming), the adults were appalled—forgetting that *they had "set up" the acceptance.*

The surburban life style also eroded "polite society." The term fell from use because society was no longer polite! People, seeking acceptance from their peers, addressed one another on a personal level. Once first names had been *limited* to family and close friends, but suddenly everyone was a bosom buddy. Colleagues at work—even the boss—were addressed as "Hey, Bill!" Last names were used only in introductions; then everyone was *reduced* to Don, Sue, Judy, Chuck, and Joan. The children picked the same approach—Dad/ Mom or Father/Mother (*archaic* in the 1950s) became Jack and Mary as children became "buddies" with their parents. "Parental control" loses impact when your "buddy" tries to apply it. "Buddies" were for "understanding," not for disciplining or directing.

The informal atmosphere was reflected in the suburban houses. Walls came down to create a family-living-dining-kitchen room where everyone assembled (when they weren't off at some group activity or meeting). Since formal sit-down dinners were replaced by potluck buffets, there was no need for a dining room anyway. Privacy, even in one's own home, became a new social disease. There was a lot of "togetherness"—unlocked doors, picture windows, and backyard barbecues all gave young and old easy access to each other's lives. Surprisingly, many adults were shocked in the late 1960s when the children from this nonprivate background grew up to be young adults who openly slept, bathed, ate, and lived "together." The communes of the 1960s and 1970s were simply extensions/continuations of the life style programmed in by the parents of the 1950s.

The young who were programmed in the 1950s were exposed to a wide variety of *group* involvement. Boy Scouts, Brownies, little leagues, slumber parties, dancing classes, etc., all "set up" the children of the 1950s to participate in the love-ins, rock concerts, be-ins, and demonstrations of the 1960s and 1970s. The young adults in all those "shocking" events had *shared* as toddlers—toys in the sandboxes, tricycles, clothes, babysitters, even parents. "What's mine is yours and what's yours is mine" was an umbrella that covered the children of the 1950s.

The community sharing of property and experiences was coupled with a growing permissiveness. The resulting behavior of young adults in the late 1960s reflected their 1950s programming. Hitchhikers *honestly* believed that others *owed* them rides, and obscene gestures communicated their irritation when adults drove by. Young shoplifters "helped themselves" with no regrets. Expectations/ values had been programmed in to create a generation of youth that believed (and *still do*) that they would be "taken care of" in all respects. Their words reflected their values: "It's *my right! I* don't have to *work* for it. *You owe* it to me! *I* don't have to *pay* for it. Give it to me—*now!*"

Diffusing Sex Roles

Still other changing values were observed and absorbed by the children of the 1950s from the changing roles of their fathers and mothers. Moms were still found at home (cooking, cleaning, raising the children), and Dads were still the breadwinners. But subtle changes occurred that would signal the first wave of change in sex roles. Families were "alone" in the suburbs, even though they were surrounded by others in their same situation. Having left their "extended" family in the city or another part of the country, the 1950s suburban family was forced to change. No longer were adults, uncles, and grandparents instantly available to help out, especially with the kids. Therefore, some fathers began to take a more active role in traditional housekeeping activities—cooking, cleaning, and diapering.

It was the beginning of a major change in traditional sex roles, but it was only a token beginning. The majority of a man's time and interest still centered on *his* job. That job, which was the key to continuing the good life, was difficult to explain to his children— he no longer *produced* some *thing,* but was part of a difficult-to-define corporate structure. "Daddy, what do you do?" produced vague answers, if an answer at all. The children who asked such questions in the 1950s later rebelled against corporations, governments, and bureaucracies of the late 1960s and 1970s—they didn't "understand" them. As young adults, they asked their bewildered parents; "What have you accomplished? A house, four picture windows, a lawn, and two cars? Why did you do it? What does it mean?" Parents couldn't explain. They had been trying to keep up with the Joneses, only to discover that their children rejected the Joneses.

The fathers of the 1950s were involved with helping a "little" at home, but their main contribution to the raising of their children was to give them *things* (toys, bikes, education, etc.), *all of the advantages*—a lot of things, but not a lot of time. In their struggle upward (for *benefits* for their families), men were aided by their women. Throughout the society, the emphasis was on the "right" woman to help her man climb up the ladder of success. Within some corporations, extremes were reached—the benevolent company provided "lessons" on how to be an effective corporate wife. That was a long way from the 1970s, when women began climbing the ladders themselves, and many corporate executives simply "didn't understand." The values changed, and with them, sex roles at home and on the job.

In the 1950s, women (wives/mothers) seemed "different," and they were. In the 1930s and 1940s, women married "later" (delayed by economic conditions, the men away in the war, etc.). Now women began marrying earlier. The age at which American women married dropped from twenty-two to twenty into the teens. Sexual awareness increased, and sex appeal became more open. For the mothers of the 1950s, "catching the *right* man" was an important value for programming into their daughters. It became very important for all children to associate with the right people. Such people populated the suburbs. Group activities groomed the young for their adulthood, and there were many groups available.

The mothers themselves became more hedonistic, self-oriented. Industries catering to the "new woman" sprang up. Metrecal became a pantry staple. Dress sizes shrank. Cosmetics, perfumes, and wardrobes all changed. "If I only have one life, let me live it as a blonde" (Clairol advertising theme) became a national "direction."

Of course, the new mothers *were* concerned about their children (and *having* them, as the baby boom verified). Like the fathers, mothers showered their children with *things*—lessons, toys, group activities, popsicles, cookies, encyclopedias. By giving their children *things that they valued* (but had not had as children), they expressed a new *form* of love. This "love" would not be repaid in kind by their children.

Some parents began using their own children in a form of competition with "the Joneses." Unwittingly, children became pawns in a game of "one-upmanship." "Susie won the piano competition,

Johnny hit a homer for his little league team, Charlie got all *A*s, and Patty speaks French and she's only seven."

Imagine the horror of these parents when Susie was pregnant at eighteen, Johnny was busted for dealing drugs, Charlie dodged the draft in Canada, and Patty joined the SDS. They came from the "nicest" homes and their parents did *everything* for them. But there were *some* things that their honestly well-meaning parents *didn't do*—"Have you hugged your kid today?"

Spoiled Brats

Another major shift in value programming of the young occurred when it became impolite to scold someone else's child. Correction had to come from his own parents, and in the permissive air of the 1950s, there wasn't much of it. Children became "special people." Whether or not they benefited from this status was a question that would later have national impact. Certainly they were not neglected —permissiveness took a lot of time and patience. The basic attitude of American parents, repeated millions of times by words and behavior, was: *"My kid's going to have it better than I had it. He's going to enjoy life—get an education."* The parents took every step possible to achieve this goal.

Children made *many* demands. A mother was "expected" to plan her youngsters' activities and then make sure they got there. Children stopped "playing" in the old sense. Now their lives were "organized." After school and on Saturdays there were all sorts of events and activities, schedules that seemed to never end. If they *were* at home, they were home just for meals and to catch a few hours of television before bed. Social critics voiced concern. Some thought that the children's chances of growing into *individuals* were being sharply curtailed, if not altogether extinguished. The parents of the 1950s weren't interested in individuality. They were anxious to raise children who could "get along" with other people. Parents admired that quality in one another, sought to develop it in themselves, and programmed it in every possible way into the developing generation.

The result was that millions of young people approached the age of awareness (adolescence) knowing a great deal about achieving popularity but very little about achieving anything else. Mothers programmed their children with the need for being liked by their peers. Then the kids practiced in sandboxes, on playgrounds, and around swing sets. The Brownies and little leagues further reinforced this "togetherness." The propaganda for good fellowship was relentless. Any child who tried to cultivate his own identity was *urged not to* by the mass media, while the last layers of "good-guymanship" polish were spit-shined in the suburban schools.

The Social "Pass"/The Educational Morass

The quality and dimensions of schools varied from one community to another. In some areas, McGuffy readers and rote memorization were still dominant. The real movement in the educational system was what advocates called "progressive education." In the beginnings of this movement, it was dedicated to freeing imaginative children from lock-step learning and encouraging them to develop their own individuality. Then, as the educators themselves became more excited about "developing social skills," teachers replaced the stress on intellectual attainment with an even greater push to turn a child into what personality profiles suggested he *should be.*

Students were no longer *told* what they must learn. They were asked to *choose* electives from a spectrum of "contemporary" offerings. There were no fixed standards of performance. Grades were limited to "satisfactory" and "unsatisfactory." "Modern" courses replaced the traditional Reading, Writing, and Arithmetic. The new educators viewed the traditional academic disciplines with undisguised hostility. The focus of the school systems was to keep children "well adjusted." Teachers aided by helping pupils choose their friends, their games at recess, even their fantasies. A trend developed to make them "better" adults—especially consumers—and they visited department stores and supermarkets instead of national monuments. The focus was not "the process of problem solving," but rather on "how to live life without upsetting the human relationships." The children were taught to be "well rounded."

Some parents wanted to go back to traditional learning—areas *they believed* were important. The educators simply shook their heads and replied "we teach the child, not the subject." They believed that in helping pupils prepare for a "consumer world" they were providing a practical, realistic approach that would be invaluable for the students' future. These are the young adults who are now "socially adjusted" *and* insecure in themselves as individuals *and* unable to deal with the world in problem-solving realities. *They're still trying to "find themselves."*

The crash in the U.S. educational system came on October 4, 1957. A small object the size of a basketball started circling the earth with its "beep . . . beep . . . beep." As Tass, the Soviet News

Agency, noted: "The first artificial earth satellite has now been created. This satellite was successfully launched in the USSR." Shock waves were felt around the world, especially in the United States, which had regarded itself as the home of scientific innovations. Americans were rudely awakened to the fact that they *did not* have a monopoly on engineering accomplishments. We were embarrassed. For the educational systems it was a shock as critical as the Crash of '29. Educators suddenly said, "Man, be an engineer. That's where it's at!"

Give/Give—Take/Take

The parents of the 1950s reinforced "progressive education." In homes it was an era of *overindulgence,* where the kids were *financially supported* BUT *emotionally abandoned.* The parents looked at their children and said such things as: "You're bored with that toy? We'll buy you another. Don't cry. Don't get excited. We'll keep you happy." To keep children "happy" became a paramount drive. Another variation was: "You broke your tricycle? We'll get it fixed. Don't worry"; or "What do you need? Want an education? How about a vacation? What do you want? Can we get it for you? When do you want it?" It became a world of *give-give, take-take.* And the young learned their lessons very well.

Think about those parents in the United States in the early 1950s. They had lived through the Depression and physically survived World War II. The good life beckoned *and* they had the money to enjoy it. Pepsi Cola commercials talked about "The Sociables"— "live, enjoy, experience." But even with the $ means, there was the slight problem of two snotty-nosed brats at home. The parents looked at their kids, looked at the good life, got all confused and frustrated, and then fell back on reassuring advice from Dr. Benjamin Spock. Dr. Spock didn't really "say" what millions of people thought he said. Through the *filters* of the media, millions of American parents *and* educators thought Dr. Spock said: "Don't worry about your children. Leave the little darlings alone. Let them explore. Let them raise hell. Let them ask questions. Let them do what they damn well want to do. They'll be better adults for it." Now, they are adults. They're *still* asking questions, raising hell, exploring, and doing what *they* damn well please.

This generation programmed permissively in homes and schools learned their lessons *very, very well.* Just a few years ago this generation began asking older generations a series of very *embarrassing* questions. In answer to those questions, generations now in their fifties and sixties responded: "Shut up! We've *always* done it this way. *This* is *the way* we're going to continue to do it. You just *shut up* and grow up and see!" Younger generations *will not* stop asking questions: it was programmed into them, it is part of them, and they will continue to question. Dr. Spock himself admitted in the 1970s that mass misinterpretation of his child-rearing philosophies in the early 1950s may have "significantly screwed-up an entire generation."

But the parents during the 1950s listened to what they "thought" Spock said. They looked at the good life . . . they looked at their kids. All of a sudden they were significantly aided in "abandoning" their children because they could plop them down in front of the new electronic babysitter—along came television. Soon it was a national phenomenon.

In the Beginning, There Were Test Patterns

TELEVISION! A lot of people today can actually *remember early television*. There wasn't much of it around. It didn't really arrive until the late 1940s. In 1947, there were only 7 stations in the entire country and approximately 14,000 sets. But with the 1950s, television exploded across the American scene. By 1954, there were 517 stations and approximately 32 million sets. Many people, recalling the early days of TV, can remember its "relative" simplicity. People were *fascinated* with those small flickering screens. When a set appeared in a neighborhood, the antenna was the first signal. For those who left their doors or windows open, the neighborhood children clustered to watch the shadowy programs or stare fascinated at the test patterns.

Remember those early sets? Those *big* cabinets with the *little* screens hypnotized millions for hours and hours. Some worked frantically to tune in a test pattern. Then, after they "got" the test pattern, they would sit and *drink* and *watch* the test pattern. They couldn't *believe* it was working! Most adults had just become accustomed to radio; then, all of a sudden, along came TV. It scared the daylights out of them. They didn't know what to do. They thought God sent it or something!

But we went a long way very quickly. From being fascinated by test patterns in the early 1950s to January 13, 1971, when that afternoon a network *dared* to interrupt a "live" professional basketball game to show the "live" launching of Apollo 14. The American public was so irritated at NASA and the network that a public relations officer for NASA *was fired,* and from 1971 NASA considered a policy that they would try not to schedule space shots in conflict with professional sports on TV. That's a long way from being fascinated with a test pattern to being "bored" with going to the moon! But then, television carried us a long way in literally every aspect of our lives. It changed the way we were entertained. It changed the way we received news. It changed the family structure. It began to erode the educational process. *Nothing escaped TV's impact.*

Of particular importance was the impact that television would have on the generation being value programmed. This was the first "TV generation." The television set assumed the roles of babysitter, mother, father, teacher, and hero creator. The myths that had earlier been transmitted by parents to children, on radio, and through comic books and school texts now were restructured on the television screen. There was one important difference that was immediately noted: television, with its direct broadcast of news and in some documentaries, was not edited. With minor exceptions, TV became the first mass medium that "told it like it was"—not always, but often enough that young minds were significantly impressed. It was one world, but there were *tremendous inconsistencies.* For example, how could Beaver ("Leave It To Beaver") go merrily on his way through his very middle-class world and not be aware that "just across town" groups of people were being harassed, even killed in civil rights demonstrations? The inconsistencies of the world became harshly real for the developing children. Massive conflicts developed between the highly fantasized world of the silver screen, the reruns of old movies, the commercials that were touting the good life, and the *reality* of what else was happening. What was taught in school began to appear irrelevant, and many students wondered why they had even bothered to attend class. Of course some didn't, and some of this group would set out directly to change a system that television had made irrelevant.

Even with its eager acceptance, television evoked considerable condemnation. It was called the "boob tube" and "the light that failed." Some of this criticism came from performers who couldn't make the switch from radio to the new medium. Other criticisms came from such nationally-known newsmen as Edward R. Murrow, one of the decade's top TV commentators. As Murrow noted, "If television and radio are to be used for the entertainment of all of the people all of the time, we have come perilously close to discovering the real opiate of the people."

Flip a Switch, Turn Me On

Television's effects on the young of the early 1950s are still being debated. The first television generation would become the first young adult generation that would directly, openly, and violently confront long-established values in the American system. To this generation television brought two major changes in value programming, discussed in more depth by Fabun in "Children of Change": (1) time collapsed as television created a world of instant satisfaction, instant gratification; and (2) the horizon disappeared as we could go anywhere at any time, if the event was important. Never before had such options been available to millions.

Sunday afternoon, November 18, 1951: Millions watched as television began to "destroy" the dimensions of time and space. The premiere of a new half-hour news show, "See It Now," simultaneously showed on a split screen two bridges, New York's Brooklyn and San Francisco's Golden Gate. Seeing both oceans together for the first time raised us to a new level of relevance in thinking and programming our young.

Television wasn't just a new score of entertainment or information. By its very nature it began to affect other value impactors in the society. Family life styles were restructed to include the flickering silver screen. Even mealtime, a traditional period of close family interaction, was changed to conform to the demands of television. The family clustered around the set with their new forms of food—TV dinners.

Before the 1950s, politics was primarily limited to the adult world, and the nominating process to only a few of those adults. But in 1952, Americans were suddenly swept as a whole into the presidential nominating conventions. Suddenly, people were being programmed directly with live and uncensored political information. No longer was politics restricted to the adult world, "closeted" in smoke-filled rooms. Now everyone, including the young, could become an active participant in viewing the complex political processes. The young who were programmed during the 1950s became a very politically active generation when they reached young adulthood. They were programmed with politics. But it wasn't just the political conventions now available for inspection by nearly everyone, it was also the first time a first-hand view was offered of congressional processes (the infamous McCarthy hearings). Further, politicians themselves soon learned that the unblinking TV eye could affect the outcome of elections. The power of the historical political bosses gave way to the glare of camera lights. A pale Richard Nixon would learn in 1960 that such scrutiny could sway voters dramatically. Television had changed forever the political behavior of the nation.

As television increasingly became the dominant appliance in American households, it began to take hold in subtle ways that are still being defined. Television became so pervasive across our society, that by the late 1970s it was estimated that 99+ percent of American households had television *but only* 96 percent of American households had indoor plumbing. As someone has pointed out:

"There's *all* that crap coming in, and not enough there to take it out!"

As the "residue" accumulated, everyone was changed! Dramatically changed were those generations that were value programmed with television as an omnipresent electronic babysitter. The first TV generation, those programmed during the 1950s, experienced new ways to "value" the world—the result of their *intense* exposure to television. As a generalization, from the 1950s, young generations seemed to seek immediate satisfaction. They wanted everything *now*. Instant gratification . . . instant satisfaction . . . flip a switch . . . turn me on! These are *real* value-oriented statements that are reflected in many ways in our society.

For example, real estate professionals across the United States report that if we go back to the pre-1950s, young couples "just getting started" were relatively content with a small home (if they could afford one). They hoped to build up their equity, and then later buy a bigger house (and some other well-earned "goodies") by the time they were middle-aged. If you ask real estate people about what has been happening over the past couple of decades, they'll tell you that young people want *all* of the "goodies" RIGHT NOW! They want *everything* as soon as they can get it, and see no reason why they should have to wait.

Where does this expectation of instant satisfaction come from? Why did the young from the 1950s *demand* immediacy in all situations? This value of "instantness" came from many sources. A major contribution was television's bombardment. TV's spies, cops, and sheriffs solved the world's most complex problems *in one hour,* with several commercial breaks for the good life. After thousands of exposures to simplified problem solving, the young came to believe: "That's it—solve any problem. Takes a couple of hours at the most. Then we'll 'rest' for a while." *That is not the way the real world works.* But *that* is the way that millions expect it to work from *their* value orientation.

The sense of immediacy, of instant solution, came to haunt us in other ways. Think back to the late 1960s and recall what college students shouted in demonstrations. They said some very naive things about the world's complex realities. They looked at very complicated problems and wanted to "flip a switch" to solve them. Typical attitudes were: "We're not doing anything this afternoon, let's get out of Vietnam." "Nothing's planned tomorrow morning, let's rebuild the ghettos." "Nothing's scheduled for the next day, let's change this and that and them." You just can't go out and "zap"—flip a switch and rebuild ghettos. But that *is* what millions wanted—instant solutions to complex reality. Television reduced problems to "highlights" covered in an hour, thus distorting an understanding of harsh realities.

Good Guys/Bad Guys—Who's on Top?

Television also gave us a whole new set of heroes. Who were *your* heroes when *you* were ten years old? If you're now in your forties, fifties, or sixties, your heroes (as you were programmed in the 1920s, and 1930s, and 1940s) were typically *great* people, *straight* people, *right* people—predominantly *white* people. The "good guys" were easy to spot—they wore white hats and rode white horses. They were people you could look up to, people you could respect. Of course, without the intense media coverage during the 1920s, 1930s, and 1940s, we simply didn't *know* that much about the personal lives of our heroes, but they *looked good* from a distance. National heroes were such people as Amelia Earhart, Charles Lindbergh, Babe Ruth, Hopalong Cassidy, Joe DiMaggio, the Green Hornet—*truly great heroes.*

Look at the heroes with which generations have been value programmed since the 1950s. Early television, with its reruns of movies from the 1940s, tended to reinforce the "good-guy" hero image. However, several programs began to show us new types of heroes. In the mid-1950s, if you were ten years old, you sat and watched such popular programs as "The $64,000 Question" and "Twenty-One." The big winners on these shows were the instant folk heroes of the 1950s. Charles Van Doren was a prime example. He was handsome, all-American, an English instructor at Columbia (at a time when teaching was fashionable), and even though he came from a "literary" family, he used his braininess to "fight" for some of the new affluence. Young people looked at Mr. Van Doren and thought: "I want to grow up and be just like him . . . have all that money . . . have all the fame . . . have it all." Teachers told students Van Doren was a living example of how hard work could be rewarding. Mothers encouraged their daughters to "marry a boy like Charlie, not like

Elvis." Later, when it was discovered that Van Doren and many others played a totally dishonest game, there was relatively little public remorse. Van Doren himself did a tearful "confessional" on national TV and then faded away. But the *basic* public reaction was: "Bad, Charlie, you shouldn't have done it (but we love you anyway)." He kept his money and went away. Columbia's students held a rally to support him, and a national survey found that three out of every four Americans believed that faced with the same situation "most people" would have done the same thing.

Wasn't the *new* value—isn't the *now* value—*"Don't not do it, just don't get caught if you do it"*? This value of not getting caught, of being deceptive, dishonest, and even being rewarded for such behavior had surfaced before (during Prohibition). But, it was now reflected again and again, not only on television, but in the movies and in real life, perhaps peaking with the Watergate affair of the mid-1970s.

Shake, Rattle 'n' Roll

Television affected all other media, especially music. Music had been predominantly sentimental, with brief swings into patriotism during the war periods. Television turned the music world upside down/inside out—new songs, styles, and stars. Music had dwelt in the relatively sophisticated "mood" world of adults, but television "hooked" teen-agers with new idols, movements, sounds, and excitement. "Mack The Knife," the number one hit of 1959, was a long way from the number one Hit Parade song of 1950, "Goodnight Irene"; "Rock Around the Clock" of 1955 was a light year away from the 1951 hit "Tennessee Waltz."

Through the 1950s, the lyrics of songs shifted far from such cutesie wonderings as "How Much Is That Doggie in the Window?" (1953, Patti Page). The big explosion erupted in 1956. The number one song that year was "Don't Be Cruel" by Elvis Presley, the new super folk hero for the young. Elvis wasn't just an overnight sensation: in just one year he became a living legend. He changed everything—country music, recording techniques, appearances, and taste. And he significantly added *sexuality* to music. This one man converted rock 'n' roll into a new national teen-age "religion." The moment he stepped to the mike and set his electric guitar bellowing, it was obvious that he was different. His voice shouted and trembled as though it too were electrified, and his way of moving was nothing short of orgasmic. Elvis' bumps, grinds, and shimmies led Ed Sullivan to pronounce him "unfit for a family audience." But in a few months, Sullivan would "eat crow." On "The Ed Sullivan Show" in 1956, nearly fifty-four million people watched Elvis (only *above* the hips) thrust his way into the lives of America's teen-agers.

But it wasn't just the songs and their lyrics; it was the *way* he sang that grabbed the youth and became a major influence in their programming. It's interesting, as noted in Alan Cartnal's article "America: 1955–1960," that when Presley was interviewed years after he became a sensation, he said: "We used to go to these religious sing-ins all the time. The preachers would cut up all over the place, jumpin' on the piano, movin' ever' which way. The audience liked 'em. I guess I learned from them." How ironic that youth's new hero had his "discussed" and "cussed" roots in Bible-belt theatrics.

The advent of rock 'n' roll not only created a new set of *prosperous* heroes (*preposterous* in the opinion of many adults), it also spawned an inevitable group of "support" people who reinforced the programming. The most visible of these were disc jockeys, suddenly elevated to new status among teen-agers within their own communities. On the national level, the king was Dick Clark, master of ceremonies of that afternoon television classic, "American Bandstand." This show reached an impressive twenty million regular weekday viewers. They mentally "joined" a parade of rock stars, celebrities, and common people. Although Dick Clark himself remained a typical all-American "square" plugged into a new "round hole" in society, he fit smoothly enough into the teen-age world to have a major effect on their perceptions of reality. "Life" for teen-agers moved further into fantasy, expressed by their dancing and music.

Every revolution has marched to a tune, from "Yankee Doodle" in the American Revolution to the tone and beat of the youth movement in the 1950s led by Presley's swiveling hips. With Presley on top as a hero, the kids began a revolution in musical taste that continued to unfold. They soaked up an endless procession of wildly assorted singing groups, styles, deviates, and variations. They ranged from the California surfers' beat to Detroit's Motown sound to New York rock to acid wails to British pop. Underlying much of it was the rhythm-and-blues and "soul" sound of the American Negro. This became another variable injected into the value programming that influenced this generation's *perception and acceptance* of those of other races.

A Gathering Momentum

And so "the beat" went on and with it the changing value programming in our society. Disc jockeys stressed the excitement of NOW! For the young, with their transistorized link to the outside world and their electronic interconnection with one another, the word was: "Something's happening! Something's happening! Life's exciting! Are you with it? Get with it!" A sense of excitement propelled them into the next decade. With the 1960s came changes that even the most extreme forecasters of the 1950s did not anticipate.

As the 1950s drew to a close, the rate of change accelerated. Civil rights issues had gained major national importance. Sputnik had stunned the educational system. Television expanded more and more in its blanket coverage of America and the world. Clark Kerr, then president of the University of California, took a close look at college students in 1959 and said: "The employers will love this generation. . . . They are going to be easy to handle. There aren't going to be any riots." But the values programmed into the young during the 1950s negated his prediction, as that generation exploded into the young adults of the 1960s.

THE 1960s:
SHOCKWAVES OF CHANGE

Of all the decades that value programmed clusters of people, the 1960s are perhaps the most difficult to analyze. During no other period of history had American values experienced such dramatic shifts and changes. Those who were programmed during the 1950s were becoming adolescents or young adults. They suddenly experienced a world in direct conflict with their relatively stable programming of the 1950s. On a well-laid foundation of affluence and technology, some major value bases began to shift dramatically as the 1960s approached. Sputnik had flip-flopped the American educational system toward a more scientific orientation. Media continued to change how we viewed the world, and television did it with a power that no one could have predicted. Glaring inconsistencies were exposed within the society—the differing treatment of blacks and whites, people starving in a land of plenty, and the suppression of "free" speech. *The 1960s changed everyone!* But the two groups critically affected by the decade were: (1) those who were *completing* their value programming, and (2) those who were value programmed *during* that decade. Both groups saw a reality filled with hypocrisies, discrepancies, and blatant lies.

The decade itself was literally a rollercoaster of experiences, contradictions, highs/lows, goods/bads, rights/wrongs, normals/not normals. It is impossible to view the 1960s in a direct chronological sequence. Wave after wave of change crashed through the society—

100

reinforcing, backwashing, overlapping, slowing, and rising once again to influence values. A raging storm of value *clashes* resulted. Sadly, these were often brutal and destructive, but highly *predictable* given the value extremes that developed during this era.

How do we understand the 1960s? Unfortunately, we're probably still too close; the changes are yet to be fully understood. Their repercussions still resound. We may never totally comprehend what happened, but there are numerous avenues for probing. The following analysis draws from three major sources: Time-Life's *This Fabulous Century* series chronicles the extremes of the decade, William Manchester's *The Glory and the Dream* brilliantly fills in details, and Tom Wicker's insights from *Great Songs of the Sixties* add some provocative interpretations. It is hoped that these three sources, combined with the experiences of living the decade, will bring perspective to those turbulent years.

The decade dawned on an emotional high. There was a new commitment across the land. All kinds of people began to show—passionately and often vocally—that they *gave a damn,* that they *cared.* The symbol of giving a damn and caring was personified in the newly elected President John F. Kennedy. His idealism and challenges to the nation particularly affected the young. Kennedy was a larger-than-life new hero for the nation. At the Democratic convention in July, he described his New Frontier as: "Not a set of promises, it is a set of challenges. It sums up not what I intend to offer the American People, but what I intend to ask of them." His challenge appealed to "the best" across the nation at that time. Elsewhere in society there were distant rumbles of the troubles that lay ahead. Yet, with the peaks of "Camelot" in the early 1960s, few could even imagine the depths to which our emotional rollercoaster would plunge in 1963–64. It rose briefly again on the Great Society's wave during the middle of the decade and then plunged to still greater depths in 1968. The feeling of commitment had shifted from optimism, to doubt, to disenchantment. It is probably truer of the 1960s than of any other decade that one had to *live* it, to *experience* it, to *believe* it, to *understand* it, to *relate* to everything that happened (especially from a value programming perspective).

President Kennedy's vibrant optimism was expressed in his inaugural speech on January 20, 1961: "Let the word go forth from this time and place . . . that the torch has been passed to a new generation of Americans. . . . So let us begin anew. . . . Together let us explore the stars, conquer the deserts, eradicate disease, tap the ocean depths and encourage the arts and commerce. . . . All this will not be finished in the first one-hundred days. . . . The energy, the faith, the devotion which we bring to this endeavor will light our country and all who serve it—and the glow from that fire can truly light the world." In a burst of enthusiasm, the youth were already trying to reshape the world as they saw it.

The liberal young "hero of the hour" had changed over time. The angry young workers of the 1930s, the GIs of the 1940s, and the youth of the 1950s (who were "misunderstood" by their parents) evolved in the early 1960s into the symbolic dedicated Peace Corpsmen, battling the world's evils with hand tools of peace. This idealism was but one of the waves sweeping the nation. Another erupted in the area of civil rights.

The civil rights explosion started in Montgomery, Alabama, on December 1, 1955, when a weary black seamstress defied the local law and refused to give up her bus seat to a white man. Rosa Parks' arrest was the last straw for Montgomery's black community. Their leaders, including Dr. Martin Luther King, met to organize a bus boycott. The first step was taken on the long road to racial equality. As the movement continued through the late 1950s, it won increasing coverage in the media. The young were paying attention.

On February 1, 1960, in a F. W. Woolworth store in Greensboro, North Carolina, four young men tried to buy coffee. They were ignored. They were black. They returned daily, bringing more students from the nearby North Carolina Agriculture and Technical College. Although taunted and verbally abused, they remained passive —and their numbers grew. A tornado started that tore across the nation. Within two weeks, sit-ins had spread to fifteen cities in five southern states. In the North, divinity students at Yale responded and marched in support. Students at Harvard, Boston, M.I.T., and Brandeis (flagships of higher education) picked up the cause and began picketing Woolworth stores. The protests expanded during the spring and summer of 1960 to read-ins at all-white libraries, sleep-ins in the lobbys of segregated hotels, and wade-ins at restricted beaches. In millions of homes the events were electronically experienced in capsule form on the evening news. Support for the demonstrators slowly spread throughout society. Slowly, in one area after another, because of people who gave a damn, the color barriers began to crumble. The civil rights movement surged across the society. Values that had never been questioned and behavior that had always been sanctioned were destroyed as the shock waves slammed into the system.

Yet another signal of change that would sweep the nation started halfway around the world. In a then little known country called South Vietnam, American army advisors were instructing

South Vietnamese army rangers in guerrilla tactics. The "advisors" were very special soldiers. "These men," said a Green Beret commander, "are the Harvard Ph.D.s of the Special Warfare art." They seemed a perfect reflection of Kennedy's New Frontier—they were specialists, perfectionists, "the best." Even though their "business" was killing, the Green Berets were really idealists. They were liberating the world from oppression, and they were convinced that the subversive tactics they had been taught would somehow set the world free. In a way, they were closely related to the values expressed by the Peace Corpsmen. They believed they were saving the world.

Still another swell of change surfaced in California. On May 13, 1960, police clashed with two hundred angry college students trying to get into a House Committee on Un-American Activities hearing on communism. The students planned no violence. But when they were denied entrance to the hearing room, they pushed their way in. Someone was knocked down, out came fire hoses and clubs, a battle raged, and as one student noted: "I was a political virgin, but I was raped on the steps of City Hall."

Suddenly, the young were shaking the label of apathy and conformity that had symbolized the youth of the 1950s. The young generation was changing the future of the world and was in turn being changed as the world itself shifted. If any one word symbolizes the 1960s, that word is *change*. "Activism" was occurring everywhere. In schools, in colleges, on jungle rivers, in military training camps, in the high reaches of government, in corporate boardrooms, a new spirit of commitment was born—a spirit of change. And the young were deeply immersed in these value programming influences.

Perhaps as much as anything, the music of the 1960s began to reflect and to interpret the dramatic changes going on within the society. Songs not only mirrored what was happening but also became a critical factor in communicating and effecting the changes. Bob Dylan's profound "The Times They Are a-Changing" talked of a battle outside that was raging. It warned that society's foundations would shake. He was right—the times *were* changing more swiftly, dramatically, and deeply than ever before. Change in itself became the battle. *Change was the central experience of the 1960s.* However one reacted to change—encouraging it, welcoming it, fighting it, regretting it, or retreating from it—it came to everyone.

Change arrived in so many ways in the 1960s that it is difficult to determine what mattered and what was superficial. The way people looked changed, especially young men. And "looks" became a major weapon in the clash of values. Perhaps the long hair and beards sprung from a rebellion against the "crew-cut" conformity and mentality of the America of the 1950s. The glitter of the good life and the "established way" of doing things were beginning to tarnish. Minor changes sometimes suggest deeper changes, especially in the area of values. Superficial behavior is rooted in the gut-level system. Even though the "hairy look" itself became a standard, those sporting it still *thought* they were different. The young had changed. They looked alike, talked alike, seemed to think alike. But, *they were different* from the older generations.

The exuberance of the early 1960s swept the value programming of the young along in a context of affluence, change, and challenge. Then it all crashed—that black day in 1963. The shock of President Kennedy's death hit the nation with immediate and horrifying impact. Millions moaned, "My God! My God! What are we coming to?" For the moment, no one seemed to know. Lyndon Johnson took the reins of the nation and tried to move us forward.

As the 1964 elections approached, a renewed spirit of optimism began. Johnson continued the New Frontier and added a few humanitarian touches of his own under a new program, the Great Society. It was an ambitious design for social improvement, perhaps the greatest in the thirty years since FDR's New Deal. The Great Society seemed to be a good idea, the direction in which we wanted to go. As Johnson swept into the White House on the largest plurality since the first presidential voting statistics were compiled in 1824, the future seemed positive. But the forces of change were already eroding the foundations of the past.

The Age of Aquarius

Change comes in many ways, both small and large. One of the most startling changes, *instantly* communicated by television, was the emergence in the mid-1960s of the "love children," the "hippies." Although the real "flower children" numbered perhaps only a few hundred thousand, their impact on society was astonishing. Some of them were confused high school kids who had run away from home, a few were hard-drug users, while others were definitely psychologically sick. According to studies conducted, more than one-half of them were reasonably mature people who had spent some time in college. Some had held responsible jobs in the business or academic world. Although they lived in poverty, the great majority came from fairly prosperous backgrounds. Nearly three-fourths reported that their families were in the middle-income or higher-range. They came from a background basically solid and predictable—a world socially respectable and economically secure, a world of values that was a breeding ground for future lawyers, doctors, businessmen, and other professionals. Yet some of these young people suddenly opted for a life they claimed was devoted to the "love" of mankind. It was a life style which outwardly appeared to be more dedicated to squalor, irresponsibility, and drugs. "Oh, my God, where did we go wrong?" their parents asked. The young who were being programmed were "watching" hippies in the media. The Pied Piper was Dr. Timothy Leary, who Manchester quotes as urging young people to "turn on to the scene; tune in to what's happening; and drop out—of high school, college, grade school. . . . Follow me, the hard way."

What emerged was a nightmare for tens of thousands of parents. For many adults, the memories of their Depression childhood was still vivid; others recalled their sacrifices in the 1950s when they raised their children. To adults, it seemed preposterous that our society would support bums or that their own children *wanted* to be bums. The kids looked like bums, often acted like bums. Many had spent their lives preparing for the "American dream." Suddenly, they rejected their dream or, perhaps more accurately, the dream of their parents.

There have always been "deviants" in our society—from the "flappers" of the 1920s to the "beatniks" of the 1940s and 1950s. With the hippies, there was a *major difference*—never had a group been so intensely covered by the media and its message distributed so dramatically to the total population. They were the first tangible, visible, irritating symbol of a new philosophy that cut to the very core of American values. For the first time in American history, our basic Protestant values of hard work, respectability, and competition for material success were being massively questioned. An entire generation—millions of young people who copied the love children's clothing, hair styles, rock music, and general outlook—seemed to find the American dream shallow and unfulfilling. In their questioning of society, some of the "gentle people" exchanged their peaceful/love approach for the more violent/political movement of the New Left. In a confrontation with "the establishment" at the 1968 Democratic convention, more than one thousand people were injured. Violent protests escalated. In May 1969, during a controversy in Berkeley over a park in a vacant lot, one person died and sixty were hurt.

Some of the flower children never abandoned their basic belief in nonviolence, and while their contemporaries battled police, they sat back and waited for love to triumph over all. Arlo Guthrie, a hippie folk hero of the 1960s, said: "All political systems are on the way out. We're finally gonna get to the point where there's no more bigotry or greed or war. Peace is on the way. . . . . People are simply gonna learn that they can get more by being groovy than being greedy."

But it was violence that had the greatest impact on our nation. The tactical approach of the demonstrators came from the mass media. They turned to the only means they understood to put their point across: the front-page headlines in the newspapers and direct-news coverage on TV. They knew the power of modern media *because they had been programmed* with such "change" tactics during the early days of the civil rights demonstrations. They knew instinctively that the way to create change was to generate enough action to get coverage by reporters and cameramen. To do this, they provoked the Establishment into response. The police, National Guard, army, federal marshals, and government officials fueled the fires by their own violent reactions. When the confrontation was great enough, there was enough action to draw the attention of the media.

In a strange way, television also "dignified" the process. If you were at a demonstration at noon and could go home and watch yourself on the "6 O'clock News," it meant that your noon behavior was lifted out of the realm of juvenile shenanigans and became a genuine historical event. In a world where your "identity crisis" was real, your "identity" was defined by being important. People on TV *were* important—they thought.

On the nonviolent side, no one proclaimed the message of love and happiness with more persuasion than the Beatles. They created a mood of childlike whimsy that seemed to captivate young people around the world. After their smash hit, "I Want to Hold Your Hand," Beatlemania spread through youth like the Plague. Millions of youths copied their clothing, their hairstyles, and memorized the lyrics of a new "religion." Filled with the hippie doctrine of love, freedom, and innocence, Beatles' lyrics promised a fantasy world in such hits as "Yellow Submarine," "All You Need Is Love," and "Strawberry Fields Forever." It was all a never-never dreamland flying on a carpet of drugs. Yet, even when they referred to such explosive subjects as drugs, the Beatles maintained their cuteness.

Although the innocence, fun, and excitement of the love children faded rapidly, the impact on millions of young people being programmed was significant. The business world capitalized on the hippies, reinforcing the new values in products, music, and experiences. Everything changed. Some changes even overlapped into the adult world. People dressed more colorfully and casually—modishly long hair was "in" and people of all ages started to "smell the flowers."

At the height of the movement, Charles Reich's *The Greening of America* eulogized the beautiful new age that was dawning. We're still waiting for it to come true.

The stumbling language of the young people of the 1960s was probably one of the first manifestations of the severe change that television had created in American youth. There were suddenly a lot of Marxists who had never *read* Marx. Slogans replaced thinking. There was a scrambling of the use of words in overlapping dialogue in a lot of movies and in the slurred lyrics of popular songs. Some tried to make a virtue of all of this, labeling it a "new consciousness." But some of the young *weren't* conscious.

Marie Winn, in *The Plug-in Drug,* and other experts have made connections between the first television generation's "addiction" to its programs and the sudden explosion in the use of real drugs in the 1960s. This was the same generation whose college-board exam scores plunged as they began to use drugs at an increasing rate. Drugs, like television, deal with sensations, not with thought or logic. Both experiences are passive; both isolate one's ego; both promise easy drama and release from boredom—escape from the "real world." Thus, the generation that was programmed first with television in the 1950s now amplified their "experience" hunger by using drugs in the 1960s.

Clay-Footed Gods

The Great Society and the love children pulled the nation in different directions. The hippies themselves divided into violent and nonviolent segments. Many signals indicated that every aspect of society was under siege.

The Supreme Court outlawed prayer in public schools. Even though religion in America had never been dependent upon schools and many denominations had actively supported separation of church and state, it was still a major indication of change. The Court's action came at a time of significant decline in church influence on American lives. It seemed to symbolize the emergence of a new way of life. The action was "rational and enlightened" to some, "hedonistic and decadent" to others. But for both it was change. So extreme was the questioning of church and religion that *Time*'s cover story for April 8, 1966, asked: "Is God Dead?" On August 5 of the same year, John Lennon of the Beatles announced: "We're more popular than Jesus." He probably didn't mean that they were more important than Jesus; he was simply trying to note that the Beatles were more *well known* around the world than Christ. He was probably correct, especially among young people. In September, Timothy Leary, high priest of the flower children, declared that

LSD was the sacrament of the new religion. And another signal of religion's decline occurred on December 2, 1966, when the Vatican announced that it was okay for Catholics to eat meat on Friday. For millions of people, this announcement came as a minor Significant Emotional Event. Having been told their entire lives that they should *not* do something, suddenly it was okay. What else could be questioned? What was wrong now became right. What was bad now became good, and vice versa. Traditional religions sank lower and lower in influence.

The New Morality: Sex 'n' Sun City

Yet another movement surfaced, and its wave began to wash across the nation. The first signals were most visible by change in the way women dressed. The miniskirt symbolized that women were changing their traditional roles. Women began showing more of themselves than ever before in many ways. Bikinis, see-through blouses, and discarded underwear all heralded a new liberation for females. Development of "The Pill" (1960) as well as legalized abortions had important implications. Women were free to enjoy sex as never before. They escaped from the historical dominance of children and the men who had fathered them. In the 1960s it became obvious that the female world was undergoing change, perhaps even more than that of the males.

Like the revolutions in dress and behavior, language itself began to change with new open use of once "taboo" words. Language became a "weapon" and a tool that reinforced the aspects of a general revolt against tradition. Words that had once appeared only on restroom walls or were heard in locker rooms were suddenly heard in public. First in popular Broadway plays, then in movies, and then in magazines and books the forbidden words blossomed. In 1953, a movie entitled *Sadie Thompson* was banned in many towns because they used one word, one time. They called someone a whore. By the mid-1960s, in such movies as *Who's Afraid of Virginia Woolf?* calling someone a whore was practically a compliment compared with the rest of the language. Profanity became "normal" in mixed company—among the sophisticated at first, but swiftly adopted by the young. *All* of the words were now used freely. In what once had been called "polite society" could be heard short Anglo-Saxon words formerly not used in mixed company. The conservative, restrained older generations were horrified.

Like the pill and public nudity, language mirrored an evolving life style and a new morality. For many in the older generations there seemed to be no morality at all. They lashed out at long hair, communes, marijuana, and casual sex. But the pleasures of the new sexual freedom seemed just as desirable to millions of young Americans as it did for the hippies in the communes. Most young people never marched in any war demonstrations and probably rarely read underground newspapers, but when the lights went out, they were as active as the most turned-on hippies. One businessman who operated in a community of "conservative hedonists," Manchester reports, told a reporter: "This is the America you don't hear about. It's clean-cut people who don't wear sandals and beards—guys and girls living very normal lives. It's almost blasphemous how American it is."

College had historically been a laboratory for sexual experimentation. But off of the campuses, until the mid-1960s, finding a member of the opposite sex who was "available" had been time-consuming and expensive. That, too, changed. Grossinger's Hotel in New York held its first weekend for singles in the early 1960s. Yet another movement had begun. The "singles life" exploded across the American scene and became a nationwide ritual for young unmarried people. Organizations sprang up which catered to single military officers, professional men, airline stewardesses, teachers, models, secretaries, and career girls—everyone! Suddenly, there were resorts for singles only. Cruise ships promised an ongoing orgy, and European tours accepted only bachelors and unmarried women. Apartment complexes sprouted across the nation catering to the newly discovered swingles. It was a long way in a short period of time from the first issue of *Playboy* in 1953. As with everything, the media gleefully reported developments in stimulating detail.

All of this was a reflection of a new "clustering" of generations. The tendency of people in one age group (and with a common value approach to life) to go off by themselves, thus insulating themselves from others, created misunderstandings that became known as "gaps," especially the "generation gap." The *real* differences weren't related to the age of the generations but to the value systems of those who had been programmed *together* as a generation.

At the opposite end of the age spectrum, the older retired people were the first to isolate themselves. The first "retirement town" was built by Del Webb in Arizona in 1960. It was a tremendous success. Grandmother and Grandfather were no longer at home helping with grandchildren. They were off to see the world or relaxing in their new "carefree" environment. In Sun City, all of the elements of the good life were available—markets, recreation centers, medical care, and the ever-present clubhouses. Lively companionship was the strongest selling point, not only for retirement villages but for swing-ing-single-sin centers.

A Tarnished Eagle

But more striking forms of change than "where one lived" surfaced in the 1960s. To many Americans—some of them intensely patriotic—the most shaking was the sudden questioning that our "defense machine" was somehow out of control. The great American war machine, which had been primarily for defense of democracy, was "good," even beneficial to the rest of the world. Suddenly, *it was a threat*—not just to foreign enemies, but to Americans and American society. This great power was suddenly questioned, and the uses of the power, especially against our own people, were challenged.

Why should we draft people to man the machine? "Hell no, we won't go!" What about the funds to sustain it? Shouldn't they be used to improve the ghettos, educate the underprivileged? What are our priorities? How should we use this valuable resource? What about the corruption, the armed forces bribing congressmen, and reporters with payoffs and preferred treatment? What about the CIA financing students, unions, and foundations and infiltrating groups of citizens? What of the contractors profiting on contracts awarded for "political" reasons? And the universities—weren't they on the take? What about their "support" of the war system? All of these questions and more challenged patriotism and the essence of the American system. The questioning of traditional power redefined patriotism. The *questions seemed appropriate* in America in the 1960s. The questions themselves did not go unnoticed by the pro-gramming young. To question, to want to know *why*, was built in to their value systems.

Twilight of "The Good Ol' Days"

One of the most sacred American beliefs and values suddenly wasn't working: no longer was it possible to "get together and work things out." From the beginning, American institutions had operated in a spirit of cooperativeness. But now in the 1960s, blacks lost whatever faith they had had in the whites' intention to work things out. When things weren't worked out, blacks "sat in" and burned down. In 1967, it was a bit difficult for an American businessman to conduct "business as usual" when snipers were shooting at his jetliner landing in Detroit. White students, many of whom had gone to the South in the early 1960s to help the civil rights movement and voted for LBJ because they thought he was against the war in Vietnam, discovered that "working within the system" was very slow and frustrating. They couldn't "push a button" and change the system. So they turned to mass demonstrations, draft resistance, campus protests, and throwing bombs. These radical actions, however positive the ends they sought, did not justify their means in the minds of many outraged Americans.

The older generations abandoned their own faith in "working things out" and began to support the police violence that exploded against demonstrators in Chicago at the 1968 Democratic convention. Traditionalists launched various forms of "backlash" against black militants. They elected reactionary public officials, approved repressive actions against such groups as the Black Panthers, opposed school integration, and moved to the suburbs to avoid physically confronting the "new enemy." All of this reached a terrifying climax in May of 1970 when the National Guard shot and killed four white demonstrators at Kent State University and Mississippi state police opened fire on black students at Jackson State University. Two died. *Don't Shoot—We Are Your Children* by J. Anthony Lukas summed up the anguish of many youth in its title. Significant Emotional Events slammed across the system. Everyone was being affected; some were actually changed.

The loss of the value of "working things out" generated a reaction of hostility in many Americans. By the end of the decade, Mr. Nixon felt it necessary to pledge that he would "bring us together." The division was real; it was critical; and it was deeper than most realized. It was the young, the black, and the poor against everyone else.

The battle lines were not even that clear. Remember, within each generation cluster there are always some whose values are "different" from the vast majority. Further, some are "changed" by Significant Emotional Events. Consequently, in the 1960s some young people *always* supported the war, hated long hair, and resented blacks, while some older people saw hope in student questions, began to sympathize with blacks, and challenged the war effort.

According to Tom Wicker of the *New York Times,* perhaps the best way to define the differences was between those who *believed on faith* in the continuance and benefits of American life and values and those who *believed on evidence* they saw that the American ideal was being perverted by such manipulators as Lyndon Johnson, Dean Rusk, Richard Nixon; the white-power structure; the military-industrial complex; such corrupt institutions as universities doing "defense" research; and labor unions that excluded blacks from good jobs.

So much gut-wrenching change had occurred in such a short period of time that millions were confused and overwhelmed, especially the older generations. Their feelings were reflected in letters like the following, from the foreword of Tom Wicker's *Great Songs of the Sixties:*

Dear Mr. Editor:

A few ideas, as we travel back down through memory lane:

If you are a native American, and you are old enough, you will probably remember when you never dreamed our country could ever lose; when you took for granted that women and the elderly and the clergy were to be respected; when you went to church and found spiritual food; when the clergy talked about religion; when a girl was a girl, when a boy was a boy, and when they liked each other.

You will probably remember when taxes were only a nuisance; when you knew your creditors and paid your debts; when the poor were too proud to take charity; when the words "care," "concern," "poverty" and "ghetto" were ordinary words and not overworked; when there was no bonus on bastards; when you knew that the law meant justice, and you had a feeling of protection and appreciation at the sight of a policeman; when young fellows tried to join the Army and Navy; when songs had a tune; when you bragged about your home state and your home town; and when politicians proclaimed their patriotism.

You will remember when clerks in stores tried to please you; when our government stood up for Americans anywhere in the world; when a man who went wrong was blamed, not his mother's nursing habits or his father's income; when everyone knew the difference between right and wrong; when you considered yourself lucky to have a good job, when you were proud to have one.

You may remember when people expected less and valued what they had more; when riots were unthinkable, when you took it for granted that the law would be enforced and your safety protected; when our flag was a sacred symbol; when America was the land of the free and home of the brave.

Do you remember when—or do you?

Every value-loaded statement and question in the above letter would probably bring a positive nod to most of those who were "over thirty" in the 1960s. Most of those who were "under thirty" probably cringed at such rhetoric, which sounded so empty to them. Even though such an idealized America probably never existed, it seemed to many older people that too much had changed too fast. Whatever your age, political affiliation, or color, if you longed for that kind of good ol' America, then what was actually happening in the 1960s disgusted, scared, and confused you.

The "yesterdays" that programmed the adult Americans of the 1960s were "different." Older generations, who had matured with different values rooted in the Depression and wars, had trouble relating to the emerging problems of the 1960s. They simply could not "compute" the horrors of living in a nuclear cloud, the ticks of a world population bomb, environmental destruction, or the frustrations of minorities long excluded from the American dream.

It is important to understand that those who marched in the streets during the 1960s were the first generation to grow up with the belief that if human life was threatened with extinction, the faults lay in man's own so-called technological achievements. This was the first generation that placed the highest importance on man's survival against himself. As Pogo so poignantly stated: "We have met the enemy and he is us." It was a message, a value-view, of such sweeping importance that the entire world was affected.

Two Steps Forward . . . One Step Back

Caught up in the chaos of the 1960s, many adults tried to justify what was happening by laying the blame on someone else. Parents were accused by the schools, who were in turn accused by the parents, who both accused Supreme Court decisions and liberal politics. Others looked to failing patriotism, still others felt the black movement had "moved too far too fast," while yet others began to criticize technology—especially the growing impact of television. But nowhere did the search find a common, definable scapegoat. Everyone was potentially the scapegoat for someone else.

In reality, positive changes were occurring throughout society. Blacks saw *real* hope in the 1954 Supreme Court decision. Suddenly, they found in the 1964 Civil Rights Act specific improvements in the legal arena. There was increased racially mixed use of public accommodations in the South and opening of housing elsewhere. Small changes encouraged rising expectations which led to further black agitation for even more social gains. This cause of racial conflict in the 1960s combined with an even greater force which had been generated in the 1950s: the then unnoticed phenomenon of the great black migration from the South into ghettos of the North and California. These blacks came looking for a better life only to find unemployment, overcrowded housing, and a white population no more sympathetic than in the South. *Unmet expectations* created *angry frustration.*

The major force fields that include all of the factors of value programming are technology, the economic sphere, the educational system, the inputs of media, changing life styles, and legal mandates. Extreme change occurred in all of these areas during the 1960s. But two of the areas are particularly critical. First, technology accomplished so many things so fast that it actually altered the means by which we (1) viewed the world, (2) were educated, (3) and were able to live and die. The problem was our own inability to control the new technology (as with the "atomic cloud" which still casts shadows).

The second factor, which was well established in its impact in the 1960s, was economic development. Our rising standard of living made obsolete the material standards by which Americans had been historically able to gauge themselves. Poverty was shifted from being an incurable disease for a large portion of the population to more of a special-interest group, like the oil depletion allowance. As poverty diminished in its impact (although millions still experienced it in the 1970s), the system was under pressure to shift from concern for a "standard of living" to the more abstract "quality of life." Suddenly with this change, millions of young Americans faced the never-before-defined problem of trying to find something productive to do with their own future. Maintaining a decent standard of living ceased to be the real problem and focus of our society. Now we became more concerned with self-gratification than contribution to the economy. The good life was in full swing.

In addition to creating changes in values because of *what* the value programmers did, there were also impacts because of *what these areas did not do.* For example, as man actually reached the moon in 1969, the question could also be raised as to why the same quantity and quality of effort, organization, and expenditure could not be focused on our earthbound problems. How could a society that was moving toward putting people in space not also focus on the growing pollution which was turning rivers and streams into sewers and clouding urban skies? Why was it easier to build super highways than mass-transit systems? With all of our affluence, high standard of living, disposable products, expanding golden arches, and increased leisure time in the richest nation that the world had ever seen, why were people still going hungry? Why were we focusing our energies and resources on creating an eighth wonder of the world like Houston's Astrodome, when within the same city browns and blacks still existed by the thousands on a poverty level? All of these questions were real and confusing, and raised conflicts in the minds and values of millions.

In a strange way, the technology and affluence of the 1960s suddenly betrayed the institutions, values, and ethics that had been based on an older, different system. Suddenly the issue of "relevance"—or, more realistically, the lack of it—became apparent in American educational systems. The generation in the streets and the one being reared before the television set were blasé towards computer technology, unimpressed by the glories and the dangers of the past, and had little if any concern for money (although this was not true for millions, since economic gain was *still* the basic thrust for older generations during that decade). Consequently, universities suddenly were seen as stuffy ivory towers that did not relate to the realities of the world around them. Insulated, isolated, and populated by teachers "out of touch," the American higher education system was directly challenged. Even though the universities had been criticizing the breakdown of training in public schools, to come under attack themselves created a crisis in its own right within our fortresses of the American dream, as recounted in Wicker's *Great Songs*.

One of the most "relevant" questions aimed at educational systems concerned the very basis of the system itself at all levels. By the mid-1960s, America was being dominated by youth, and these youths in many cases believed that they were not receiving from the schools what they should be receiving. Most adults thought the students were too young to know.

Primarily because of affluence, there was no need for young people to contribute actively to society. Adolescence evolved into a cult that was to be extended, enjoyed, and commercially catered to as no other generation had ever experienced. *Self-expression* and *child-centered* became part of the permissive jargon. In the schools, students chose from "elective" subjects. Even some grade-school students were expected to use computerized schedules to create their own "best" learning experiences. Many of them were too young to know what they were electing or should be electing. Teachers became pals, not authority figures. Elementary school teachers regressed to working with limited vocabularies and endless repetition.

In homes children were told that they were equal to their parents in nearly every way and that they should take part in decisions. This meant, at a minimum, *participation* in any decisions that affected that person. Since the kids would ride in a car, they now helped *select* the family car. This was perhaps the peak of children being seen *and* heard, in contrast to the past where they were *sometimes seen* but *infrequently heard*, if at all. Visitors faced the hazard of children who were treated as "pets" and who were not "put away" when company came. The family structure, the *primary* programming unit massively disrupted in the 1940s, further deteriorated in the 1950s, and reached a low-tide mark in the 1960s. Teen-agers were bound together by an antiauthoritarian, antiadult compact. Parents had lost control in their own homes. Society was conspiring against them, and one of the greatest offenders of all was television.

Television's portrayal of the American family was anything but inspiring. Wives dominated husbands by talking louder and knowing more. The fathers, as they had done in the 1950s, continued to work in ill-defined jobs. Families responded to their children by continuing to lavish the good life on them. The young had become the *now* generation, the new people, the Pepsi generation. Overindulgence of the young accelerated. Values slammed into the young from their rock-star heroes. Janis Joplin, who promoted a basic don't-give-a-damn attitude, killed herself with whiskey and drugs. Popular song lyrics pushed drugs, free sex, and "if it feels good, do it."

The emergence of a pampered youth population across the nation took unusual turns. Violence and vandalism became a common part of the teen-age scene. "Don't not do it, just don't get caught if you do it" was reinforced again and again. A Gallup poll found a startling difference between the values of parents and those of their children, Manchester reports. The poll reported that three out of four youngsters said they knew that cheating on tests was common, but it didn't seem to worry them. Drug usage grew and was soon accompanied by an increasing use of alcohol. In many homes fathers did the bartending (after all, it was better to drink than smoke "funny" cigarettes). Everything was changing, and the rate of change accelerated. By the late 1960s, X-rated movies tried to outdo themselves in their portrayal of explicit sex. *I Am Curious Yellow* was thought shocking, but it soon paled in comparison to *Deep Throat's* orgasm of living color.

As the educational system, the family unit, and relationships with friends underwent dramatic changes, no area was immune. The political system was a natural target for attack. The state subdivisions of the United States had been organized basically for the needs of the nineteenth century. Now faced with the onslaught of change in the twentieth century, they appeared outmoded, inefficient, under-financed, overlapping, jealous, and antiquated. The "umbrella" federal system collected massive tax monies, but it could not effectively redistribute them against an impossible variety of problems. The political system created gigantic federal building projects and technological leaps forward, but could not seem to protect teachers in urban schools or people walking their dogs. By the end of the 1960s, it was becoming very clear to many people that the United States—wealthy and intelligent as it might be—was simply not organized to cope with the twentieth century or to control the things that affluence and technology had made possible. For those people born in the post-World War II period who were programmed through these rapid changes, it was simply impossible to blindly accept on faith the "traditional" American system. Further, they became basically distrustful of its workings and claims.

As our institutions seemed to falter and fail, ethical standards and values were not far behind. Government officials tried preaching nonviolence to radicals and blacks, but they could not restrain the violence of their own agents. Perhaps the height of the inconsistency was the 1968 Democratic convention in Chicago, when Mayor Richard Daly, operating in fear, distrust, and hate, launched a violent police attack on passive demonstrators. The U.S. presidency itself was challenged as the recent occupants of the office were caught frequently misleading and lying to the American people. Political rhetoric about the glories of the nation's history sounded even more hollow when it was used to respond to those who tried to point out obvious current deficiencies. A sense of hopelessness began to sweep the nation. What good were affluence and technology if they could not solve the problems that were so real?

In fact, the changes that were going on in the United States made the traditional values of historic America—hard work, self-discipline, personal material success, and productivity—all seem irrelevant. Obviously, conformity to the old values was not the *only* norm of respectability and social acceptability in the world of the 1960s. Those values seemed more irrelevant and the conformity to the old values more stifling. It is little wonder that those who were programmed during the 1960s—and, in fact, everyone—were confused by the contrast between Richard Nixon's 1968 campaign theme of "Bring us together" and Broadway's rock musical hit, *Hair*. They vividly portrayed how far apart the generations really were.

The thrust of America throughout history had been toward creation of the good life, a better life for all. Although, admittedly, many had been denied that better life, it still arrived on a massive scale, and progress was being made in bringing deprived groups into the mainstream of society. But now with the 1960s, suddenly everything was open to question. What was the value of affluence? What were the rewards for this value, if, in fact, it meant the destruction of the family, increased teen-age pregnancies, drug abuse, alcoholism, and vandalism? Something seemed wrong with the entire system. Basic questions occurred repeatedly: What values could be erected in the place of the old? What had our material overachievement brought us? Technologically we seemed to have become slaves. Although the technology itself was useful, helpful, even interesting and entertaining, it seemed that we were on a course of climbing new scientific mountains simply because they were there. The Americans programmed in the post-World War II period moved away from the god of technology and the overindulgence of affluence toward social involvement, personal and intellectual development, preservation of the environment, constructive use of leisure, and better public services for all. These were in direct contrast to the values that had historically challenged the youth of America. The values of the past eroded under the pressures of the realities of the 1960s.

Electronic SEEs

One of the decade's realities was television's evolution from an instrument of entertainment in the 1950s to an electronic injector of Significant Emotional Events in the 1960s. It was one of the most unique aspects of change ever experienced by humans. With unrelenting intensity, it slammed the changing world against the value fortresses of the older generations. For the young, TV was the primary programmer. Television was uniquely important in value programming because of the major changes occurring: the civil rights movement, the assassinations, the Vietnam War, and the conquest of space. Each of these events dramatically altered gut-level values in our society. Thus, in four major areas—social change, awareness of *real* death, acceptance of those who were "different" as normal, and boredom with extremes—our values changed.

Social change usually occurs slowly within a society. Occasionally, a major event will trigger its acceleration—the French Revolution, the American Civil War, and the Russian Revolution. Sometimes, a single event becomes a benchmark for major change throughout society.

Do you remember May 17, 1954? That was when the U.S. Supreme Court said in effect: "Thou *shalt* integrate thy school systems."

In some schools across the country, teachers broke into tears. They knew it was the beginning of the end of the world as they had known it. What they didn't know, couldn't know, was how unbelievably rapidly we could change with respect to relations between the races in this nation. We have a long way to go before relations are truly smooth, but in a relatively short period of time, giant steps have been taken.

By the late 1950s, Martin Luther King was well on his way to becoming a national, soon-to-be-international hero. Civil rights had exploded in the South and were erupting in the North and West.

Why the late 1950s? Why Martin Luther King? There had been other great black heroes in the past.

Why, did you ever ask yourself, did this nation *really* experience the intensity of the civil rights eruptions? Probably . . . *primarily* because of *television*. Think about it very clearly. Let your mind go way back in time.

We *knew* what had been going on! Harriet Beecher Stowe wrote *Uncle Tom's Cabin* in 1852. It was *all* there—the bigotry, the hate, the prejudice. *Roots* was *real*—and *they all knew it*. For those who bothered to read the newspapers and magazines in the 1920s and 1930s, it was there—the whole bloody mess. But, as a nation we had ignored it. It was *unpleasant,* and we didn't want to do anything unpleasant. Did we, white America?

As a nation, as individuals, we didn't *want* to get involved. We didn't *have* to get involved—so long as it was *just* in print, so long as we could "turn it off" emotionally. With *television*, whether we liked it or not, *we were there emotionally.* We were *there* with George Wallace at the schoolhouse door barring black children. We were *there* with Bull Connor's snarling police dogs and fire hoses. As a nation, we "sat" at lunch counters watching people order hamburgers (that probably weren't worth eating) while others came in and attacked. As a nation we *finally* began to say: "Wait a minute. What do I believe? What is *right, wrong*? How do *I* stand in in this situation?"

Significant Emotional Events—a whole series of them were electronically injected, changing us. Television had that power, the *power to change.* You don't think so? You don't think this very second as you sit reading this book that you're not "different" because of television?

Where were you on November 22, 1963?

The day John Kennedy died in Dallas, Texas.

Remember that day?

What did you say? Did you cry?

What was the color of the sky?

That moment, that event is perhaps one of the singularly most significant points in the history of human beings. The planet Earth "froze" emotionally on that day. That is the *first time,* that around the world, hundreds of millions of people were *simultaneously, emotionally involved in a single event.* An event so powerful, so intense, that whomever you meet for the rest of your life, if they lived that day in time, can talk to you in amazing detail about it. Those who lived it, experienced it, were value impacted by it, would never forget it. Even for the very young, the memory of the drama of those few days is still very real, very important.

Remember the funeral? Jackie, with her veil blowing in the breeze; the lone caisson going down Pennsylvania Avenue; little John saluting; the sound of the drums—The Day of the Drums.

That day, that moment, those events were intensely critical for the young generations. For those now in their twenties and thirties, John Kennedy had been a *major hero.* He was *elected* on television. They lived in "Camelot" on television. He *died for real* on television. His death wasn't fake like on "Bonanza" or "Gunsmoke." *It was real death, emotionally felt.* For older generations, *real death* wasn't a part of their value programming. When older generations were ten, they didn't know the *violence* of death. Death's violence was part of the adult world; the young were shielded, insulated. But those now in their twenties and thirties were *value programmed with violent death.* They watched their heroes die for real, one by one— John Kennedy, Martin Luther King, Bobby Kennedy. Death came again and again as those now in their twenties and thirties value programmed. The blood, the guts, the gore, the violence of the Vietnam War were "electronically mainlined" into their thought processes, day after day, as they sat in their own homes trying to eat their evening meals. These generations *are* different—honestly, sincerely, *completely different.* As a generation, they've had a lot of trouble articulating those differences. But the *differences* are there, and they are *real.* They even "hate" differently.

Remember how people "hated" in World War II? They *loved* it. They practically had fun hating. It's easy, it's fun to hate a *group of people.* They looked at thirty thousand people screaming "Heil, Hitler" in a plaza in Berlin and thought "Get the Krauts, get *all* the Krauts. Wipe 'em out." "Look at all the Japs. Press a button, *vaporize* the Japs." It's *fun,* it's actually *easy* to hate a *group of people.* But it's damn difficult to hate an *individual* Vietnamese mother holding her war-torn child. And that's how young people in the 1960s and 1970s thought about *those people* all along— as *individuals* to be dealt with, not as *masses* to be vaporized. The young people were different—very different in their gut-level reactions to other people and their problems, to death, to war, to excitement, and to what was interesting.

Excitement. . . . We craved it!

We became "bored." Unless things were truly dramatic/spectacular, as a nation we seemed not to care. The young sought increased intensity in rock concerts, their language, the underground press, and their extreme demands on the good life. The older generations were also affected. An excellent example of changing American values, rapidly shifting under the intensity of television's unblinking eye, can be found in the American space program. If you think back over time, you can see the amazing shift from the "beep . . . beep . . . beep" of Sputnik to that hot night on July 20, 1969. The world stayed awake to watch as Neil Armstrong became the first human being to actually *touch the moon.*

We were there, live, emotionally, and in color. With his first step—whomp—millions thought, "My God, we've *reached the moon.*" Two years later, millions of people in this nation said, "Oh what the hell, why are they gathering all those *rocks?* We don't care about *that!* Let's see something *interesting. Let's be entertained!*" Young people? Their initial excitement rapidly faded to an attitude of "Big deal, we'll watch a rerun—they're *only* going to the moon." Think about that from a value-programming point of view. From the beginning of time man had dreamed of flying, reaching the moon. Now we could do it, sense it, "feel" it! But America's reaction became "To hell with it; let's see something exciting!"

Television jaded us. Television taught us to be bored. Boredom has continued as one of the major problems in all areas of society. Educational systems reported that their students were bored. Classes were an interruption of their "real" education. Within the family unit, talk became impossible. Television took over. Studies indicated that children were spending more time with television than with anything else. The content of television increased its intensity. The gun-fight westerns of the 1950s gave way to the detective blood baths of the 1960s. New extremes were reached in sex, violence, and language. If you don't think America isn't jaded and bored unless something is extremely intense, go to the movies. Movies are but a reflection, a mirror of the values being programmed and expressed in society.

During the late sixties, the movies reflected the shifting values within our society. Three were especially popular among the young: *Butch Cassidy and the Sundance Kid, Easy Rider,* and *The Graduate.* In the first, the heroes killed people and robbed banks for a living. Everyone thought it was great fun. In the second, drug dealers became martyrs—it was "the way to go." "Bad guys" became "good guys," and vice versa. Finally, *The Graduate* summarized the chasm that had developed between two major groups in our society: those who were programmed before the late 1940s and early 1950s and those who were programmed after that period. With lots of sex, profanity, and social commentary, it symbolized, perhaps more than any other popular movie, the value conflicts that existed during the 1960s.

Pluses and Minuses

As the 1960s drew to a close, it was obvious that several major value shifts had occurred. We had moved from a predominantly agricultural society to a largely industrial one, although more people were employed in white-collar than in blue-collar jobs. We had evolved from a primarily rural and small-town society to a largely urban and suburban one. The economy had shifted from one of scarcity (in which productivity and production were the primary goals) to one of abundance and affluence (in which consumption was the main goal and distribution the main problem). We had changed from a geographically stable society before the 1940s to a highly mobile world. Our relatively primitive communication systems had evolved to a highly sophisticated level, where time delays had given way to "instant emotional involvement." We had moved from a labor- and job-oriented society to one increasingly concerned with the use of leisure time.

During all of this time, the major institutions of our society—schools, industry, government, church—had remained very much the same. During the 1950s and 1960s the institutions were being run by generations that found it increasingly difficult to be in tune with the technological environment that had developed. The young people, on the other hand, had never experienced any other world but the very complex one through which they had been value programmed. What was good/bad, right/wrong, normal/not normal to the younger people was very confusing, even threatening, to many of the older people.

In sorting out the gains and the losses of the 1960s, one can readily recognize the importance of the changes that had occurred. Whether one agrees or disagrees or likes or dislikes them, the shifts were reality. American youth had established a new place in our society. It was a force to be reckoned with at every level and had an impact on a worldwide basis. Although the flower children had faded rapidly, they had affected society by moving it from a drab sameness into a riot of color and sound and lights. People were beginning *to enjoy and have fun without feeling guilty about it.*

Within the educational system, some positive gains were fairly obvious. Much had changed, not only for those who were programmed through the school systems, but for the generations that would follow them. In many places, what amounted to puritanical rules of conduct had been discarded. Students were given at least a small voice in campus decisions. They influenced the curricula and began to participate. The forces of our political system redirected attention to social and economic inequalities. Minority groups developed a sense of purpose and direction that they did not have before, in addition to a place within the society beyond the menial skill level. The forces of the 1950s and 1960s made *very clear* the illogical contrast of "pockets of poverty" in the midst of our affluent society. It became increasingly difficult for anyone to ignore these problems.

While the Vietnam War did not end until the 1970s, during the 1960s millions of people began to examine and question the policies and the politics of American involvement. Change came through demonstrations and publicity. There was a massive re-examination of the draft, America's commitment, and our historical role in the world as "protectorate of the underprivileged."

The political process itself was closely examined. Historically, the American political system of conventions and the electoral college dated back to frontier days. Suddenly, with communication networks readily available, it was technologically possible that more citizens— in fact *every* citizen—could participate directly.

Television, the major communication linkage, brought coverage of disruptive activities to the attention of millions. Although there was difficulty in understanding *what was happening*, it became obvious that there was a *difference* between law enforcement and justice. Or if there wasn't, there should be. The whole concept of law and order began to be reexamined. Although the underground press that sprang up during the 1960s was extreme in every respect, its existence reminded our traditional press that the right of free speech is *dependent* upon the *responsibility* to correctly inform the people. Freedom and responsibility in our society were examined head-on. Finally, the massive changes that occurred during the 1960s caused many adults to reevaluate their own way of life, their gut-level values, and how these related to their world. The basic question seemed to be not what or how, but *why?* Unfortunately, during the 1960s the best answer seemed to be: "Because that's the way we've always done it, and by damn, that's the way we're going to continue to do it!" That sort of comment, rooted in the value programming of the adults, was simply no longer adequate for generations that had been programmed since the 1950s. "To ask a lot of embarassing questions" was programmed into the gut-level value systems of the young.

The negative dimensions of change during the 1950s and 1960s were also apparent. There was considerable destruction and loss of life. Violence was being condoned as a means to an end, even though violence itself was in direct conflict with the ends sought. Historically, this *has* been a country of violence. During the 1950s and 1960s, television *reinforced* the concept that violence solved problems.

The violence of the 1960s, which seemed "correct" to many at that time, probably programmed the very young at that time to be more passive, more resistant to the use of such tactics. Perhaps because the rebels were so caught up in their own rapidly changing world of values, they failed to recognize the historical threads of our nation. They thought *they* were the first generation to really challenge the old order, but there had been sincere efforts by millions of people who protested, went to jail, and gave their lives in the enormously painful task of creating the world that was possible for the young to enjoy. Those who had faced each day in perhaps a humdrum existence of getting up and going to work had helped to *create* the world of affluence that made the changes of the 1960s possible. In their burst of enthusiasm to create further change, the young were terribly inconsistent. On the one hand they would say: "We're against the war. Stop the killing." In the next breath they screamed: "If you're not against war, we'll kill you." Although they held pollution rallies trying to clean up the environment, it took two dump trucks to haul away all the trash they left behind. Such inconsistency justifiably irritated and confused the older generation.

Sadly, many young people in the 1960s seemed to lack a sense of humor. They made fun of the older generations, and in that "fun" tried to make their point. But they seemed incapable of laughing at themselves. In its own way, the generation that finished its value programming and began to actually participate in society during the 1960s was as rigid and conformist as the system it sought to change. They were too intense, too committed. When you laugh at yourself and not at others, the world is much more manageable.

Overall, the 1960s saw the greatest changes in the shortest period of time that any society had ever experienced. It *all* changed —politically, legally, economically, socially, commercially—everything flip-flopped. It was difficult to keep up, frustrating to the extreme, and led to the phenomenon of the 1970s that Alvin Toffler so aptly labeled *Future Shock*.

127

THE 1970s: IN THE EYE OF THE STORM

As we entered the 1970s, those who were in their fifties and sixties (programmed through the 1920s and 1930s) looked at the world they had created, the good life, and found that it seemed to be falling apart. What was happening in the early 1970s was not a realization of the Great Society or the challenge of a New Frontier, but what appeared to be a massive disintegration of the good life born in the post-World War II period. There were seemingly endless reasons for feeling frustrated—inflation, pollution, crime, the war, the stock market, the generation gap, immorality, riots, traffic, strikes against the public, racism, skyjacking, and bumper stickers that insulted everybody. Nothing seemed to be working right. It was increasingly evident to social observers that major areas of our entire society had shifted. However, such shifts were still being ignored, or even fought, by large segments of the population. Parents couldn't understand their own teenagers because the parents hadn't been paying enough attention to what happened to their kids while they were being value programmed in the 1960s.

The publication in 1970 of *Future Shock* by Alvin Toffler offered a massive coverage of the impact on the future of the changes already well under way within the society. The fabulous 1950s had sizzled, the soaring 1960s had crashed, and the 1970s looked challenging, confusing, and frustrating. Toffler's book looked at " . . . the roaring current of change, a current so powerful today that it overturns institutions, shifts our values, and shrivels our roots."

According to Toffler, "future shock" was a *time* phenomenon. It arose from superimposing a *new culture* on an *old one*. Unlike the past (where we had time to get used to change), or culture shock (where one knows deep down one can return to "the old familiar way of doing things"), future shock meant that we were suddenly confronted with a diversity of values, institutions, and subcults within our own society. But there was no way to go back. The present was with us so overwhelmingly that we couldn't ignore it, try as we might.

A 1970 Associated Press report read widely in newspapers across the country seemed to summarize how we felt with its title "Snap!— The Plastic Life Cracks at the Seams." The following material is from that article by Saul Pett. As you read it, remember that while it is his view of what was happening in 1970, it is a view shared by millions.

Quality of life? You could start anywhere.

With a new car that won't start or an old war that won't end or a dollar that won't stretch or an optimism that won't revive. Or a lake too dirty to swim in or a plane that is late or a supermarket checkout counter that resembles an exercise line for the catatonic. Or the phone bill you can't understand and the computer you can't fight or insult or the traffic that boils your bile or blacks whose progress is too fast or too slow or just right for no one. Or the two-way generational guilt a man can feel today, toward the young who get away and the old he puts away, or that vague unspoken feeling that life is cheating us these days, or the single fact that poor old square dad has to hide in the cellar to hear his Tommy Dorsey records and what in the hell ever happened to simple nonpolitical, nonissue-oriented, noncrisis-connected, nonecological romance in the U.S. of A.?

"New Equation"

Quality of life? You could start anywhere. With a crack by comedian Woody Allen: "Not only is there no God but try getting a plumber on weekends." . . . Or with the feeling of . . . Archibald MacLeish, that "someone has written a new equation somewhere and our lives have changed without our changing them. . . ."

We walk safely among the craters of the moon but not in the parks of New York or Chicago or Los Angeles. Technology and change run berserk, headlights hide by day and moral values shred overnight. The unthinkable multiplies until it seems "things fall apart; the center cannot hold."

The standard of living rises while the satisfaction of living declines. Hunger haunts our prosperity and minorities circle the conscience of the majority with louder cries. The young mock our past, robbing us of the comfort of our victories in depression and war; and inflation, the ubiquitous pickpocket keeps lifting the pay raise in our wallets. The planes are faster and the cars are faster, but we have fewer unspoiled places to go and more people who want to get there. Problems beget solutions which beget new problems. . . .

No Longer Immune

But America, we seem suddenly to have discovered, is no longer infallible or, as Arthur Schlesinger notes, immune to history. We are no longer the good guys who win all the wars and at home and abroad we are caught, Schlesinger says, in the "collapse of our pretensions." America, we seem suddenly to have discovered, is no longer infinite in space or resource or hope. There is no next valley of quiet or virgin forest to treat. Beauty diminishes and tastelessness and flatness abide in neon lights and urban sprawl. Beer cans now litter the beach of our beginnings, at Plymouth Rock, and 6,000 miles away, at the other end, Polynesia turns plastic. The hotel sign in Honolulu says, "Aloha Congoleum dealers."

Each year seems like another year of the locusts, another tear in the national psyche, and there is now a special terror, a flashing feeling of here we go again with the words, "We interrupt this program to bring you a special news bulletin." Another assassination or riot, or massacre in Vietnam? Or an accident in those mysterious mountain arsenals where we have enough bombs and germ weapons to kill the race of man?

Everyday Thing

We live with the trauma of the present and apocalyptic visions of the future. Every day, it seems, serious experts tell us that our society may become a series of armed camps between black and white, urban and suburban. Every day, it seems, serious experts surround us with doomsday predictions of a shattered ecology, of babies dying from pollutants in the soil, of lakes and oceans dying, of a population too vast to feed, of the atmosphere warming up enough to melt glaciers and drown cities. City noises, we are told, can damage our ears, constrict our blood vessels, and increase our blood pressure, and laboratory experiments show that prolonged exposure to excessive sound has made homosexuals out of rats. Will the cavalry never come?

We live in an expanding theatre of the absurd and the unreal. Between beers, we watch real men dying on television and, same station, same network, we get a poetic message about the dangers of smoking and a poetic message about the joys of smoking.

In Santa Barbara, California, a seabird is unable to take off because of the weight of oil on its wings and a man in a plexiglass helmet steam-cleans the black sludge off the rocks and a bitter resident predicts, "Next thing, they'll be putting plastic crabs on the beach to make it seem natural again." Elsewhere, a deadline proclaims, "Aleutian Bomb Is Fired Without Setting Off Earthquake." Look, ma, no earthquake.

Numbers Game

Much of the quality of life in America today is related to numbers, lopsided numbers. "In the United States," Gertrude Stein once wrote, "there is more space where nobody is than where anybody is. This is what makes America what it is."

In the United States, two-thirds of the people live on one-fiftieth of the land. In the United States, trends persuade experts that we will be 300 million by the year 2000 and, to accommodate the added 100 million, we will have to crowd them in where we are or build the equivalent of a new city of 250,000 every 40 days for 30 years, 35 more Los Angeleses or 250 more Newarks (N.J.) or 1,500 more Levittowns (Pa.). The mind boggles.

Where we already are, we are crammed and cranky.

Every day it becomes harder to remember the smug satisfaction we once took from pictures of those godless Communists lining up for scarce consumer goods in Moscow. Now we God-fearing Capitalists are lining up all over America.

Lines for Everything

We line up for our pleasure and our pain, for ski lifts, trains, planes, license plates, school lunches, tax payments, college registration, golf courses, movies, supermarkets, restaurants, and popcorn. We line up to buy and we line up to pay, to vote, to get into the Army and out of the Army, into debt and out of debt. We line up, too, in those dandy turnpike restaurants while there are empty tables and after a plastic meal line up for the privilege of paying. We line up our cars, bumper to bumper, for the privilege of working in cities and the need to escape them.

Deeper into Mountains

We save our money to buy boats and car trailers and in the great rush to see nature as it is, we see it as it never was; all those other boats give the sea an unnatural chop and all those other cars give the land an unnatural glut. If you live in Denver, you have to go deeper into the mountains every year for solitude, and if you live in Los Angeles you have to go farther for a deserted beach, and if you live in New York, forget it.

We have come a long, long way from those days and nights on the prairies when, in Sherwood Anderson's words, men alone in the fields sensed a "bigness outside themselves . . . a mystery whispered in the grass . . . a deep semireligious feeling . . . it had taken the shrillness out of them. They had learned the trick of quiet." Where do we learn it now?

We have polluted the land and the air and the water, defaced the horizon with commercial clutter and blurred our history and our symbols with dollar signs. We have left Lake Erie beyond redemption and Lake Tahoe beyond recognition. We have pasteurized our milk and put strontium 90 in its source and enough waste in streams and lakes to kill 15 million fish in one year. We have turned the New England farm of Robert Frost into an auto junk yard, and built highrises that block the view of Mt. Rainier near Seattle and the bay in San Francisco and the surf in Waikiki and countless other vistas that nourish the soul of man. We have put enough smog in the air over Los Angeles to warn school children not to play too strenuously or breathe too deeply on the days of the amber cloud and enough toxics in the air over New York to make a day's walking and breathing equal the intake of almost two packs of cigarettes. And between the two coasts we have made eyes smart in mile-high Denver and not-as-high Phoenix and countless smaller places once idyllic.

DDT in Atlantic

We have put DDT in the shellfish off Martha's Vineyard in the Atlantic and frenzy in Hawaii in the Pacific and human excrement in Sugar Creek, Charlotte, N.C., as well as the streams of tiny Peterborough, N.H., where Thornton Wilder based his bittersweet tale of *Our Town*. We have mined enough coal and iron to sag and crack two million acres of land and strip-mined enough to bring floods in Kentucky and West Virginia. We have made parking lots out of houses older than the American Revolution and rumpus room bars out of trees older than the discovery of America. We have taken the view looking south on Park Avenue, New York, where views are as scarce as free rentals, and filled it with concrete and glass, like a mottled monster dam, and this was called "air rights." We have broken the serene blue line of the Pacific off Santa Barbara with crablike monsters of metal, and this was called "oil rights."

We have paved valleys with giant shopping centers and blanketed meadows with dreary housing developments and scarred mountains with utility poles. We have shaken our ecology with technology, our houses with huge diesel trucks and our teeth with monster jets and we have put enough cars on the "freeways" of California to tie up, in a single accident, 200 vehicles, like uncut sausage.

We have suffered, in Lewis Mumford's words, "disorder, blight, dingy mediocrity, screaming neon-lighted vulgarity. . . . We have ceased to respect ourselves . . . we have ceased to cherish our own history and to enlarge our own prospects, by promoting character and variety and beauty wherever we find it, in landscapes or in people."

Scene From *Our Town*

In the play, *Our Town*, editor Webb falls in step one evening with the town constable.

Mr. Webb: "Oh, Bill, if you see my boy smoking cigarettes, just give him a word, will you? He thinks a lot of you, Bill."

Constable Warren: "I don't think he smokes no cigarettes, Mr. Webb. Leastways, not more'n two or three a year."

Mr. Webb: ". . . I hope not. Well, good night, Bill."

Constable Warren: "Good night, Mr. Webb."

In another scene, reference is made to two women who "cooked three meals a day—one of 'em for 20 years, the other for 40—and no summer vacation. They brought up two children apiece, washed, cleaned the house—and never had a nervous breakdown."

In that play, Thornton Wilder mostly had Peterborough of early in this century in mind. Today Peterborough is a town of 4,000, snug in the valley of two lovely hills, dominated by church steeples, still postcard-pretty and relatively serene. Only relatively.

Like most of America today, it is more affluent and more nervous than it was. The women have washing machines and vacuum cleaners and regular vacations, some as far as Florida and Europe. And the high school seniors, whose annual class trip used to be to Washington by train, now fly to Rome or Paris or Rhodes. Today, Peterborough has its share of nervous breakdowns. Today it is highly doubtful any father would expect an errant son to listen to a cop. Use of drugs among the young has begun to creep from outlying cities and colleges into *Our Town.*

Change, Change

Change, change, change. Will nothing hold still?

Kids sleep together before they are married and marry before they can support themselves and poor old Dad is regarded as oppressively square for asking, "When will you find yourself?" Today's new jet is obsolete tomorrow, today's new superhighway is a bottleneck tomorrow, today's new clothes dryer needs a repairman tomorrow and today's new mini is maxi tomorrow. A war to stop the spread of communism, which was credible in Korea, becomes a credibility gap in Vietnam; liberals exchange postures with conservatives; and yesterday's interventionist talks isolation today. Teachers close down schools by strike, police and firemen threaten to walk out, soldiers circulate underground newspapers denouncing the Army, priests quit to marry and the Pope has his troubles with his bishops.

TVs and Hunger

Baseball and football teams switch franchises, leagues subdivide like amoebae, widows outnumber widowers, women turn jockey and the star quarterback of Harvard quits because the game has become "too mechanistic and too violent." Candidates for president are shouted down, and presidents of the United States cannot travel without screaming pickets, and young men with beards and bullhorns take over faculty meetings and business meetings and science meetings. Stalin's daughter finds escape from Russian oppression in the United States and thousands of Americans find escape from the draft in Canada and the last secretary of state finds difficulty getting a routine job in his home state. The work week grows shorter, leisure time grows longer, and the sale of sleeping pills rises. But for a quarter you can make the bed vibrate. A man making $20,000 moonlights to make ends meet, the Salvation Army turns down gifts of working stoves and TV sets because it has too many, and the poor are hungry.

What do we tell the young? Where do we go wrong, where do we miss?

"We've been as good parents as we could possibly be. We've done everything you do according to the book—taken vacations together, gone on pack trips together, traveled all over the world. We've been a good Christian family. My wife and I have tried to set a good example by being a good example."

Thus, the poignant cry of Art Linkletter, a wealthy television entertainer, whose 20-year-old daughter, youngest of five, experimented with LSD and went out a window six floors up. The cry of one father at the extreme tragic end of a national spectrum called the youth problem.

At the other end, the wistful regret of another father, a reporter in Louisville: "We like the boy she married. He's fine. But she dropped out of college early to get married. And you know, I had kinda looked forward to going to those homecoming games with a pretty coed waving a football pennant. For just a little while. Now all I hear is the high cost of pediatricians and playpens."

Parents' Questions

Two ends of a spectrum of concern, and in betweeen, in many different places large and small, are many different kinds of parents, rich and poor, progressive and conservative, worried, confounded, outraged by or disappointed in their young.

No-problem days grow fewer, new-problem days come faster, complexity multiplies with a sense of helplessness, of things not working, of everything hitting the fan at once. One senses that if a single man could speak for 200 million Americans, that man, any day now, will slap his newspaper down, turn off the TV, kick his checkbook and ills and credit cards aside, elbow his way roughly through an insistent family and an insistent world until he climbs the highest mountain on earth and there, into the howling winds, screams, "I am goddamn tired of coping!"

Tired and numbed.

A president's commission tells us we are a racist nation. Another presidential commission tells us we are the most violent nation in the world. An historian tells us the streets are less safe these days than during the Depression when millions were hungry and jobless. The phone operator tells us the circuits are busy.

Runaway Arsenals

The General Accounting Office tells us that our major weapons systems are costing at least $20 billion more than original estimates and that no one in the government knows the total number of systems being acquired or their costs. Wives tell us the checkbook is unbalanced, and teachers tell us about the new math, and ministers tell us the kids will have no faith unless we go to church regularly, and doctors tell us you can get cancer from smoking and hungry from not smoking and heart failure from overeating. Editorialists tell us that responsible citizenship requires we understand the issues but no one tells us how in the hell a man today thinks his way through the ABM or MIRV or SST or LSD or HEW or DNA. The President tells us we must lower our voices, and the vice president calls peace demonstrators intellectual eunuchs. The phone operator says the circuits are still busy.

The Supreme Court says integrate and black militants say they want their own institutions. The blacks in Gary, Ind., which is 60 percent Negro, tell publisher Walter Ridder of the *Post-Tribune* that he is a "racist" for not publishing enough black news and the whites tell him he is a "nigger lover" for printing too much black news, and all over America readers complain to editors, "Why don't you tell us what is good about America?"

Unreconciled Facts

The President of the United States tells us we will have all our combat troops out by and by and the president of South Vietnam, a junior partner, says no, not all. The moralists tell us we must do something about pornography and the civil libertarians warn us about censorship. The builders tell us we will have planes big enough to carry 400 at a clip and fast enough to cut two hours off the ocean trip and no one asks us if we want that. Science reminds us that science has made it possible for more babies to survive birth, more people to survive disease and more old people to live longer, and environmentalists tell us we are running out of space for ourselves and our garbage.

The airline tells us the skies are friendly and the friendly stewardess tells us, after that damned little paper creamer squirts milk all over us, "I don't know why they give us those things." But nobody tells us who "they" are, either they who are the silent majority or they who want those huge tail lights that blind the driver behind. And the CIA tells us they can't tell us anything. The tailors tell us you can't lengthen the hem of the new miracle fabrics because the permanent creases will not come out. The flip kids with the lapel pins tell us, "God is not dead; he just doesn't want to get involved." The phone operator says the circuits are STILL busy.

A full catalogue of our miseries serves a purpose other than masochism. "If we could first know where we are and whither we are tending," said Lincoln, "we could better judge what to do, and how to do it."

Unknown Needs

Where we are, most thinkers agree, is an untended garden, overgrown and wildly seeded, in which human purpose has been obscured. We have much of what we don't want and have almost forgotten what we do want. "It is not so much that the pace is fast but that it is somebody else's pace or schedule," says Paul Goodman, social philosopher. The poets and the philosophers and the psychiatrists agree: Men must somehow regain control of their lives.

There is among many Americans today a yearning for new prophets. "We need some great statements about what America is about and what we can do about it," says the Rev. Theodore M. Hesburgh, president of the University of Notre Dame. "We need leaders with a large vision of what the world needs. In a sense we're almost like the Jews were when they needed a prophet to come down from the mountain and tell them some hard things and what to do about them."

But government has its limits, says a man of government, presidential adviser Daniel Moynihan. "It cannot provide values to persons who have none, or who have lost those they had. It cannot provide a meaning to life. It cannot provide inner peace. It can provide outlets for moral energies but it cannot create those energies."

People, we are being told, must find these things themselves. The oratory and literature of the day are, in fact, full of reminders for many different kinds of people. The minorities are reminded of the progress already made toward more justice and equality. The young and the old are reminded of the need to seek such wisdom that each possesses. The majority, silent or otherwise, is reminded that a flag decal is not the limit of patriotism, that the American Revolution was led by a minority of intellectuals and scholars and politicians.

Pain Shows Way

And the all-out pessimists are reminded that the beginning of the cure is the pain of the illness, that people who become aware of their troubles have thereby taken the first step toward solutions. It was, after all, an official commission appointed by a president of the United States which said this is a racist nation and another presidential commission which documented the full extent of its violence. A majesty clings to a system which says these things about itself.

Progress there is. The government is committed to ending the war, or at least the combat. There are nuclear disarmament talks. There is a commitment to equality and justice. Arguments there are as to method and speed and even intent, but there are commitments. The physical world around us is no longer the exclusive concern of poets or eccentric bird watchers or old ladies in tennis shoes. More and more people actively seek to conserve a tree, a lake, a view. More people question the biblical injunction to be fruitful and multiply. More people question the old American faith in growth and expansion and suggest that maybe what we don't need is another factory in town. More middle-aged people have begun to sense a validity in the young who scorn the plastic life. Congress has appropriated funds to fight air and water pollution. People have made a difference. It was people—individuals before they were groups —who by marching or just answering Dr. Gallup's questions began to turn the country around from war toward peace.

But awareness and commitments, we are constantly reminded, are only beginnings that guarantee nothing.

"We will not find a way out of our present troubles," says John Gardner, former secretary of Health, Education and Welfare, "until we have the courage to look honestly at evil where evil exists, until we foreswear hypocrisy, until we call injustice and dishonor by their right names, and until a large number of Americans from each sector of opinion—right, left and center— are willing to acknowledge their own special contribution to our troubles.

". . . There is no middle state for the spirit. It rises to high levels of discipline and decency and purpose—or it sags and rots. We must call for the best or live with the worst."

This verbal portrait evokes the myriad of confused feelings that ran rampant in this country as the 1970s began. The confusion seemed to center on values, those personal and internal issues versus those at work externally in the society. The new decade suddenly *compressed* the changes that had been mounting into one period of *intense change* in value programming. The feeling that gnawed at millions was one of disillusionment, irritation, and confusion. Many of the problems mentioned in Pett's article are still with us and have intensified; others are being reversed, solved, or eliminated. The scars and the value impact of these events were felt by those who were programmed during the 1970s. This young generation experienced a programming period of more complexity, diversity, and confusion than perhaps any other generation in our history. It is little wonder that young adults today are wary of the adult world they have entered.

In 1971 campuses were quiet, reflecting the impact of Kent State. In effect, we had said: "If you do it again, we'll kill you." Four young people died. And that was truly tragic. But the historical reality was that an entire generation experienced a Significant Emotional Event via the media coverage of Kent State. The number of riots on college campuses dropped to nil. The protests moved to Washington—the war was still going on.

The young in the early 1970s were programmed daily watching the war in "living color." The impact on these young children was profound, but not so great as the impact on the young adults who had just been value programmed through the deteriorating 1960s. Their protests and embarrassing questions caught the federal administration and the military complex off guard. The officials lied, they distorted, they were confused, they could not justify. Consequently, the young soon began to curse the officials and the system itself. Publication of *The Pentagon Papers* vindicated their beliefs. Their worst suspicions paled in harsh realities. The momentum grew until finally the United States withdrew from Vietnam. *For the first time we had not won a war*: psychologically *we had lost* a great deal. The psychological losses were important for those who remained at home, but perhaps even more so for those who returned shamed, not heroes. There were no Audie Murphys returning from Vietnam. The war and the end of the war, the disgrace of the war, were some of the most significant programming events of the 1970s. The value of war and the value of patriotism had changed dramatically.

Some would say that had the Korean conflict received the same intense media coverage as the Vietnam War, we would have never been involved in Vietnam. Television had been too technologically "primitive" to bring the grotesqueness of Korea directly into American homes. There was no "living color" or satellite transmission as there was for Vietnam. Although the geographical distance to Vietnam was great, the close *emotional involvement* created hideous psychological scars within the United States. The real and tragic horrors of war could not be hidden from us.

There were many "casualties" beyond the dead, and each of them influenced basic gut-level value systems. Public esteem for the presidency, which led the country into the war, reached an all-time low. *Congress*, although purporting to represent us, had continued to appropriate vast sums of money to support the conflict, even though public opinion had moved well away from such support. The *courts* had failed to find the war unconstitutional. *The institution of democracy itself had proved ineffectual* in attempting to influence the policymakers and had degenerated into chaos and anarchy in our streets. James Reston said: "There has been a sharp decline in respect for authority in the United States as a result of the war. . . . a decline in respect not only for the civil authority of government but also for the formal authority of the schools, the universities, the press, the church, and even the family . . . something has happened to American life—something not yet understood or agreed upon, something that is different, important, and probably enduring."

Watergate: Up the Potomac and Off to Jail

Even as the war ebbed in late 1972, yet another note of discord was beginning to surface, one that would shake the foundations of our total system. A seemingly minor break-in into Democratic party offices in the Watergate complex in Washington became a cancer that created the gravest crisis in the history of the American presidency. Although Richard Nixon would win the election and end the war, the final days of his presidency were at hand. Less than two years after the actual break-in, the President of the United States would be forced to resign in one of the most tragic scenes in American political history.

Even though the initial break-in received some publicity, Gallup polls reported in October (before the 1972 presidential elections) that barely half of the voters had heard of the break-in, and of those who had heard of it, four out of every five did not see it as a good reason to vote Democratic. Only 6 percent of the population thought that the President was involved. It was inconceivable to most Americans that the highest officials of the land were involved in anything so blatantly illegal and dishonest. But on June 25, 1973, John Dean's testimony before a congressional committee became a Significant Emotional Event in the American political process. We were swept into the denials, the payoffs, the deceptions, the reality of a political world that *few had ever acknowledged* (much less understood or been forced to look at in detail).

Initially, millions of Americans seemed to be irritated—their soap operas had been taken off the air! They were beginning to see, whether they realized it or not, the beginning of the end of the Nixon administration. That end came officially on August 9, 1974, with the resignation. As *Air Force One* carried Nixon and his party away from Washington, the belief in and acceptance of our federal system sank to its lowest credibility level ever.

Think about Watergate from a value-programming point of

view. By the late 1970s we had become irritated, bored with Watergate. After all, it had started in June 1972 and ended with Nixon's resignation in August 1974. Watergate is behind us. Right? *Wrong!* Watergate will probably influence this nation politically for the next one hundred years. Many political observers around the world have indicated that Watergate is unique in its political significance. Yet for most of our population, Watergate has been reduced to reading and relishing the gory details in such best-selling books as *The Final Days* and *Blind Ambition.* Some of the scenes seem right out of the soap operas. One had Nixon drunk, crawling around on the floor praying. Pat was "hitting the bottle" across the room, and the girls were crying. We avidly consume such theatrical details, whether they are true or not. We don't care about the issues, just the drama.

But, *think about Watergate*—the events that actually occurred. After the break-in, only a *handful of people* in this nation *seemed to give a damn!* The rest of the nation, our government itself, said: "Oh, it's just a few million dollars. They're just 'bugging' one another. Let's not worry about that. *That's just politics.* Let's see something exciting. Let's be entertained!" Millions flipped their dials away from history unfolding.

What do you think the young children who were being value programmed with Watergate are going to be like politically as adults? They watched, *experienced emotionally,* the Vice-President and the President of the United States resigning because they were "crooks."

But then came the pardons. We seemed to say: "Don't worry. We'll forgive. We'll forget. Play like it really didn't matter anyway." The very clear *value message* was: if you have the *power,* if you have the *money,* if you have the *pull,* and if you have the *position,* you can do whatever you damn well want to do. You can live in a mansion in California, make $600,000 on a television interview, and make a "political comeback" a few years later. *You can thumb your nose at the United States Constitution!* We don't care—we just don't want to know about it. We don't want to be concerned. Watergate is an ultimate expression of *"Don't not do it, just don't get caught if you do it."* But if you do it, and you get caught, and you have the 'power,' "we'll let you off easy." *We have just programmed an entire generation totally differently than any generation has ever been programmed* in this or any other society. What will they believe about *honesty, cheating, trust,* and *responsibility?*

When Gerald Ford took over the presidency from Nixon, he found a nation that had been through more in a relatively short period of time than perhaps any other nation in history. Cataclysmic changes had been wrought in institution after institution, and the very foundations themselves seemed to be sinking.

There was a growing distrust of American leadership and its major institutions. A Louis Harris poll published in December 1973 showed that, with few exceptions, confidence in major American institutions was down sharply, sometimes drastically, from 1966. Higher education, long a Rock of Gibraltar unchallenged by the masses, had declined in a confidence level from 61 percent in 1966 to 44 percent in 1973. The executive branch of the government had dropped to an all-time low confidence rating of 19 percent following Richard Nixon's downfall; the Supreme Court had dropped from 51 percent to 33 percent; and major American companies were down to a low 29 percent, as compared to 55 percent in the preceding decade. Increasingly, *Americans distrusted everyone*—churchmen, scientists, businessmen, bureaucrats, police, and educators were all under attack and suspicion.

This skepticism generated an erosion of beliefs and values—religious, political, and social. Dr. Robert Goheen, former president of Princeton University, put the dilemma this way: "We would know how to build a good country if we were confident what 'good' means . . . . We want to do the right thing but too often have trouble agreeing on what 'right' means." Goheen had put his finger directly on the *value crisis* that had developed within the society. The breakdown in law and order, the collapse of family and religious supports, shifting roles for women, inflation, urban blight, and the looming energy crisis would all further contribute to the decay of stable value guidelines throughout the 1970s.

The Spiritual Search: Heaven and Hell

Certainly religion wasn't the traditional stable foundation it had once been. Many Christians simply could not believe God was a bigot. They were deeply troubled when the new president of the Mormon Church said, "There is a reason why one man is born black and with other disadvantages, while another man is born white with great advantages. The Negro evidently is receiving the reward he merits." At least *one church* had not caught up with the civil rights legal decisions of 1954 and the Civil Rights Act of 1964. Many others practiced active racial segregation within certain congregations. Episcopalians were shaken in a controversy over women being ordained as priests. Worst of all, there was growing anti-Christianity. "Strange" new religions, brought initially by some of the young from the East, were creating turmoil. Satan himself was now openly worshipped. A Houston sorceress who cast spells said that there were perhaps 8,000,000 initiated witches in the world. Astrology boomed. Our fate might be written in the stars, but the view was obscured by the smog.

The roots of the religious upheavals in the 1970s lay in a phenomenon of the 1960s that had been called the "Third Great Awakening" by a number of scholars (the first two were religious revivals in the early eighteenth and nineteenth centuries). The new movement had two distinct stages. First, the enemies weren't perceived as Satan and evil, but rather as The Establishment, reason, and technology. Establishment America's spiritual rituals often included such uninspiring activities as church socials and bingo games. In the 1960s, numerous new religious alternatives and "head-trips" mushroomed: Buddhism, the mysterious wisdom of Carlos Castaneda's Don Juan, Transcendental Meditation, speaking in tongues, primal screaming, bio-feedback, and Zen and the art of practically everything. Millions used psychedelic drugs to buffer the situation once described in graffiti on restroom walls: "Reality is a crutch." New religions and drugs offered alternative crutches. The problem was that these new movements, rather than attacking the well-entrenched, traditional establishment, were largely symptoms of its collapse in the storms of Vietnam, racial strife, generational misunderstandings, and rapidly shifting values.

Certainly many young people desperately and sincerely sought answers to what life was all about. They watched their parents become alcoholic, divorced, or neurotic, and knew they had to look quickly for "another way," a better way. Most kids were ill-equipped for the search. Pampered and naive, they fell prey to "instant answers." Drugs and cults could change their world in one weekend.

When the second stage of the so-called mind-control cults began to emerge with many of the popular esoteric trappings but without the horror and chaos, the change was actually greeted with relief by millions. In the mid-1960s, the Hare Krishna cult had arrived and took "doing your own thing" to a conformity extreme: they dressed in identical robes, shaved their heads, and chanted incessantly with drums and finger cymbals. They were treated as an irritant rather than a threat, and many felt sorry for them because the cult members, like most cult members, seemed to look tired and undernourished, but ecstatic.

Most traditional Americans probably never came to terms with the spiritual upheaval and cult phenomenon that was growing out of the disarray of American society in the late 1960s and early 1970s.

We were so concerned with preserving the threatened good life that most people ignored the messianic cults and their persuasive techniques. Further, we had forgotten the terrible lure of absolutism, especially in an age of uncertainty.

The quest was for certainty. Just as religions throughout history have sought to flee absolute determinism, the new cultists sought an escape from chaos. They even tended to stress some identification with middle-class American values. Some groups dressed conservatively and on the surface worked actively for community improvement. It was all a charade covering their underlying goal of total control of the individuals who joined them. Cults promised to provide—and in fact *do* provide—for the convinced convert the assurance and absolutism the larger society so conspicuously lacked. Once someone decided to join, the rest came prepackaged and ready-made. What is right, what is wrong, who shall be saved and who shall not, how to eat, how to dress, how to live, and even whether to live were all neatly laid out.

Modern-day cults represented what anthropologists have long seen in cultures around the world: a revitalization movement that follows a period of cultural value distortion. Such periods are often marked by increases in alcoholism, extreme passivity, violence, disregard of relatives, extremes in sexual behavior and irresponsibility of public officials. This historical pattern was clearly in evidence in America in the late 1960s and early 1970s.

Most Americans had never heard of a country named Guyana when the events of the weekend of November 18, 1978, stunned the world and brought the awesome power of cults to center stage. Led by their beloved but deranged Rev. Jim Jones, hundreds of adult Americans, supposedly immune to madness by virtue of their twentieth-century education and backgrounds, watched their own children, spouses, and friends die in foaming cyanide-induced convulsions. They waited their turn, happily joining the piles of dead. The horror story lasted for days, with revelation after revelation increasing the intensity.

Millions ask how this could have happened. Could it happen again? The answer is yes. So directionless were these people, so *devoid of usable rudders* in their lives, that their vulnerability destroyed them. Anyone with a "blissed-out" look, charisma, and a handbook could be a messiah. Jim Jones was one of the most successful and evil. He "got hooked" on his own power.

From a sociological point of view, any group can move its members toward extreme horrors like those in Guyana if it possesses the following characteristics: (1) dependency upon one person, usually a zealous leader; (2) activities that focus on ritual and repetitive actions; (3) knowledge of mind and thought control; (4) the requirement that a group member give up his own identity, stripping him of his name, his possessions, and his former ties to reality; and (5) use of fear to control and create isolation of its members from such critical value links as family and friends. Realistically, the only way cults will lose their appeal is if society provides the "benefits" they offer their converts (security, value direction, certainty, and support). These qualities seemed sadly lacking for millions of Americans in the 1970s. As widespread frustration developed, many sought release through sexual expression.

Victorian vs. X-Rated

So-called Victorian attitudes toward sex and resultant repressive sexual behavior actually existed in this country from the day the Puritans landed. When the twentieth century (technology, mobility, etc.) caught up with these values, old barriers were broken. Social *repression* of any kind, when finally released, will create an *outburst*. Guidelines for sexual behavior and attitudes were lost in the flood of pornography and teen-age promiscuity. Young people in the 1970s were being programmed with America's new *obsession with sex*.

The rise in the sale of obscene material was seen by many as a real bellwether. Explicit sex invaded Main Street theatres with such X-rated films as *Sexual Freedom in Denmark, The Minx,* and *What Do You Say to a Naked Lady?* Such themes as male homosexuality, only hinted at before, received direct and open coverage in *The Boys in the Band.* A Broadway play, *Futz,* dealt with the problems of a country yokel who enjoyed making love to a sow. Americans could go to any corner drugstore and buy pornographic works that a short time ago were unattainable for any amount of money. A 1970 presidential commission found that the average purchaser of so-called pornographic material was male, thirty to forty-five years old, Caucasian, educated, and most likely married.

For all Americans in the early 1970s, especially those over the age of thirty, the changes were mind-boggling. During the programming of older generations, the word "ass" had been forbidden in mixed company. The older generations could remember the uproar when the Hays Office decided to let Clark Gable say "Frankly my dear, I don't give a damn" in *Gone With The Wind* in 1939. People left theatres to show disapproval of the language. By 1970, Hollywood approved "horseshit" and "piss on you" in movies that were rated for the whole family. After the Supreme Court's 1957 decision that to be obscene, material must be "utterly without redeeming social value," millions wondered what were the values expressed in the movies and on stage that were so positively social.

The children themselves were probably more advanced in their dating customs than their parents had been at a similar age. Since medical evidence showed children were reaching puberty at an earlier age than their parents, millions felt that sex education was a necessary solution. A Gallup poll found that 71 percent of the people approved of it, with 55 percent in favor of courses that explained birth control. Even the majority does not rule in such value-loaded issues. At the peak of the controversy, sex education was an explosive topic in twenty-seven states during 1970.

Across the nation, school board after school board (dominated by the older members of the community) said in effect "Thou *shalt not* have sex education in the classroom. The kids can't talk about it." Lots of people wondered why they couldn't talk about it when in fact some of them were *doing it* on the playground during recess. Anyone who doubted the sexual liberation of the young needed only to look at the spiraling statistics in teen-age pregnancies and abortions. For the young being programmed during the 1970s, sexual activity became a part of their lives earlier and earlier. By late 1978, national statistics concluded that there were eleven million sexually active teen-age boys and girls in the United States. More than one million girls between the ages of fifteen and nineteen were becoming pregnant each year. Further, one-third of all United States abortions were performed on teen-agers, yet only 10 percent of the sexually active kids were enrolled in any kind of family planning class. One-half of the girls who became pregnant, according to a John Hopkins University study, didn't want to be. Thus, there was a real question as to whether sex education was extensive enough. Venereal disease was rampant, and the incidence of gonorrhea reached epidemic proportions. A new strain brought back from the Far East was immune to vaccination.

What was offered by schools as family planning or sex education seemed to be coming too late anyway. At an unusual gathering of two thousand teen-agers and counselors in Atlanta in the summer of 1978, the discussion of sexual decisions and issues by adolescents startled many. The young people casually remarked that sex education in junior high school was frequently after the fact. They were streetwise long before then. Yet as in the early 1970s, in the late 1970s censorship groups across the nation were objecting to any educational material that was concerned with sex. Many librarians found themselves under attack over books with "vulgar" language, although such language and behavior were completely consistent with the life styles and values of modern teen-agers portrayed in the novels. *That* reality was totally ignored by do-gooder censors. Also ignored was the importance of frank discussion and changing family patterns and social problems. It was as if we had retreated to an ostrich era of "hide one's eyes" (or hide the book or the movie) and it will go away. But it didn't, and during the summer of 1978, millions of teen-agers went repeatedly to their favorite movie, *Saturday Night Fever*. They watched star (and new hero) John Travolta in scenes with detailed violence and explicit sex using *all* the four letter words throughout the movie. Parents who saw the movie (usually over their teen-agers' objections) rarely perceived that it was the bickering, empty home life that had driven this teen-ager to seek "happiness" in his disco world.

The Good Times . . . Went That-a-Way

As the mid-1970s and America's two-hundredth birthday approached, it was clear that profound shifts had taken place. There was an obvious slowdown in the forces that had been propelling us forward in the headlong pursuit of the abundant life during the previous three decades. Although there had been economic dips in the post-World War II period, the general trend had been an upward movement in affluence throughout the United States.

Now the occasional dips seemed to be turning into a trend. The economic system (that had been "created" in size and scope during World War II) depended on unlimited sources of *raw materials* and *fuel*. Suddenly both of these areas faced critical *shortages*. Americans experienced inconveniences and anxieties that they had never known. Adjustments were necessary in a world of rising prices. The old style dream of endless growth had been fueled by naive optimism. Americans could no longer afford blind faith in a tomorrow that would be better than today. There were obviously limits. As inflation cut deeper and deeper, Americans began to worry. People couldn't necessarily improve their life style each year. The cost of living rose 25 percent in five years. The economic dilemma was not creating hard times in the classic sense, yet people found themselves changing the way they lived. Housewives passed up steaks in favor of cheaper meats, cars became smaller, some affluent families scaled down college plans for their young. Parents who had vowed that their children would get a good education even if they went broke paying for it suddenly realized that they just *might*!

Remember when there was no limit to what you could buy if you could afford it? In the United States there was plenty of everything for everyone, right? In 1974, we watched that myth die as we sat in our cars waiting for the gas lines to move forward, hoping to get a glimpse of the pump before it ran dry. The good life that had flourished for nearly three decades was definitely slipping. The following article, "The Good Life: Dead at 28, But Mourned by All Survivors," by Russell Baker, describes that event.

The meaning of 70-cent gasoline, $250 electricity bills and 10 percent mortgages is that the good life is over, kaput, dead. Its obituary follows:

The good life was born in the autumn of 1945 and died in a gasoline line in early March, 1974. It was 28 years old. It began with a free college education for every man who had worn a uniform and soon afterwards moved to the suburbs where it settled in a split-level house with a picture window in the living room and rain water in the basement.

In 1947 it discovered television and beef, which, with the 4000-pound car, constitute the bulk of its estate. At the age of 2 its chief joy was to consume a huge quantity of roast or grilled beef, then go to a saloon to watch wrestling on seven-inch television screens.

Soon, however, it began producing babies and had to change its habits. By age 7, it had quit going out altogether and sat at home eating beef and spoiling babies. To ease its life it invented the 17-inch home television screen and diaper service. On Saturday evenings it loved to sit in the dark, digesting beef and watching cigarette packages with legs dance on the 17-inch screen.

By age 9 the good life had discovered the back yard and gin, which gave rise to the cookout. Now it took its beef to the back yard with a martini pitcher, which ruined millions of tons of beef and several tons of marriages.

In the meantime, Matt Dillon and Perry Mason were born in the living room.

The babies, being stuffed with beef, grew prodigiously while watching "Ding-Dong School" and learning that happiness was instantly getting whatever they craved, preferably from an aerosol can.

Then came a startling day in the history of the good life. The babies all disappeared. Everybody looked at the screen where the babies used to sit watching "Ding-Dong School," and the babies were gone. In their places were huge, muscular, beef-fed people and they were no longer watching "Ding-Dong School," but listening to astounding noises on the hi-fi.

The good life was impossible with these immense people all

crowded into one split-level, but the challenge did not stymie the good life. It simply re-created the babies as kids and shoveled them all off to college.

By the age of 15, however, the good life was showing signs of middle-age fatigue. It began grousing about the rat race. It went to Europe for the weekend and complained that the beef was no good. It invented color television and griped because Matt Dillon was green.

Then the babies-turned-kids took up politics and grew hair and said, "To hell with the gray flannel suit."

It was a bad time for the good life. "What more is there?" it asked the gray-flannel-suit haters. "Haven't I given you twice-as-much anti-perspirant power from an aerosol can to quell the odor of grilled steak fat which would otherwise give offense in the amatory clinches?"

"WE WANT THE even gooder life," came the reply. "Preferably instantly from an aerosol can."

Thus it discovered the generation gap, blue jeans at $29 a pair and the science of kidnapping the dean.

Within the past few years it had begun to show the crotchets of age. It no longer enjoyed breathing the chemical fumes with which it had replaced the air of its youth.

One day in early March it walked into the back yard. It was wearing the now fashionable faded jeans and felt only silly in them, realizing that they were after all the clothing of now-gone babies. There may have been a moment of yearning for the old gray-flannel-suit. In the back yard the smell of cooking beef was many years gone.

It went to the beloved car, two tons of Detroit glory, patted it sadly on the dashboard, turned the ignition and headed out for the last time in search of 70-cent gas.

It is survived by Matt Dillon, the interstate highway system and hair spray in an aerosol can.

Whatever was happening to the American life style in the mid-1970s, it was definitely a temporary suspension of the American dream.

The generation being programmed during the 1970s was looking forward to a future that by *material* definition could not be significantly better than the present they experienced. The good life had peaked, at least in a quantitative sense. Perhaps the time had come to make our lives "good" in other ways, to see the possibility of a *new* American way of life that would be more limited in material ways, but more beneficial in human relationships, the quality of living, and basic values. Dr. Edward C. McDonagh, chairman of

Ohio State University's sociology department, said: "We are all going to tend to be less optimistic and a bit more pessimistic about the future than we have been. But at the same time, we are going to be a whole lot more realistic. . . . The dreams of the future will dim. But what dreams do come true will mean so much more."

Social changes boggled minds. Millions felt they no longer knew who they were or what life was all about. Tensions, neuroses, and psychoses raged. Our traditional refuge of support, the family, was itself under intense pressure. Family structures seemed to disintegrate before our eyes. No study of the 1970s is complete without looking at what happened to this critical value source and all of its members, both living and electronic.

As the 1970s moved on, millions of Americans seemed to be yearning for the past, a more simple past where the rights/wrongs, goods/bads, normals/not normals were more clearly defined and life itself was more predictable. A strange phenomenon occurred. *Nostalgia* became big business. Anything from the past seemed to offer reassurance for the present. People attacked attics and basements looking for things that Granny couldn't wait to throw away. Wooden ice boxes became bars or stereo cabinets. Junkyards became antique hunting grounds. And if you couldn't afford the *real* old thing, then reproductions were desirable—thousands of *plastic* Tiffany lamps glowed. Coeds "discovered" ankle-length dresses and steel-rimmed granny glasses. Hippies wore Mickey Mouse watches. Hundreds of radio stations across the nation rebroadcast Orson Welles' "War of the Worlds." In the 1970s it didn't create chaos, but it brought back poignant memories. The sounds of the big band era returned, and millions of albums were re-recorded in stereo to bring back the swing hits of Glen Miller, Tommy Dorsey, Les Brown, and Benny Goodman.

Very clearly Americans were yearning for the past because they were threatened by the present. Tangible items or sounds that had survived from the past seemed to offer some sort of emotional security to millions. Certainly emotional security was getting harder and harder to come by. The idealized family life shown on "The Waltons" (nostalgia at its finest) was especially fascinating to young people. Perhaps they saw in the Waltons a family life style far more rewarding and supportive, *more emotionally secure,* than the reality they were experiencing. The Waltons were loving, caring, and totally supportive of one another. While each family member had a distinct personality, there seemed to be a common bond that was often missing in modern families.

The Family: Shrinking, Splintered, and Scattered

Before the 1950s most Americans lived in families where the roles were clearly defined. Mom stayed at home cooking, doing the housekeeping, and raising the kids (the little ones all day, and the big ones after school). Dad worked, then came home at night, and the kids (more than two!) were under "relative" control. The expression "children should be seen but not heard" was generally real and operational. Nearby clustered an assortment of relatives willing to help or to pass on advice based on their past experiences. In the 1950s, television joined the family. The relatives were left behind in a series of moves related to the job and upward mobility. By the 1970s, the family had lost Mom (along with Dad) to the work force, but television was still there. And the *traditional* family unit lived on in TV shows with Mom, Dad, the kids, a few pets, and assorted relatives—laughing, loving, and playing together in a harmonious, reinforcing cluster.

Obviously this was no longer the norm. But current experts disagree about what has happened to the stability of the American family and the long-run implications of the changes that have occurred. Studies present contradictory information. Blame is placed everywhere, yet no one is willing to take responsibility.

To see what *has* happened, let's start with the U.S. Census Bureau's review of marital status and living arrangements in 1977.

The spiraling divorce rate, as calculated by their statistics, has risen from .9 per 1000 population in 1910, to 2.0 in 1940, to 5.1 in 1977. The implications on a more personal level are that four out of every ten children born in the 1970s will spend some time in single-parent homes, of which at least 90 percent will be headed by women. Not only are marriages ending more often, but a critical portion of the American population is choosing to remain single or postpone marriage. In 1978 it was estimated that there were fifty-two million single adults in the United States and that record numbers of them were opting to stay that way. If the current trends for staying single continue, according to a New York securities firm, then people who live alone may well account for 25 percent of all United States households by 1985.

David Riesman, professor of social sciences at Harvard, believes that the trend in living alone is an expression of the new narcissism. Thomas Wolfe's *The Me Decade* reflected this new concern with self, particularly among those who had been programmed through the individualism of the 1950s and the 1960s. "Doing your own thing" became the new value. "Awareness" programs like *est* threw all responsibility on oneself—you and you alone are totally responsible for your life: you created it, you did it, you live with it, you clean it up. Many people are choosing to do that *alone.*

In those marriages that survived this onslaught, the very core of the family, "the homemaker," was trying to bake her cake and eat it too. Some found homemaking tedious and boring, and they sought a fulfilling "career." But more often than not they found it tough to stretch their husbands' paychecks so they joined the work force chiefly for the money. Whatever the reason, the increase in the number of working mothers is staggering. The Campbell soup commercials show us a young man dashing in after work to start preparing the family meal, while his working wife enters later, a common scene of the 1970s. Twelve percent of the women with children under six years old were working in 1950. By 1975 that rate had jumped to nearly 37 percent; and of the women with children under three years of age, 33 percent were working in 1975, double the 1960 rate. As soon as the children are of school age, the number of women who work increases even more. In 1975, of women whose children were all of school age, 52 percent were actively employed. The Census Bureau concludes that the roles of wife and mother are seemingly becoming more compatible with work. The Census Bureau's quiet "conclusion" belies the jolt that has occurred in critical mother-child relationships during the early programming years.

In some homes, traditional roles have completely reversed. The women now work full-time (are the breadwinners), while the men are at home as house-husbands. Although somewhat common in certain European countries, this phenomenon is a new and growing part of the American family scene. In American families where husband and wife are together, more than one-half of those with children under age eighteen have both parents working full time. In families headed by only one adult, more than three-fifths of those who have children under eighteen have full-time working mothers. Such statistics further negate the old pattern of the father at work and the mother at home raising the children.

The number of working parents of both sexes has created a new subgroup within our society: "latchkey" children. These children arrive home after school and find no parent present. They turn to the media, especially television, or to their own peers. This, in turn, increases the importance of one's peer group and the media in providing information and contact. While simple time exposure is not necessarily the critical factor in creating values, it certainly is one of the major influences. The more time one spends with friends or media, the more one is likely to absorb from them rather than from one's own family. Millions of latchkey children have turned to nonparental sources for their value programming information.

Looking at such changes in a slightly different way, Jane Howard, in her best-selling book *Families*, found that only 16.3 percent of this country's fifty-six million families are conventionally "nuclear" (breadwinning fathers, homemaking mothers, and resident children). According to Howard, that leaves 83.7 percent making other arrangements, which are often so noisy that the resulting clamor is easily mistaken for the death rattle of the family unit. In addition, Howard notes that parenthood for the first time in human history has become optional for most people, at least for those who know where and how to obtain contraceptives or abortions. Currently, one baby is aborted for every five born in the United States. Nearly five million American men have volunteered for vasectomies. For whatever the reason—better education, more affluence, more self-centeredness—the option of having children is certainly out of the hands of Mother Nature and in the hands of the individual.

Still other factors have influenced the American family unit. The growing use of alcohol and drugs by *all* members of the family and the increasing rate of suicide among young people reflect frustration and alienation within the family. High mobility separates families geographically from blood relatives, and older members are shuffled off to Sun City. The extended family is being lost, and our roots are eroding along with it. Schools, the legal system, and religions have either failed to support the traditional family unit or have contributed to the decline in the family's relationships by pulling its members away for extra-family activities.

Still another tear in the family fabric has been observed by Christopher Lasch, who notes that the family has become a victim of the rise of the "helping professions." The proliferating flock of teachers, doctors, psychologists, counselors, social workers, and juvenile court officers claims expertise. They have assumed the family's main function: raising children. According to Lasch, parents who are increasingly uncertain about what it is they want to transmit to their children or how to bring about certain results are necessarily dependent upon expert advice. This professional advice is highly questionable in many areas.

From every source—both hard Census Bureau statistics and soft, interpretive sociological data—the American family does appear to be undergoing massive changes in *form, function,* and *purpose.* The results of this major programming change will be seen in the future behavior of the young.

"Love, Honor, and ERA"

When changes occur in broad areas of influence (the legal sphere, technology, the educational system, the economic environment, etc.), the relative position and behavior of groups of people within a society change. However, there is a time lag before the gut-level value reactions are incorporated in *actual behavior*. For example, before the passage of the nineteenth Amendment on June 4, 1919, women (as a group) were below men in their ability to participate in the democratic process. But even with the legal right to vote providing the potential power to create changes for themselves, it was many years before large numbers of women actually became *active political participants* in this country.

Similarly, when the Federal Drug Administration approved the Pill for public use on May 9, 1960, there was not an immediate surge in sexual freedom, even though technology now provided to millions *the choice of conceiving*. However, the ultimate impact of the Pill on sexual freedom did occur faster than the nineteenth Amendment brought women into political power. Why the difference? Could it be that sex was more *fun* than voting? Possibly, but probably more critical was the media of the 1960s. If the Pill had been introduced in the 1920s, it would have taken much longer to disseminate information about it. Also, most women during the 1920s would have been operating with their ancestors' restrictive Victorian values, programming which inhibited sexual freedom and exploration.

To understand what has happened to any group of people within our society, *one must examine that group as it moved through time and look at the major influences of change that affected the group.* Historically, the roles, the positioning of people within all groups of society (work, community, family, educational system), were well defined and stable. Change occurred slowly. A new law or new technology might take years, even decades, to affect the majority of the population. But mid-twentieth century mass media, mobility, and social homogenization speeded up changes. When a change affects a group (blacks, whites, gays, Jews, Catholics, Protestants, Buddhists, etc.) it *now* impacts most members of that group broadly and quickly.

Throughout Western history men ran things and women tended the hearth and had babies. Their roles were unquestioned. Suddenly in the 1970s all of the potentials for change in the status and behavior of women compressed against reality. Militant feminists attacked every vestige of unequal status from corporate boardrooms to locker rooms. Women with "older" programming perceived their "protected" and "sacred" roles to be under attack. But the vast majority of women were somewhere in the middle, ranging from hopeful to confused about their future roles in life. Younger women began to expect instant equality.

Sex discrimination had existed for years in every area of our society from the professional levels in the adult world down to the first year books for school children: "Run, Dick, run. Look, Jane, look." By the early 1970s millions of people began to realize that "Dick" was still *running*—the corporations, businesses, bureaucracies, universities, religions. "Jane" was still *looking*—for a place, a "role" in modern society.

Most Americans were probably first aware of a new wave of feminism when a TV actress from "I Remember Mama" marched into the 1968 Miss America pageant pulling a train of blazing bras. By the early 1970s women were using the publicity techniques developed by the demonstrators of the two preceding decades. They had learned the value of mass meetings and protests. The "bra burners" antagonized millions of women, but when the smoke cleared, they too found that their relationships to others in society had shifted. From getting the vote in the 1920s, women, as the ad says, have come a long way. They have ceased to be the "property" of their husbands and have achieved more equality in the eyes of the law.

By 1970, women's liberation arguments for equality in employment and education were finding more support among men. But free abortions and free day-care centers were more controversial. The proposed twenty-seventh amendment to the Constitution, the Equal Rights Amendment that ensured women complete equality under the law, was a dream of the 1970s. But even after Congress passed it on to the states, millions of people could not decide whether the founders of our country *really* wanted the sexes to be equal under the law. ERA triggered a backlash among those who were persuaded or programmed to view it as unnecessary or undesirable. Just how equal *should* women be?

Equal work with equal pay was not even possible for women until quite recently. History seemed to conspire against them. During the 1930s, legislation focused on putting men back to work. Women were "held down," expected to keep the family together and the hearth fires burning through the very stressful Depression times. During the 1940s, women showed that they could participate in the work force on equal footing with men. When "Rosie the Riveter" became a national heroine, many attitudes changed toward women who worked in traditionally male occupations. But value programming is strong. Many men who appreciated Rosie during the war still reject modern career women, except perhaps the loyal secretary without whom they would be lost (as women "served" their husbands at home, secretaries "served" their bosses at work, coffee included). These men who are now making corporate personnel decisions often feel at a gut level that women are simply not capable of doing many jobs which by necessity must be done by men because of their superior strength and emotional stability. How easily they forgot Rosie! How strong are the values!

When the men came back from the war, women went home and the baby boom kept most of them busy throughout the 1950s. But more changes began to affect the roles they could play. A woman was no longer completely subservient to her husband. She could own credit cards in her own name and make purchases herself. Laws began making women equal participants with men in most of the areas of our lives. This equal participation on the job, in the credit bureau, and in the voting booth also generated demands for equal participation in decisions affecting the family.

Technological advances created significant new options for women. Sex without pregnancy was only one of the many. Power equipment gave them equal "strength" on more and more jobs. On the home front, modern appliances meant more free time. Food storage and preparation, cleaning—all those chores that had saddled women with hours of tedious homemaking—were made simpler. Automobiles provided easier personal transportation, greater mobility, and "escape" from their homes.

While TV took over as a babysitter, other *media* did their share to promote change. Historically, women's books and magazines stressed the homemaking role, offering advice on how to create better homes and gardens and a warm family circle. In 1963, Betty Friedan's bestseller *The Feminine Mystique* angrily blasted American women's domestic bondage and helped to trigger what would be labeled the "women's liberation movement." Helen Gurley Brown, author of another bestseller, *Sex and the Single Girl*, took over *Cosmopolitan* magazine. The implications that women were changing and were now liberated led to dramatic changes in the contents of that publication. Others would follow suit until we had magazines like *Playgirl*, which in the vernacular of the times "let it all hang out." By the 1970s, Mary Tyler Moore could appear in a *real* job setting showing that single women could survive (although still slightly stereotyped) in the very demanding work world.

Before women could make substantial inroads into male-dominated positions of power, restrictions on their educational opportunities had to be eliminated. Before the 1950s few of them went to college and their dropout rate was high. They were discouraged from scientific study and certain professional schools such as law and medicine. The educational value bias existed in all sorts of ways, from "one-sex" schools and "finishing" schools in the East to the educational materials themselves. Dick and Jane *still* romped on separate paths.

By the 1960s women's educational opportunities were changing drastically. While the Census Bureau indicators of educational achievement (attainment, enrollment, field of study, and degrees awarded) showed that women had not reached the *same* levels as men, in most of the areas the educational gap between the sexes *narrowed significantly* after the 1950s. "One-sex" schools were suffering financially. Even those bastions of femininity, the Seven Sisters of the East, began to look longingly at *male* tuition payments. Texas A&M, the all-male agricultural military "base," accepted females, and Harvard Business School acknowledged that it was *possible* for women to move into the world of business.

They were soon proving that they could in fact climb very high on the corporate ladder and elsewhere. In the world of advertising, Mary Wells spearheaded changes in how Americans bought products. Madison Avenue would never be quite the same. In 1976, Dr. Mary Francis Berry became the first female Chancellor of any major state university campus. The fact that she was a woman and *single* and *black* signaled further unrest in academia. Rising to such a high position was not simply a reflection of a desperate search to bring women and minorities into key decision-making positions; rather it was a reflection of the fact that one's race or sex no longer preordained one's position in an organization. It didn't matter how long one had been around "breathing" or how much vested interest one had in the corporate steps; the *competence* of the individual was becoming important.

National "signals" broadcast loud and clear changes taking place throughout society. In 1972 when Barbara Jordan, the black female representative from Texas, addressed the Democratic National Convention it was a Significant Emotional Event in politics, impossible twenty years earlier. Now we have female mayors, governors, and members of Congress.

How people behave in their social roles reflects how they were programmed and affects young people (for whom they are role models). The traditional behavior of married women was that of loyal "helpmates" for their husbands. The 1950s bestseller by William Whyte, *The Organization Man*, told women how they could reinforce and help their husband's progress on the job. The wife's *expected* social behavior and graces, even conversation and dress, were detailed. She was the "little woman behind the great man." In her wedding ceremony she had *promised* to "love, honor, and *obey*." By the 1950s, some wives were beginning to question the "obey" part, especially if they didn't like the orders. This change "registered on a seismograph" in the family unit.

During the 1950s divorce laws were being rewritten. Previously, many states did not allow women to sue for divorce, and if they did, it was only on the grounds of adultery or abandonment. Suddenly *incompatibility* became a valid reason, and the laws began to support women who wanted out of their marriages. Before the post-World War II divorce explosion (when a lot of those "quickie" marriages suddenly became unbearable), most women who were unhappy in their marriages stayed with their mates for the "benefit of the children" and because they had *no other options*. They did not have the education or job possibilities to support themselves (and their children). They were not equipped to compete and survive in a male-dominated world. Suddenly all of this changed. By the 1950s and 1960s, women began to realize that they could lead productive lives on their own. They began to initiate pressure for no-fault divorce laws.

The dramatic value shifts that had taken place among women by the mid-1970s first occurred primarily in middle-class America. But the impact was soon felt at all levels of our society. This dramatic shift was measured in a series of studies on the attitudes and values of so-called working-class women, wives of men who work in nonprofessional, non-white-collar jobs. These women clung longer to the values that were established before the 1920s and reinforced during the Depression and war years. From the mid-1960s to the mid-1970s their values shifted substantially. In a study called *Working-Class Women in a Changing World*, Social Research, Inc. compared the working-class women of the mid-1960s to the same type of women in the 1970s (see next page).

Clearly, by the 1970s *most* women had changed. The younger women will continue to function differently with respect to *themselves*, their *husbands*, their *children*, and their *homes*, and to an increasing degree, their *jobs*. In a very short time most women had come so far that they would never go back to the old ways. However, the repercussions have not yet played out. The old stereotypes are not gone and old behavior will clash with new as long as old programming exists. As shown in a recent *New Yorker* cartoon, startled expressions register on the faces of middle-age businessmen seated for takeoff in their 747. Over the intercom a female voice broadcasts, "Ladies and gentlemen, this is *Captain* Dorothie Miller. Flight 491 will be departing today. . . ." Have a good flight, baby!

Changes in Working-Class Women

	Mid-1960s	Mid-1970s
Typical broad characteristics	Somewhat dull and uninspired	New spirit
	Protective and closed	Frank and open
	Rather humorless	Greater sense of humor
	Rather insecure	More confident
	Satisfied with their lot	Less readily satisfied with their lot
Relationship with husband	Dependent and passive	Believe they could go it alone
	Clearly separated roles	More shared experiences
	Suffer in silence	Demand changes
Attitudes toward housewife role	Satisfied with confinement to home	Dissatisfied with confinement to home
	Concerns limited to caring for children, husband, and home	More active in neighborhood and local community (PTA, volunteer and recreational groups)
Attitudes toward motherhood	At a loss to think of themselves as anything but mothers	Children less the center of their attention, current goals, and long-term aspirations
	Self-sacrificing	More self-centered and self-indulgent
	Three or four children is the ideal number	Two or fewer children is the ideal number
Social contacts	Limited almost exclusively to relatives	Less dependence on relatives, developing many more friends
Fundamental change in outlook		You have a right to become a "new person"—in appearance, personality, and occupation—if you want to

Men—The Decline of Macho

While the changes in men's roles may not seem as significant as those in women's roles, they are important. The women's movement, the disillusionment of Vietnam, and the general loss of faith in major national institutions have all confused men about their place in the world. Changing parental relationships, the decline in white male supremacy, and shifting attitudes toward work have further left men in a real transition period. What will eventually replace the traditional macho role has not yet been determined.

As with all groups, new laws affecting American men created new values and behavior. The impact of the post-World-War-II GI Bill on our society, especially on the role of millions of men, is perhaps one of the most overlooked legislative changes in this century. Before its passage, higher education had been virtually inaccessible to all but the sons of the moneyed. To millions of young men who had never dreamed of going to college, new paths were now open for upward social movement.

When intelligence and ability were found to exist among these masses, a "new elite" was born. Intelligent, educated men who married intelligent, educated women they met in college went off and formed clusters with others of similar experience. They based their "elitism" on intelligence and achievement rather than money. Insulated from other levels of society, they raised their (usually intelligent) children with life styles and values quite different from the rest of the population. These are the people who would rather have a Volvo than a Cadillac. Some fear has been expressed that this "new elite" poses a threat to democracy. These people think they know what is best for the rest of society and wield disproportionate power in this country, says David Lebedoff in his article "The Dangerous Arrogance of the New Elite."

Civil rights legislation further eroded the old male dominated social and economic order. In 1954 millions of Americans suddenly found their children's educational systems being changed in spite of their objections. During the early days of the civil rights upheavals, those who seemed most opposed to improving the status of blacks and other minorities were those who seemed to be most threatened—a lower income and lesser educated group. The people "at the top" were also opposed; they were just more subtle in their reactions.

Throughout the past sixty years, upward mobility and economic change influenced the way men worked and led their family lives. A song from World War I first asked the question, "How You Gonna Keep Them Down on the Farm After They've Seen Paree?"

In the 1920s and 1930s, the shift was from blue-collar, rural/agrarian jobs to white-collar, urban/professional occupations. World War II further encouraged mobility and change for men who before the war had not expected to venture far from their own birthplace. Even in 1954, 15 percent of the adult population had not been more than 250 miles from their point of birth.

With mobility and the move to urban areas (and then out to suburbia), men continued to change their relationships to their jobs and the actual jobs that they performed. While young people could easily observe and understand their fathers' blue-collar, rural/agrarian jobs, the commute to urban "white-collarization" ended this. The work of millions of men in city offices no longer had meaning for their children.

Conflicts with their children created challenges to the traditional role of men. The draft of World War II took men away to fight for motherhood and apple pie. They were defending democracy. When these men returned and the good life emerged, their service to their country seemed more than justified. But in the late 1950s, this good life began to crumble. By the 1960s the baby boom, which had been created by those World War II fighters returning home, suddenly erupted in a fight of its own. This time, youth fought against the traditions of the society itself. Not only did they not understand what their fathers did for a living, but when they did find out they didn't approve. This conflict created enormous stress in many fathers who not only had fought physically in a war but had fought daily on their jobs to provide the good life. They suddenly found themselves with children who rejected everything that their parents had built.

Certainly television in the 1950s and 1960s did nothing to reinforce the masculine traits of the typical American father. Although macho cowboys and virile detectives dominated the thrillers, such family-situation shows as "Leave It To Beaver," "Ozzie and Harriet," and "Father Knows Best" portrayed mostly inept fathers. There was no idea of what these people really did on their jobs; they went away and came back and nothing seemed to happen to them while they were gone. Children couldn't relate to the role models portrayed. On those shows mother seemed to direct, in fact even manipulate, the family.

As more women began to enter the work force in previously all-male occupations, their mere presence began forcing men to revise their sexual stereotypes. Even if men were only giving lip service to equality for women, the very fact that they recognized such changes verbally ultimately affected reality. With more women working, the men were forced to change the way they performed at home. They made at least some gestures toward sharing the housework with their working wives, and they became more involved as fathers.

As men's roles changed at home, their attitudes toward work changed. American men seemed to be under stress, and while it was difficult for them to talk about their feelings, they were beginning to do something about them. These changes were noted in the work world. Executive recruiters and corporate officials began reporting in the 1960s that the upwardly mobile male "workaholic" of the past was harder to find. The earnings of working wives allowed men to throttle down, work less, and think more about the quality of their own lives. They began to turn down overtime, transfers, and promotions in favor of more time at home and a more stable family life. Workers once demanded overtime opportunities as a consideration for taking a job. Now young workers rejected late hours and weekend work, even if the pay was doubled. Fewer men seemed willing to take promotions to managerial spots from the production line if it meant cutting into their own "discretionary" time. Across the nation personnel officers lamented: "The values of the work force have changed."

Although males may be just as dedicated to their job and company (some seriously question the dedication of younger age groups), they all seem to seek more *balance* between it and their outside activities, family, and recreation. Even single men are not willing to dedicate their whole life to their job. They are balking at transfers and out-of-town travel assignments. Ten years ago, rising young executives with 2.4 children and a "captive" wife seemed ready to go anywhere anytime for advancement. Now, according to many corporate recruiters, "We rarely see that man." Part of the reason men seem to resist jobs that involve travel or frequent moves is that their wives are demanding a bigger say in such decisions. Companies began to woo wives by the late 1970s, taking them to lunch and asking pointed questions about proposed changes. Even with such wooing, perhaps 25 percent of prospective employees are turning down highly mobile positions. The wife's new veto power is a radical departure from the world of the pre-1950s.

The real change of the 1970s may be in the creation of so-called "fifty-fifty" marriages among younger couples who have been programmed with women's liberation. More young couples in their twenties and thirties seem to be taking turns accommodating each other's interests and professional responsibilities. Housework is divided, and decisions are made with *both* partners taking an active role. Recent college graduates were programmed through a period where they were very conscious about changes in male/female relationships. They were no longer "boys on one side of the room checking out the girls on the other side." Contemporary males seek females as *friends,* but not necessarily as "girl-friends." They accept girls asking them out and tend to be unflustered when the girl pays for her movies and meals. It is not even uncommon for more liberated women to ask men to bed, a role reversal that makes "macho" males seem totally out of phase with the reality of today's world.

This new fifty-fifty arrangement is causing men to assert themselves in strange new ways. Before the 1950s, it was common in divorce that the children automatically went to the wife. More recently, men have begun to assert *their right* to have the children, often noting that the woman was in error and that the man could provide a more stable home situation. This male demand for parental rights resulted in a series of breakthrough cases that since 1970 have directly challenged the legal assumption that the mother is automatically "the appropriate custodian" for young children. By 1978, fifteen states had passed parent-equalizing statutes that said both parents were to be judged on an equal basis in determining the custody of the children in a divorce.

Carrying parental rights one step further, a recent court decision upheld the rights of *unwed fathers* in custody cases, with the court saying: "Today's sex roles are becoming more flexible, and unmarried fathers are both willing and capable of being competent parents." In a 1978 book, *"Kramer vs. Kramer,"* the author deals with the growing love of a father for the son he wins in a custody battle. Avery Corman, the author, questions whether the book could even have been written a few years ago. At that time, he said: "There was no forum then for a man to express loving feelings for a child. These things have been kept from us like a dark secret. We've been lean-jawed and macho all these years, and the women's movement has created a climate that allows us to express our feelings."

The social structure itself and the programming being passed down to the young seem transformed by the evolving sex roles. While there are fundamental changes in the relationships of men and women at work and at home, it is in the *process* of these changes that turmoil is being created. This is especially true for men who were value programmed with traditional assumptions about male supremacy. Many of them now seem confused to the point of anguish about what their roles should be.

Kids: The Bottom Line

Today's children, the adults of tomorrow, are "collecting the data" on which they will base most of their life-long values and behavior. If it is true that all of history adds up to the *present,* then it follows that the present will produce the *future*. Look at today's ten-year-olds. They are amazing little people, standing there growing up in the most amazing way. They know so much. The adult world, for the most part, has not been paying much attention to *them* or *their* value *programming*.

Mostly it's a matter of coping—their parents with them, and vice versa. From the late 1940s, children were programmed in a world totally different (and often alien and hostile) from the world in which their parents and grandparents had been programmed. The generation gap has been broadening. The things children are trying to cope with today are *more complex* than their parents faced. Likewise, parents seem to have lost control over their families; they feel inadequate and overwhelmed.

The financial costs of raising children have increased so drastically over the past few years that for the first time a majority of American mothers hold jobs outside the home. As the economic pressures build, social and psychological pressures generate a decline in the desirability of parenthood. This is especially true among career-minded young women. Now many wonder whether having kids is worth the sacrifices. Furthermore, schools and other institutions that once helped program parental values and authority are now contradicting them. What can the parents possibly do, faced with rebelling children and nonreinforcing help?

As the traditional family structure changed, a great deal of parental anxiety developed toward children. According to Harvard psychologist Jerome Kagan, the fundamental cause of parental anxiety is lack of consensus on values: "Parenting means implementing a series of decisions about the socialization of your child—what do you do when he cries, when he's aggressive, when he lies or when he doesn't do well in school." In the past, such decisions were relatively simple to make because most Americans shared a common agreement concerning what "good parents" should do. Today, Kagan asserts that "there is no consensus in America today as to what a child should be like when he is a young adult—or about how you get him there." By the 1970s, the real questions were: Who is raising the kids? How are they doing it? Why are they doing it? What is happening? What is going wrong?

And something *is* wrong, Kenneth Woodward and Phyllis Malamud report in "The Parent Gap." Things *have* changed: divorce, suicides, drug abuse, alcoholism, vandalism, and delinquency. While the media may exaggerate their coverage of these areas, upward-trend lines point to a future that is even more disruptive for the traditional family unit. These problems are not found just among the poor, the non-white, or the uneducated. They exist throughout all levels of society. The middle-class family seems to be approaching the level of social disorganization that was characterized by the lower-income, lower-educated families of the 1950s and 1960s. Anthropologist Margaret Mead took an even bleaker approach: "We have become a society of people who neglect our children, are afraid of our children, find children a surplus instead of the *raison d'être* of living."

While all American families are not collapsing, all parents are not creating major errors, and all children are not out of control, it certainly seems to be true that the family unit is under a tremendous amount of pressure. From America's earliest days through each successive generation, parents were challenged to find new ways to raise their children in a constantly changing society. In today's world, trying to instill traditional values into the modern family life setting can be a real struggle.

Today's children find themselves growing up in a family which, even if still together, has become "isolated." No longer can the nuclear family depend upon relatives, neighbors, or other caring adults who used to share in the socialization of American children. The children themselves have been influenced by forces that center on their parents but affect the children: occupational mobility, the deterioration of neighborhoods, the separation of residential from business areas, consolidated school systems, separate patterns of social life for different age groups, and the delegation of child care to outside institutions. *Who is raising the kids?*

Parents still exert some influence, of course, but more and more, their time with the children is decreasing. If time alone is a measure of control and influence in value creation, American parents are rapidly shifting their respective roles to schools, television, and the children's peer groups. Parents express a great deal of concern and frustration with school systems. Administrators and teachers express a great deal of concern too—about *how* the parents are *failing* to raise children "correctly." Neither group is right or wrong. The schools are caught in the same values shift/crunch as everyone else.

The schools of the 1970s were pulled in many directions: parents demanded a return to the "basics"; courts disagreed on how children should be disciplined; teachers struck for higher pay and *protection* from the students; taxpayers refused to approve bond issues; special-interest groups fragmented resources; inner-city school populations dropped, suburbs were overcrowded; busing proved more frustrating than effective; violence and vandalism made schools more dangerous than the streets; and discipline became virtually nonexistent, certainly no deterrent. Competence test scores continued to drop (*if* any tests were even given); the energy shortage darkened classes already gloomy with ill-prepared students, the Bakke decision infuriated minorities; affirmative action policies hung in the balance; students were promoted on "social passes"—great people at parties, but they couldn't spell their own names. Educators had not conspired against them; the schools merely reflected the changes, pressures, and crises throughout society.

With the deterioration of authority and the ability to discipline in the schools, many children don't even bother to go. Parents go away to work and never realize that nationally there are two million school-age children who are not attending school. Another million more are latchkey children. Studies of child development indicate that the number of children who are without adult supervision for a large portion of the day is growing at all age levels. These children seem to be less satisfied with themselves, their parents, and society as a whole. It is perhaps not a problem of parental negligence, but rather that parents have been pulled out of the family by social, economic, and institutional forces over which they have little control.

Help is widely available, but often in inadequately funded social-service programs. Some parents are aided by seminars, programs, and books with such titles as *Father Power, How to Deal with Hyperactive Children* and, of course, the more traditional child-care approaches of Dr. Spock. For parents experiencing a crisis, there are networks of hot lines and tot lines, Parents Anonymous, and Families Anonymous. According to a nerve center that coordinates several family activities in the Chicago area, "The people we service have no sense of parenting because they weren't parented themselves. There's a vicious cycle operating here." The parents of the 1970s were the children of the post-World War II boom. They were programmed in the radically changing family environments of that period and now find themselves seriously deficient in their abilities to deal with their own children.

As youngsters, today's parents were "left on their own" and turned to early television's portrayal of "model" family life. Unlike those TV shows, real-life scripts do not always have a happy ending, and lacking effective cues programmed in earlier, today's parents are blowing their lines.

Clearly, parenting is one of the most critical tasks of the human race. An inadequately parented child has great difficulty becoming a fine human being or operating at full potential. Not knowing how to parent, today's young adults deal with their own small children as if the children were adults. Mom and Dad have now become Sue and Bob, and Sue and Bob try to *rationalize* with their four- and five-year-old offspring. Children are incapable of such interaction and understanding. Sadly, millions of parents have lost touch with the true nature and needs of their children. In his illuminating *Magical Child*, Joseph Pearce describes the tragedy of this loss and attempts to reintroduce awareness of these needs inborn in every child.

The Omnipresent Blinking "People Sitter"

No discussion of the American family unit and its interactions in the 1970s would be complete without a more specific look at the impact of television, which has grown with each generation. It is perhaps now the only member of the American family that significantly influences *all* of the other members. The power of this electronic medium has been praised, cursed, discussed, and analyzed, and still remains only partially understood.

Television is like a double-edged sword, cutting both ways through the family. Its potential good is through programs such as "Sesame Street," which can improve the cognitive skills of preschoolers or trigger a chicano child in a migrant labor family to direct his future towards an education that can help his people. But the overwhelming body of evidence points to the negative. More than 2,300 studies and reports have shown that television has many negative aspects, especially in the area of video violence. Without a doubt, the overload of violence on television has a substantial desensitizing effect on the young. The prestigious American Medical Association says that the weight of medical opinion backs up the belief that television violence causes mental and physical traumas in children.

Is it television's *content* of violence, sex, instant satisfaction, and overblown reality that is critical? Or is it the *process*—passive, hypnotic, noncreative—that is the most critical? Television is a modern enigma and a major, critical variable in our value-programming processes since the 1950s. In less than thirty years it has slammed America and the world with Significant Emotional Events that altered basic value structures and created new attitudes in youth —assassinations, demonstrations, man in space, "Holocaust," "Roots," "Centennial." History was presented, created, changed, and rechanneled.

We are still attempting to understand television's full effect on the young. In a *Newsweek* article, "What TV Does to Kids," the following opening gives some indication:

> His first polysyllabic utterance was "Brady Bunch," he learned to spell Sugar Smacks before his own name, he has seen Monte Carlo, witnessed a cocaine bust in Harlem, and already has full color fantasies involving Farrah Fawcett-Majors. Recently he tried to karate chop his younger sister after she

broke his 6 million dollar man bionic transport station (she re-
taliated by bashing him with her Cher doll). His nursery school
teacher reports that he is passive and non-creative, unresponsive
to instruction, bored during play periods, and possessed of an
almost non-existent attention span—in short very much like his
classmates. Next fall he will officially reach the age of reason
and begin his formal education: his parents are beginning to
discuss their apprehension—when they are not too busy watching television.

Only recently, with the first TV generation well into its twenties, have many social scientists, psychologists, pediatricians, and educators begun to study its influence seriously. It became the *major
value-programming* unit in terms of *time exposure* alone. American
parents using television as a hypnotic babysitter have failed to be
really concerned about the implications it might have on the future
lives of their children. According to Stanford psychologist Alberta
Siegel, "We have been astonishingly unconcerned about the medium
that reaches into our homes. Yet we may expect television to alter
our social arrangements just as profoundly as printing has done over
the past five centuries." Dr. Siegel is saying that although five-hun-
dred years of printing changed the world, only thirty or more years
of television have changed it just as much, if not more so.

The "statistics" of television are overwhelming. Many educators
maintain that by the time a child reaches the age of five, he has
experienced as much intellectual growth as will occur over the next
thirteen years. So the first five years of a child's life are critical for
the entire future of that child. In modern America, a child under
five may watch an average of thirty hours of television a week. While
that is less than the time adults spend (they view up to forty-four
hours per week), its effects are potentially much greater. If that rate
of viewing is multiplied over seventeen years, the average high school
graduate will have spent more hours in front of a television screen
than in school, or on any other activity except for sleep. At current
levels of advertising, he will have seen nearly 350,000 commercials,
participated in more than 18,000 murders, and not even the network
executives know what else has happened. The time factor alone
leads to an inescapable conclusion: television has become an extremely potent influence on the beliefs, attitudes, values, and behavior of those who are programmed with it. It profoundly affects the
way in which members of the human race learn to become human
beings and how those human beings will function and behave as
adults. It shapes their loves, hates, likes, dislikes, beliefs, opinions,
even "gods."

One of the most complete coverages of television's influence on all of us, especially children, is Marie Winn's *The Plug-in Drug.* The *Los Angeles Times* described this book as "Extremely important. . . . ought to be read by every parent." Not only parents, but *everyone* can benefit. From a value-impact perspective, *The Plug-in Drug* gives lucid insights into *how* television affected those generations who have been (and are being) programmed with it.

So important are the changes wrought by television's intrusion in the lives of the young, that future social commentators may suggest a change in the way we calculate our history—BT (before television) and AT (after television). BT children were programmed *first* by family, *then* by churches, schools, and friends. AT children spend more time with television than with *any* other value influence, including their own families. This is especially true for preschool children, who are in their *most* formative period.

During those critical early imprinting years, the major foundations are laid for a child's mental, social, and emotional development. Consider the AT child who has spent thousands of hours transfixed before a television set during this critical stage. Might the AT child not emerge from childhood with *fewer social and verbal skills* and with a diminished sense of self than the BT child, who spent the *same critical* hours actually playing, touching, drawing, and, above all, talking and listening, questioning, responding, and reacting with words in interaction with the *real* world, not with an electronic image?

In the AT child's world, *skills and resources* once developed during early childhood play, and *interests and hobbies* that were used by BT kids to entertain themselves simply never have a chance to develop. BT children enjoyed a far *more involving family life* than AT children—the talks, games, arguments, fights, festivities, rituals, and traditions all enriched children's learning and character development. As television replaced these interactions, the AT child's *opportunities to explore and understand himself* were limited.

Verbal development, so necessary for a child learning to read, write, and *express* himself clearly and effectively, was diminished by television for the AT child because TV is *passive intake* requiring no verbal or physical participation. By the late 1950s, "Johnny couldn't read," not only because of faltering schools but also because he had grown up with TV. By the 1970s, as achievement test scores plummeted, such phrases as "like man," "you know," "it's our thing," and "far out" reflected AT youths' inability to communicate with meaning. English teachers virtually gave up on teaching writing skills. These kids couldn't even talk.

The BT child's intellectual and creative stimulation was infinitely better than for most AT's. BTs *learned* by actually manipulating, touching, exploring, smelling, and creating—they were actively not passively, involved. The AT child is like a mechanical robot: he can spew forth words and numbers, but without the *experience of usage*, the meanings are limited. Such educational programs as "Sesame Street" revolutionized early childhood by providing sophistication and awareness. *But* the sensory overload TV approach created superficial and false expectations. Pity the poor schoolteachers who, *after TV*, were trapped with students who *expected* "dancing Ks" and a chorus line of singing numbers. There is now conclusive evidence showing that television *does not* lead to significant learning gains. Parents *and* many educators accepted educational TV programs with false hope. The programs were "delightfully entertaining" but sadly lacking in any measurable learning experiences.

Perhaps the saddest effect of television on children is how it perpetuates their *dependence* on others, actually limiting their ability to develop as *independent* human beings. At around two or three years of age, just as the child "is achieving independence as a little person"—able to navigate, beginning to talk, discovering his world—he is *thrown back* to dependency much as he experienced as an infant. Why? His parents "discover" that now "he'll watch TV—and some of the programs are 'good' for him." So, *before the child develops his independence,* he is entrapped by his well-meaning (and happy-to-have-him-out-of-their-hair) parents in front of the TV set. The AT child really never had a chance even to approach having the same values as his BT parents.

And now, AT children have become AT adults with "second-generation" AT children. We "turned them on" to television in the 1950s, honed it with "living color" in the 1960s, and "fine tuned" it further in the 1970s. Little wonder that these children grew up into young adults who "turned on" to drugs, authoritarian religions, and other experiences that perpetuate *passivity* and *dependency*.

In the late 1970s, still more inroads were made by television into our lives and the value programming of the young: (1) multiple-set homes have become common—now *each* family member can immerse himself in the program of his choice, furthering the individual's isolation; (2) videotape recorders offer control over *when* you view, *but,* for the young, they instill another value—I want *what* I want *when* I want it. What will happen to the values of patience, tolerance, and expectation? (3) QUBE, an experimental cable system in Columbus, Ohio, promises "something for everyone"—participation.

You electronically "vote" on the local "Gong Show"; you express your opinion on social/news issues; you can watch X-rated movies; you shop, take lessons, etc. Why do you need other people?

Newsweek projects the "scene":

> The year is 1985, the setting a typical Video Communications Complex (formerly known as a "home"). As the "CBS Evening News with Roger Rather" fades from the 84-inch screen, Dad switches to the local pay-cable channel and sits back to enjoy "Jaws 4." No one disputes his choice, for everyone is off on a different electronic trip.
>
> In the den, Mom has flicked on the video-cassette recorder and is engrossed in the soap-opera episode she missed last week. That will be followed by a homemade-for-TV movie of the family's recent trip to Disney Cosmos. Upstairs, meanwhile, Sis has slipped a plastic disk onto a turntable device wired to her own TV set. Now she is grooving along with a transvestite reggae group, this month's R-rated selection of the Vidiary Guild. Down the hall, Junior has tired of playing Super Pong and has dialed in a baseball game. Suddenly, the announcer interrupts to ask the audience: "What do you think the next pitch should be?" By punching some buttons on a small console, Junior informs the system's computer that he would opt for a slider—and, sure enough, it is a slider that ends the inning.

Consider how distorted the young may become as they become a "post" of the electronic systems—"wired-in" with headphones and control swtiches, dependent on video "games" for action. "The Six-Million-Dollar Man" tied it all together: as today's children become adults, where will the machine end and the man begin, and vice versa?

Undeniably, Americans must take control of this monsterfully powerful medium before it takes control of them. Its educational and entertainment value can be utilized judiciously but it *must not raise our children.*

A Vortex of Values

The decade of the 1970s saw the *ends* of some chains of events that had altered our values: the Vietnam War, the "worship" of technology, the violent protests of social injustices, the belief that more-bigger-faster was good-desirable-inevitable. The old guard was besieged. Many "movements" *continued* and some *gained momentum*:

human rights—equal employment opportunities, gay liberation, abortion/right-to-life, child abuse, reverse discrimination, international political oppression; *human potential*—transcendental meditation, transactional analysis, *est*, biorhythms, born-again Christianity; *consumerism*—rights of customers, patients, clients, students, investors, and retired people; *ecology*—endangered species, polluted air and water, industrial wastes, nuclear proliferation, wilderness areas; *health* —jogging, exercise, organic foods, carcinogenic additives, smoking, obesity, noise, radiation; *special-interest groups*—handicapped, *all* of the ethnic minorities, unions, farmers, oil companies, veterans, taxpayers. Virtually *everyone* got on some sort of bandwagon, verbally, if not physically. We were pulled in hundreds, perhaps thousands of *different* directions.

Other societal-change forces crystallized and promised to continue into the next decade: *inflation* threatened the very basis of the good life; *tax revolts* became a reality; *credibility gaps* widened in government—the CIA and FBI were publicly censored, Cleveland and New York City went bankrupt, many prominent political figures were exposed in moral and financial scandals, but we forgave and forgot; *winning* in sports, both scores and profits, became more important than sportsmanship; *living beyond one's means* became commonplace; extreme *self-centeredness* was cultivated; old international *enemies* became new "good" friends; and America's *self-sufficiency* changed to international interdependency.

As the decade of the 1970s moved into the homestretch, anyone who paused to review our population would be struck by the diversity of values held *across* the generations. The programming events/ processes for the 1970s had added on another layer of uniqueness to the spectrum. After the 1950s, it was true that American society possessed a variety of values that was unique in all of history: never before had a population brought to adulthood such a uniquely "different" group of young people whose values differed so much from the values of their elders. Until this point in history, there was a remarkable *continuity* of values between the generations (like father, like son). The same values were passed on, and change evolved very slowly. The programming of the 1950s changed *all* of that predictable continuity. The 1960s changed it even more, and the 1970s were so volatile that even greater variations were created. Never before in the history of this or any society had so much real, honest diversity existed in the operating gut-level values that directed the behavior of our people. These were very *unique* times and, above all, *misunderstood* unless one pulled back and looked *objectively* at other people and asked one basic question: "Where were they *when* they were value programmed?"

If we do this, if we try this, then we *can* understand. Because *what we are now*—how we feel, what we believe, what we want, what we condemn, what we value—*is directly related to where we were when—when we were value programmed.*

Part IV

VALUE PROGRAMMING ANALYSIS: MAKING IT WORK FOR YOU

Okay, so where do we go from here? We've looked at how values are programmed and how major events cause clusters of people to hold highly similar values. We've reviewed from a psycho-historical perspective the past six decades of our nation, examining each generation's critical programming influences. If we accept the premise that most individuals are now using many of the gut-level values programmed during their formative period, then we can use such insight to improve our relationships with other people in the world—all those people out there who are "different."

Value-creating or value-changing events (SEEs) are ever present. As parts of this book were being completed, four major world events occurred that have potential long-range value implications: the mass suicide in Guyana, the overthrow of the government of the Shah of Iran, the opening of diplomatic relations between the United States and China, and the loss of control of a nuclear power plant. These events may alter values of young generations who are programming right now. These events may also affect millions of adults who already hold well-established values. Even as you read this book, other events are occurring that will have value programming implications.

Let's stop, pull back, and look objectively at the current spectrum of people in our society and their gut-level values. We begin to see *clusters* of people that may be defined as generations. Much has been written and discussed about so-called "generation gaps." Those gaps are real, and they are evident in major value differences between clusters of people. The *Random House Dictionary of the English*

Language defines a generation as "a group of individuals, most of whom are of the same approximate age, having similar ideas, problems, attitudes, etc." A generation includes all those people who experienced common programming events. Although some individuals may escape the impact of events, life styles, trends, depressions, or wars within any given time period, most people in a generation are affected by common life/value molding forces. Thus, when we talk about the Depression generation, we mean those people who were value programmed during the 1930s. Even though some observers suggest that two-thirds of our nation was *not* brought to its knees economically by the Great Depression, those two-thirds were affected to some degree by what was happening to the other one-third. People who programmed during those years or who had an SEE *were* affected, some to a greater extent than others.

Generally, major changes in value programming stem from four major areas: the legal sphere, technological changes, educational processes, and the economic system. Some changes occur with sudden and direct impact, i.e., the Great Depression and the beginning of World War II. Other changes occur more slowly. When a law is passed that forceably alters people's behavior, the real value impact may take years to evolve. Still other changes proceed with a degree of speed, such as quickly accepted technological innovations (television and the adoption of the automobile for private transportation).

By using value analysis in our daily lives, we can look at another person, know where he was when he was about ten years old, and then use that knowledge to understand him. Realistically, we can look at that person as part of a group. If you are a manager dealing with a fifty-five-year-old employee and a twenty-two-year-old employee, it is not necessary to know *exactly* what happened to each when he was being value programmed. However, it's extremely useful to know that the fifty-five-year-old is a member of a generational cluster whose members hold many common value views of the world; and understanding those value views allows you to communicate, motivate, and interrelate more effectively. The same would be true for a twenty-two-year-old. Therefore, what we really need is knowledge and information about the generation of the fifty-five-year-old and the generation of the twenty-two-year-old.

Since our concern is primarily with people in the United States and Canada, our focus is on those events which created definable generations within this North American society. However, we could use the same approach for any society or culture. For example, if we look at Western Europe or Japan, we could make the same *type* of analysis but would have to be aware of the variations in influences that created values unique to those societies. As the world becomes more and more Westernized, we will find an increasing similarity among young people around the globe. Young Europeans, Japanese, Americans, and Canadians are now very similar because they are sharing common experiences, especially through the media.

One additional variable is worth noting. Within a given generation, there are variations in values because of differences in ethnic background and sex. Recognition of these variations leads to a more accurate fine tuning of our basic model. The time line that moved from the 1920s to the 1970s in our psycho-historical examination represented white, male, middle-class Americans. Obviously, blacks, chicanos, Indians, women, and other sub-groups within the society were not being influenced in the same way as the so-called mainstream." We can look at each of these groups and place it in a *relative* time line position. For example, blacks were obviously not traveling along the same time line because of technology, legal restrictions, educational limitations, social patterns, and economic constraints. They were positioned lower in the total society. We might represent them in the following manner.

Relatively speaking, as a group black Americans were held below the mainstream line until the 1940s, when there was a great

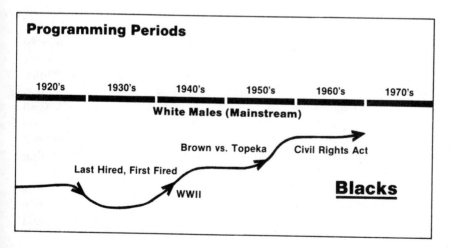

demand for them to fight and to contribute to the production needed for World War II. After the war, they sought to maintain their position, and in the 1950s legal changes bolstered their attempts, moving them into a position closer to whites. The civil rights movement and further legal changes during the 1960s moved blacks even closer to the mainstream line of white, male, middle-class Americans.

In a similar vein, women changed their position over time with respect to the mainstream, as we see in the following diagram.

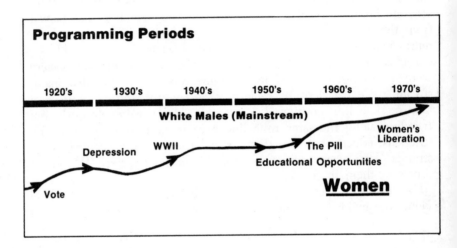

Women's position rose slightly during the 1920s after they received the vote. It dropped during the 1930s when they were "pulled back" mose closely into the family in order to preserve it during the lean years of the Depression. The advent of war demands in the 1940s brought Rosie the Riveters into the force. They gained economic clout. Although there might have been some tapering off after the war, educational opportunities improved and laws were changed in the 1950s and 1960s. Gradually, women received more nearly equal pay (although still sadly behind white males). The women's liberation movement further spearheaded the move toward equality. By the 1970s, women were approaching the mainstream line, at least legally, economically, and educationally.

Chicanos stayed lower than the mainstream line until the late 1950s and early 1960s, when the chicano awareness movement began to move these people closer to the mainstream. Indians, the true native Americans held down so long by the major factors, began their movement toward equality in the late 1960s and accelerated during the 1970s.

Now we can easily see that if we are dealing with a young black who was programmed in the early 1960s, we are dealing with a very different individual than a black who was programmed during the 1920s and 1930s. Likewise, a female employee programmed during the 1960s is dramatically different from females who may have been working since the 1930s and were programmed earlier. Age is a determinant because of forces that impacted that generation, but the actual behavior and value reactions of people in today's world will also be based upon the sub-group of which they are a member.

THE BUILDERS, THE CONFUSED, THE UPSTARTS, AND THE CONCERNED

Now let's examine the major generation clusters currently existing and analyze the gut-level values characteristic of these groups. If we look at the total age spectrum, we find that it may be broken down into four broad categories of value differences. People now around forty and older tend to fit into a traditional mode of values. These *traditionalists* are neither right nor wrong—they simply are what they are. They are programmed with values expressed in statements, beliefs, customs, and legends handed down mostly unchanged from generation to generation. They continue to hold and use their traditional values in relating to the modern world confronting them. While there are obviously some differences within this cluster, the traditionalists exist as a large group that shares many common values.

The next distinctive cluster includes those who are around forty years old down to around thirty years old. These people are *in-betweeners*, programmed from the late 1940s to the late 1950s. This group was caught in the middle. It really doesn't know which way to go. Basically, members of this group hold the traditional orientation, but they have also heard, experienced, felt, and related to a large number of the new values that swept in during the 1950s. This generation is perhaps one of the most difficult to understand. They are literally caught, torn in several directions. They might be categorized as "searchers." In fact, if you look at sales of recent

Contemporary Generational Clusters

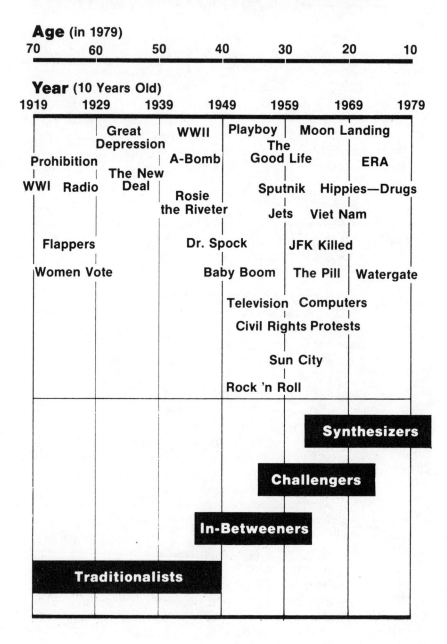

Age (in 1979)

| 70 | 60 | 50 | 40 | 30 | 20 | 10 |

Year (10 Years Old)

| 1919 | 1929 | 1939 | 1949 | 1959 | 1969 | 1979 |

Great Depression WWII Playboy Moon Landing

The Good Life

Prohibition A-Bomb ERA

The New Deal

WWI Radio Sputnik Hippies—Drugs

Rosie the Riveter

Jets Viet Nam

Flappers Dr. Spock JFK Killed

Women Vote Baby Boom The Pill Watergate

Television Computers

Civil Rights Protests

Sun City

Rock 'n Roll

Synthesizers

Challengers

In-Betweeners

Traditionalists

popular books you will find that in-betweeners are the major consumers for all the "answer" books (how to find yourself, who you are, how to be happy, etc.). The in-between generation is a pivotal group, for they can communicate with either side. What role they choose to play in the future is going to be instrumental in the way our total society moves. Programmed by traditionalists, but accepting values of those younger, they could serve as effective mediators and communication links in today's world. Relatively speaking, there are fewer of these people than traditionalists or younger generations. Yet their function will be increasingly important in our society.

Behind the in-betweeners are the *challengers*, a rejection-oriented generation of people who are around thirty years old to around twenty years old. They have challenged the older establishment for several years. They were programmed to challenge; they have asked embarrassing questions and they will continue to ask embarrassing questions. The challengers rejected many traditionalist institutions and values. They were rejected in turn by the traditionalists. The challengers are perceived as a threat, a thorn in the side of established ways of doing things. Their needling frequently expresses human-based values they feel have been ignored. Love, caring, communication, self-esteem, happiness, fulfillment, creativity, romanticism, self-expression, beauty, and equality are all included in their concerns. They truly believe the greatest resource is people, as opposed to capital, technology, material goods, political pressures, or cost controls. Their emphasis is on psychological satisfactions ("what we grow up without").

Due to sheer numbers, the challengers can't be ignored. They are the bulk of the "baby boom," which has already altered education (schools were overexpanded to accommodate them, and now we have a glut of classrooms and teachers). Now their numbers are pressuring business for jobs and government for services. Our society is like a boa constrictor that has swallowed a pig—there is a huge bulge moving through the system that creates stress wherever it is. When the pig squeals, things are even more uncomfortable. The challengers are a force to be reckoned with now and in the future.

The youngest group, those now being programmed and finishing their programming, may be thought of as *synthesizers*. They are around twenty years old and younger. They are unique because of the diverse information bombarding them from the three major groups preceding them. The traditionalists tell them to beware, pay attention, become conservative. The challengers tell them not to listen, the world is fouled up, everything's going wrong. In-betweeners, taking their typical mixed stance, give conflicting directions or plead to be left alone. The synthesizers are emerging as a skeptical but concerned, even conservative, group. Yet their conservatism is dramatically different from the conservatism of the traditionalists. Synthesizers are conservatives not because they know of no other alternatives (the in-betweeners and challengers can show them a lot of alternatives); the synthesizers are conservative because they are concerned and pessimistic about their own future. All the older groups (traditionalists, in-betweeners, and challengers) might have anticipated difficult futures for themselves, but they felt they could overcome obstacles and improve the status of the world. The synthesizers aren't so sure. Faced with the reality of shrinking resources, rising energy costs, and inflation seemingly out of control, synthesizers look forward to their future knowing that it may well be worse than the present they are enjoying. They see the world declining in a *quantitative* sense, even though there is some hope that the *quality* of life may go up. Anyone who doubts that the world is not changing quantitatively need only compare the size of American automobiles from the late 1950s to the late 1970s. They are indicators of the future. The trend is inevitable and it signals new life styles for the synthesizers.

Certain segments of each cluster must also be considered as different from the "norm" of the group. For example, some people in their early- to mid-forties, who are chronologically in the traditionalist group, are really "lead in-betweeners." Likewise, some whose chronological age makes them in-betweeners are really traditionalists. No one generation can be defined as absolutely starting at a given point in time and ending at another point. There are always people caught between major changes because of their particular birth date. Those who are in an overlap, the borderline gray area between generational clusters, experience frustration because they lean in both directions. Their values include some that are strongly held by one group and some that are strongly held by the other group. These people are likely to be primary candidates for self-help courses such as Arica, Transcendental Meditation, *est*, and Scientology. Books such as *Passages, Your Erroneous Zones,* and *Looking Out For #1* are especially attractive to those who feel a sense of frustration because they have composite value systems. Also, some people who fit generally into the basic value set of one generation may also have some value characteristics of another group. On certain issues they have been receptive to change, at least in their superficial behavior. Some traditionalists sport longer hair styles and wear puka shell necklaces—not all of them by any means, but some. In-betweeners may maintain their three-piece suits in perfect order, but wear voguish sneakers and gold necklaces. Even some challengers may have the appropriate wardrobe to move in traditional business circles, but their personal free-time life style may be totally alien to that of the traditionalists.

Others may change at a deeper level because of SEEs. Some accept "new" values from other generations because they are sensitive enough to not be threatened by "different" ideas and behavior. Further, they are secure about themselves and are able to be objective in their evaluations. Still others come from a background/environment that blended diverse values in a unique mixture.

However, we are interested in the basic values strongly held by the majority of each generation. As we examine the four groups, we find that we can't comprehensively define the values strongly held by the synthesizers. They are still forming their values. We have some indication of how they will behave, but because they are still being programmed, we can only project what they are likely to value. The in-betweeners are a composite of traditional- and challenge-orientation, and consequently will attempt to walk a tightrope between the two extremes. The traditionalists, however, have a series of very clearly defined values related to work, family, religion, play, and the way life should be lived. Likewise, the challengers express a defined set of values. Many challenger values are in direct opposition to the values held by traditionalists, so that we can examine values held by the traditionalists versus values held by the challengers. In many cases the values differ to the degree that real conflicts are created. Understanding these two contrasting sets of values gives us a key to becoming better human beings: parents, children, educators, managers, employees, citizens, politicians, clergy, all of us.

A profile of values strongly held by traditionalists versus values strongly held by challengers would look something like this:

Traditionalists	*Challengers*
Group-Team	Individualism
Authority	Participation
Institutional Leadership	Questioning
Formality/Structured	Informal/Unconventionality
Puritanism	Sensuality
Social Order	Equality/Ability
Work for Work's Sake	Work for Self-fulfillment
Problems	Causes
Stability	Change/Experiment
Materialism	Experiences

There is some overlap among the values. For example, the traditionalists view work from a "work for work's sake" perspective. Their attitudes and performance on the job also reflect a problem-solving orientation; acceptance of the social order (where minorities and women fit into the work scheme), the acceptance of authority figures such as bosses, presidents, executive committees; the overall acceptance of the institution as more important than the people who comprise the institution; etc. In a similar vein, challenger values overlap in their work, play, and consumption. The challenger generation propelled vans into the product mix of American automobile manufacturers. Traditionalists have used vans as a utilitarian tool: florists drive them, telephone company repair men ride around in them, and plumbers need them for equipment. Challengers looked at vans a few years ago and decided that with minor modifications the van could become something more than a utilitarian, work-related product. After making their changes, they found that vans expanded their potential for experiences. They provided a place for sensual interaction, with a lot of experimentation, participation, and individual satisfaction. The once utilitarian van became a much more human-oriented product. The challenger consumers changed the product in response to *their* values and needs. The traditionalist automobile manufacturers were forced to "catch up" with the needs of the consumers.

If we examine the values held by the two main groups, we can see where conflicts exist because of real differences between their values. We should remember, of course, that neither side is right or wrong. Values are simply appropriate in their expression through behavior for each group. The following explanations are not intended to be complete, but rather to give an indication of how one might use value analysis to understand others more effectively.

GROUP-TEAM VS. INDIVIDUALISM

Traditionalists place a great deal of emphasis on the group–team concept. This important value is expressed at home, in leisure activities, on the job, and in the community. Traditionalists accepted a group–team orientation because "people working together" was a necessary ingredient for winning wars, getting out of the Depression, and creating the complex economic system that would eventually provide for the good life. Within his group, each traditionalist became a specialist. Each member of the team had a specific function/contribution that was necessary for the end result of the team's effort. Such cooperation and coordination among groups of people dates back to our early history. Although emphasis has always been placed on the "rugged individualist," the reality is that America was founded and built by *groups* of people working together. From the first pilgrims to modern corporate structures, accomplishment depended on the group/team. In fact, physical survival often hinged on the support of groups. The American West would have never been won without people cooperating in exploration and development. America's history is filled with physical and economic *interdependence*. It is natural that traditionalists would stress such relationships and place great importance on being a member of the team.

Although challengers were placed in team–group situations in their programming experiences (parents enrolled them in endless classes, the Boy Scouts, little leagues, etc.), the challengers were also told that they were unique *individuals*. They received this information from most sources. Challengers were programmed through a period that created different values in them (the 1950s and 1960s), and their own feelings about being "different" reinforced the information that they were unique.

Educational systems began to *equalize* challengers, giving them more flexibility in their own lives. As more people became elevated in social status and position because of their educational background, they began to demand acceptance on their own *individual* merit, as opposed to depending on membership in a group. Groups themselves began to break down due to lack of interest in membership.

The general economic system added yet another influence on the challenger generation's drive for independence. Mass affluence allowed greater independence for many individuals. Children grew less dependent on parents and other groups within the society. They began to function in their own right, often encouraged by permissive parents. The net result of being told that they were different, actually experiencing different options opened by education, and enjoying the independence provided by relative affluence created a generation that sincerely believes in individualism. Although challengers may appear highly similar—same hair styles, dress, entertainment, expectations, etc.—these people *think* they are unique, distinctive individuals. It is this viewpoint that is critical. They will not accept conformity to group demands or standards *unless* such conformity seems to coincide with their own personal goals. Similar on the surface but believing in their uniqueness at the gut level, challengers now demand individual treatment and recognition of their personal importance.

In-betweeners, of course, are a composite. They accept the importance of the group–team efforts and accomplishments, but they also feel that individual rights and needs must be taken into account. In-betweeners believe that individual growth can be achieved in a group–team context.

The operation of these values is readily seen in many work situations. On the job, traditionalists often lose their identity to the group. The group (or the organization) and its needs become more important than the individual's needs. The importance of the team is stressed in marketing plans, sales quotas, production demands, and all the planning processes common to our industrial, bureaucratic, governmental, and educational systems. "Let's *all* do it for good ol' _____!"

Whenever possible, traditionalists love to form special groups in addition to their standard work units. Groups such as committees and task forces pop up for every problem. Traditionalists *love* committees. They can all get together, re-invent the wheel, generate a report, and feel very satisfied that they have brought together the best minds. All of this is contrary to modern management literature, which contends that committee decisions are the weakest, most ineffective kind. Yet so ingrained is the orientation toward *groups* working on problems that committees reign and members easily shirk their personal responsibility for making decisions. Traditionalists' acceptance of the group as more important than the individual is reflected in where they work, what they do at work, the way they dress, and even their outside life—where they live, their social contacts, where they go and what they do for recreation. All of these things create rather predictable conformity patterns. Although traditional individuals *do* have choices, their *real* choices are limited to those sanctioned by their group. Try to get a fifty-year-old telephone company executive to go to work in a caftan and sandals—there's *no way*! "What would other people think?"

In contrast, challengers frequently don't care what other people think because *they* are thinking, almost exclusively, about themselves. On the job, their needs, not the organization's, are the most important needs. If their biorhythms are off, if it's a good day for skiing, or if some other personal demand is pressing, then challengers simply may not show up for work. Their needs take precedence over the needs (the demands!) of the organization. They are less conformist in their dress, behavior, and leisure, and they certainly have far less allegiance than traditionalists to the company, the organization, or the nation. This lack of loyalty is now being expressed by challengers who leave jobs where they have a great deal of security to explore new avenues for their *individual* expression and/or development. Also tied in is their tendency to bore easily. Lacking a challenge on the job, they move around geographically, socially, and occupationally. The result is that younger challenger workers feel they can pretty much call their own tune on a job. If they don't like what they see or the demands that are made of them, they will simply pick up their marbles and play somewhere else. They assume they can always find something else; after all, we've *always* taken care of them. Maybe they'll just collect unemployment insurance. It's a viable option from their point of view. There's certainly no stigma attached to taking time off to "find oneself."

One major U.S. chemical company recently discovered that all its engineers (challengers) hired for a solar energy project between 1969 and 1975 had left for other companies that offered more advanced technological opportunities. Many companies report that their challenger computer technicians drift with the hardware. If one company gets a more sophisticated computer, that company suddenly has more appeal as an employer. The challenger's popular expression "doing your own thing" sums up their allegiance to individualistic independence. As this group moved through educational systems, teachers noted that as students they simply didn't relate to deadlines. Deadlines were for others; they had *unique* problems that had to be considered.

When traditionalists were growing up, their families reinforced the value of the group–team. Families were *expected* to stick together through hardships. They worked problems out and settled differences. The laws, religions, and economic system reinforced family cohesiveness. Challengers have rejected "sticking things out," as attested by their volatile divorce and remarriage rates. Divorce laws have also become more liberal and the social stigma of divorce has diminished greatly. All in all, challengers reflect a very protective attitude toward their *own* happiness. They seem to say, "I don't have to put up with this hassle; I have my own life to lead." As they drive away from divorce court, their car tape deck plays "I Gotta Be Me" and "I Did It My Way."

In recreation, traditionalists emphasized the team. Some traditionalists can proudly remember all the members of the 1941 pennant champs. "Making the team" was the goal of every young boy. Non-team members were social outcasts in some schools. Students enthusiastically suported their teams: wearing their colors, singing songs, and cheering them on to victory. While there were a few stand-out heroes, most individuals were simply part of the team. Babe Ruth was a Yankee. Traditionalists are presently the most avid supporters of professional sports, as indicated by their purchase of season tickets. Challengers will follow a sports team *if* the team is winning, but they relate best to individuals on the team. Reggie Jackson and Pete Rose can play on any team, but the emphasis is on them as individuals, not on the team of the moment's affiliation. When playing on teams, challengers want to be the superstars or they aren't interested. In their own sports preferences, challengers often look at themselves as their own competition. *Their* time, *their* distance, *their* ability is the concern. This is reflected in challengers' mushrooming interest in jogging, skiing, hiking, biking, climbing, etc. They shun being spectators in favor of their own active participation.

Heroes of the traditionalists were team players not only in sports, but in the military, politics, and business. Individuals who did not "play along" with the group were stifled, as George Patton and Douglas MacArthur quickly learned. In politics the bosses ran the show, but they didn't rule without the party's blessing. Heroes for challengers stand out in their individuality. Ralph Nader successfully attacked the ultimate corporate team, General Motors. Joe Namath flamboyantly did his own thing in training, on the field, and at play. Julian Bond slew numerous traditional political dragons.

Even heavily tradition-oriented trade unions face the same dissension between members with traditional values and the more individual-oriented young rank and file of today. Union boss power weakens in direct proportion to the emergence of the new challenger union members.

Individual self-expression is confronting traditional conformity. Some play the in-betweener role, shifting from conformity on the job to individual expression in personal life. Increasing self-awareness and identity are replacing the old dependency on the group.

Conflicts between the group–team orientation and individualism abound, especially at work. A top level production executive (65 years old) for a large brewery expresses his continuing frustration with younger workers. He gets so furious he practically foams at the mouth. He doesn't understand their casual attitudes and lack of allegiance to the company. As an example, he cites a breakdown on the production line. A filter blew out. Potentially, they could lose thousands of gallons of beer. Everyone started working frantically, from the executive himself all the way down to the youngest employee. They worked all day. Then, late in the afternoon the younger employees looked at their watches and said "Well, it's four-thirty. That's the end of our shift. See you guys tomorrow." "Wait a minute, what the hell are you doing?" demanded the older workers. "Where're you going? We've got to stay here and fix this damn thing." The quick reply was "Not us. Our contract calls for us to work eight hours. We've done that! Catch you later." And they left. The traditionalists stayed on and fixed the problem about midnight. The next day challengers thought that was really "neat," but they had had other things to do *for themselves.* Sense of responsibility (to oneself or the company), sense of commitment (to production of a product or to one's personal life), and employer-employee relationships (do it for the good of company or do it for the good of self) are *all* different in today's world. The sixty-five-year-old executive is *right* as he views the world, condemns the world, and damns the young workers. He is absolutely 100 percent correct because he views and filters their behavior through *his* gut-level value system. His system tells him that people should have a commitment to the group-team, not to themselves as individuals. Of course, the younger workers are also correct. They just relate to the situation with *their* different (and normal) value system. If *both* are correct, then today's management requires a real juggling act to work out effective compromises.

AUTHORITY VS. PARTICIPATION

Until the 1960s authority figures were readily accepted by most people. Although occasional "palace revolts" reflected questioning of the established system, on the whole there was relatively little dispute with those in authority positions. Having aged into their positions and bearing the appropriate titles (President, Boss, Professor, Judge, Captain, etc.), those in authority rarely saw their decisions challenged. It was a "natural" part of the system that someone was "in charge" of the various groups and teams. These "leaders" lived in a somewhat rarefied atmosphere. No scandals were exposed; no human weaknesses were shown. For example, through common agreement the press rarely showed FDR in his wheelchair—photos were carefully shot to present him in a complimentary manner.

Institutions directed our progress, and their leaders simply echoed the values inherent in the churches, universities, businesses, and governments. The institutions always reinforced one another. So pervasive was traditional acceptance of the institutions and their leaders that rare was the serious challenge to their right to give us directions. Even at home, the father was the central authority figure (and then at work his boss took over). Marriage vows included promising to "obey" and, because the father was the breadwinner, other members of the family were economically dependent upon him and his blessings. Surrounded by a general acceptance of authority, the traditionalists inevitably accepted the value of authority. Challengers were value processed through a very different time period where their allegiance to authority was not nearly so automatic.

Rather than accept authority, challengers were programmed to expect, in fact demand, *participation*. First, they were allowed to participate in family decisions. Prior to the 1950s, children were "seen and not heard." With the permissiveness of the 1950s, children played a more active role in family decisions. Where do we go on vacation? Do we get a new car? What kind will it be? What about the color? Should we move from Ohio to Washington? Which channel shall we watch? At an early age they learned to take part in decision-making processes and not to accept being told what to do. In schools, permissiveness eroded the authority of teachers. Perfectly well-meaning parents contended that it was not the role of teachers to discipline their children, although they themselves refused to accept the responsibility at home. The net result was that educational authority dwindled. The children were actively engaged in making their own decisions about what to study, when to study, and how to study, *if* they studied.

By the 1960s and into the 1970s, inquisitive media exposed national figures and their human frailties. Sensationalism blossomed and no one was shielded. Lyndon Johnson's gallbladder scar was placed on view for the world. Gerald Ford was seen stumbling, falling, and hitting people with golf balls. President Carter's hemorrhoids became a topic of national concern. Business leaders, religious officials, and university presidents were all bathed in uncomplimentary media glare. People in authority positions, long traditionally revered, suddenly became *very* human. It was more difficult to accept their directives when they were seen as equally human to those being directed.

As children, many challengers were programmed in "empty" homes where fathers were frequently absent and mothers were also active and away. When the parents were there, rather than holding children responsible, they seemed to give into every passing whim. From this background, it was inevitable that the challenger generation would demand participation. Not only was it built into them, but also it came to be seen as the *right* of an individual to participate in decisions that affected him. Some of these rights gained legal sanctions. The civil rights movement with its unique blend of human needs and active participation gave further validation to the expectation of participation as a major value. As authority crumbled and active participation increased, our society seemed to be going out of control. Traditional law and order broke down under the pressures of participation.

Many traditionalists still cling to the old authority structure. In corporations, titles are bestowed instead of some tangible reward. Executive perks remain critical and a title on the door often still rates a Bigelow on the floor. However, more organizations are finding that many people don't want an authority position because of the decay in respect for such positions. In today's world, being "at the top" is often more trouble than it seems worth.

Given the opportunity to participate, a lot of the challengers failed to pick up the ball, but they weren't playing on the team anyway. After the national voting age was lowered to eighteen, an upheaval in politics was predicted. Surprisingly, in the 1972 presidential election millions of young voters avoided exercising their new option to change the system. In the post-mortem, analysts theorized that young voters looked at elections as ineffective solutions, since results were not quick in materializing. Perhaps the act of voting was too symbolic of the system that was being challenged.

On-the-job demands brought on flex-time, individualized benefit packages, and Management By Objectives. MBO proposed to mesh the objectives of the organization with the objectives of the individual. However, the reality of many MBO applications saw the objectives of individuals being subordinated to the larger objectives of the organizations. What was offered as a token remedy by many traditional authority managers failed when tested by workers. As the challenger generation moved into junior executive levels, traditional managers were confused when the young executives refused to abide by directives from the corporation. "No, I don't want to move" they would respond to the dangling carrot of a better title, more money, and a new location. "I want to stay here; it's a good place to live; I want my kids to grow up here." They frustrated the decades-old tradition of climbing the corporate ladder according to directions from above.

Challenges to authority ran rampant across the system. Hundreds of thousands of young people ran away from home rather than bow down to demands of their parents. On college campuses students seemed to show no respect or deference to their elders. A receptionist in a Dean's office, secure in her mid-fifties, bristled when the students popped in and said, "Uh, can we see Bill?" Her icy response was, "The *Dean* is not available." "But, we see him hiding around the corner," they responded. "The *Dean* is not available to *you*!" she snapped. In all her years, she had never referred to him except as the Dean, Sir, or Doctor. Characteristic of her generation, titles were very important and respect was owed to those in such positions.

On the national level, the directives of both President Johnson and President Nixon were greeted by dissenters who replied, "Hell no, we won't go!" Such open and massive revolt was unheard of in the memory of anyone in this country.

Watergate may well have been the watershed between the acceptance of authority and the demands for participation. Interestingly, it was in-betweeners who held the key to the downfall of the Nixon administration. John Dean and Jeb Magruder on the inside and Bob Woodward and Carl Bernstein on the outside were pivotal figures in bringing the authority of the presidency to its lowest ebb. When the nation finally realized that the ends of power and authority were being justified by such means as bribery, corruption, and payoff, the response was an overwhelming dilution of traditional authority.

All challenges to authority did not have such serious overtones as Watergate. In the early 1970s, a Southwestern town built a brand new community college. Boom—instant campus. All of the town's leaders were justifiably proud of their new educational facility. The Chamber of Commerce just loved it. The traditional administrators hired to run it were most impressed, and the students seemed to take it at face value. Now, every good traditionalist knows that a school's colors and its mascot are extremely important. So when the time came for their selection, the students were told, "OK, you want to participate? You participate; you vote on our school colors and mascot." The students, concerned with other more important worldly matters, responded that they weren't interested. The reaction of the traditional administrators was, in effect, "You get out there and vote right now!" So they voted. They voted in pink and white for the colors, and for the mascot they chose an artichoke. Pacemakers practically short-circuited among the traditional authority figures. Community leaders were livid. How could such a quality community be represented by pink and white artichokes? The school administrators were embarrassed, but the students held firm. As the controversy raged, the incensed traditionalists filed a law suit against the student government. The suit went all the way to a Federal Court, which ruled if they wanted pink and white artichokes they could have them. The traditionalists are *still* upset. Many administrators have come and gone, but none have swayed the students.

On the surface it's a trivial story about tongue-in-cheek college student humor. At a value level, it shows very clearly some major differences between traditionalists and challengers. *What is important to us and what is not important to us is directly reflected in our behavior and our response.* For the traditionalists, school colors, teams, authority figures, and respect are extremely important. They simply do not compute as critical in the value systems of the challengers.

INSTITUTIONAL LEADERSHIP VS. QUESTIONING

Major institutions (and their authority figure leaders) have long reigned unchallenged in the control of our society. If the government said do it, or the university said it was OK, or business needed it for a profit, or the church thought it was wrong, then no one questioned. A well-entrenched establishment operated with systems that were structured to perpetuate the institutions. So basic was the acceptance of directives from these sources that no one even questioned when something seemed ridiculous. For example, there are probably millions of pieces of furniture in the United States (primarily in traditionalist homes) that still have tags attached which say "Do not remove under penalty of law." People have obediently left the tags hanging on their furniture, fearing perhaps that removal would bring in some sort of secret "tag patroller" who might be lurking outside waiting to hear that ominous rip. We're not sure why we should leave them on, but we just know the law says that we can't take them off. No questions asked.

Although most of them probably never consciously thought about it, traditionalists generally agreed with a misquote from the 1950s that said something like "What's good for General Motors is good for the USA." While General Motors certainly has an impact on the economy of the country, most people would agree that General Motors should not be allowed to determine the course that the country takes. The challenger group saw a lot of inconsistencies between the directions in which our major institutions were leading us and more human-oriented concerns. They saw inconsistencies when an organization publicly professed to be concerned about people, but then arbitrarily discriminated in its hiring practices. Others publicly stressed the importance of safety, while their products maimed and mutilated consumers. Confusion over these blatantly hypocritical situations resulted when the media openly presented issues of conflict. Many people, especially the challengers, began to feel that they were no longer in control, but were in fact being controlled by impersonal institutions. When they raised questions about decisions and directions, the frequent response was "That's the way it is. That's the way it's always been. And that's the way it's going to be." Yet *these ways* were sometimes dangerous and often perpetuated bigotry and prejudice and denied opportunities to millions. When one major corporation advertised "The System is the Solution," a lot of challengers thought that the *system was the problem*. They had ample evidence to back up such beliefs. When traditional institutions seemed slow in adjusting to the demands of the 1960s and 1970s, the challengers created alternatives in education, food supplies, diets, amusements—as many dimensions of their lives as they could modify. They expressed their options in a blitz of bumper stickers that made statements such as "Make Love, Not War"; "Do Not Fold, Spindle, or Multilate. I am a Human Being"; "War is Not Healthy for Children and Other Living Things"; and "Take Time to Smell the Flowers." The traditional institutions and their leaders bristled and labeled the challengers as rebels, radicals, dissidents, and perverts.

When the challengers didn't receive what they thought were adequate answers to their questions, they not only created options such as free schools for education, but they also used direct action (which they had instinctively picked up during their value programming as they viewed the civil rights demonstrations on television). Boycotts and protests were fashionable. Don't eat tuna fish if the tuna companies refuse to stop killing porpoises. Stop the building of a nuclear power facility if the utilities cannot prove the safety measures are fail-safe. File suit against an automobile manufacturer if its designers for a small car covered up a defective gas tank arrangement that created explosions on impact. In effect, the challengers coupled the value of direct action participation with the value of questioning. And their questions were not readily answered.

FORMALITY VS. INFORMALITY

Americans have never been saddled with the extreme rigidity found in many other cultures; but because our roots reach back into those cultures, it was inevitable that certain symbolic relationships, rituals, and structures were incorporated into the American system. However, our institutions created their own *unique* structured behavior. Freedom of opportunity theoretically meant that people could rise as high as their capabilities would allow, but they still had to rise through the established systems. All of the major institutions reinforced one another. Once their ways became internalized, everyone knew and generally agreed what was appropriate, proper, and right and what was *not*. Such a system was formal and rigid. There was relatively little gray area.

A system of etiquette developed, prescribing ways people could relate in social situations. This system was complemented in other types of relationships: business meetings, religious ceremonies, the way people dressed, the way they approached work, the way they played, ate, married, faced tragedies, etc. The American system created self-perpetuating rules and regulations. When some rules and regulations were challenged, especially in the 1960s, it was a direct threat to "the system" (which really was the ultimate target). Formal, customary ways of doing things were seriously disrupted by rebellious in-betweeners and emerging challengers.

One of the first areas noticed by large numbers of people was personal grooming. Prior to the 1960s, dress codes were fairly rigid, if sometimes faddish. Those in business wore dark suits, white shirts, and striped ties that labeled them as part of the appropriate team. This button-down mentality extended throughout the system in various forms, whether it was the pinstripe suit of the Chairman of the Board, or the blue work shirt of the laborer, or the aproned housewife. Although there had always been some token *avant garde* dressers, it wasn't until the 1960s with the election of Jack Kennedy that we saw major shifts toward informality at the highest level. The entire Kennedy clan was informal in the way they interacted internally and with other people. Of course, Jackie set a very stylish model for millions of American women. This was an abrupt break from the dowdiness and stiff collaredness that had existed in prior administrations.

In the 1960s, dress (whether at work or at play) became symbolic of the challenge to formal structures. Out of this and other challenges to "the rules," a general confrontation developed between formal and informal behavior patterns. The casual, informal approach to social, business, and religious relationships by the challenger generation was rooted in their programming. Their suburban lifestyles had been basically unstructured; therefore, as they neared adulthood they saw no real reason to accept arbitrary rules. Dress and fashion became weapons in the challenge to the old establishment institutions. Once the heroes of the young pushed informality in dress it became a viable symbol of rebellion throughout society—a weapon that instantly, visibly needled and flaunted new values at the older establishment. In addition to the symbolic nature of the more informal approach to life as a stab at tradition, the new styles also reflected what to the challengers appeared to be a very logical assessment:

their personal comfort was more important than doing the "right" things at all times. They honestly didn't feel that they should have to put up with being uncomfortable. Further, colorful dress showed that they were unique individuals (which they so desperately wanted to prove). A strange thing developed, however: as more challengers became informal they became conformists in their own informality.

For the traditionalist, the group rules of how one should behave were clear, predictable, and "comfortable." These standards all communicated something about a person, who he was and how he was to be treated. One really didn't have to think creatively, one simply had to follow established patterns. Even though we professed equality for all, dress and behavior maintained social class distance between groups of people within our society. One's position (and possible authority) were reinforced by the way he dressed, how he talked, whom he interacted with, what he did for recreation, where he lived, what car he drove—all those arbitrary but real indicators of position.

The formal rules for behavior created a structure that often seemed to demand an excessive amount of time and energy for what many challengers deemed insignificant things. There seemed to be an excessive emphasis on empty form—form for the sake of form. The National Anthem and intoned prayers opened most functions, but probably did little to further real patriotism or communication with a Higher Being. For traditionalists, at hundreds of thousands of meetings head tables set an elite few apart from the masses. The program itself was predictible, ritualistic, and often tediously boring. Most institutions encouraged blind obedience. The military was especially good at demanding obedience, operating in an extremely structured form, and reinforcing discipline (the idea was that if people were to obey during war conditions they must obey under peaceful conditions).

The swing to informality among the in-betweeners and challengers resulted in the alienation of many older traditional people. There were heated confrontations about the way children looked, groomed themselves, and what they did. Some ultra-traditionalists even physically attacked "hippies" with long hair, shoring them with sheep shears in the best Old West tradition. Men's hair is one of the simplest and best examples of real value conflicts across our system. Since the 1960s, more furor may have been created over the length of hair than virtually any other issue in society with the possible exception of war and major political scandals. Men have been fired from their jobs simply because of the length of their hair. There have been cases of corporate personnel directors informing their college recruiters, "Don't you hire any of the long-haired freaks." Right behind

them on the wall equal opportunity rules and regulations hung
ignored. That was inconsistency, that was hypocrisy, but they didn't
want any of those long-haired creeps messing up their nifty little
corporation. Across the land subtle and not-so-subtle pressures were
applied to young workers to conform to grooming codes. The military
generated volumes of directives on how long hair could be, how
trimmed the moustaches, and how full the sideburns. The idea that
something so simple as a beard could be so threatening to the status
quo seemed incredible to the young. Yet, in formal institutions and
around dinner tables across America the battles raged.

Public school systems took up the challenge and issued directives concerning hair length effective all the way down to the kindergarten level. Children were expelled from school and denied access
to education *just* because of the length of their hair. In the early
1970s the school board of Pasadena, Texas, received world-wide
media attention when it kicked a kindergarten student out of school
because his hair covered his ears. The attitude of the school board
was expressed when one member proclaimed, "That little kid is
going to *morally corrupt* the entire school." To millions, such attitudes seemed ridiculous, asinine. But to millions of others, programmed with different views, it was a real and very normal response.
That's the way they were programmed to look at the world; that's
the way they have always looked at the world; and that's the way
they will continue to look at the world.

Look at the way we have been programmed to respond to hair.
Way back in time, most men had long hair and beards. Good cutting
equipment wasn't available, and it hurts to scrape it off. So they let
it grow and kept it trimmed. Around the turn of the century modern
shaving equipment was introduced and a lot of people began to
trim up. World War I created a real need for short hair. You can't
effectively fight a war with long hair. It gets in your eyes. Bugs live
in it. But most critically, you can't *mass produce* helmets to head
and hair variations. They settled on standard head sizes for the
production of helmets. Look at what happened—millions of *good
guys* got short hair.

In the 1930s they cut it themselves. It was scruffy, but short.
The 1940s? Go look at a high school annual from 1945. All across
America, the guys were standing around with shirt sleeves rolled up.
You could see scalp all the way across. Why? They were modeling—
imitating their heroes, GI Joes. Then we moved into the 1950s.
There was less and less need for short hair. It began to creep down
a little bit. How could that nice man Ed Sullivan let that sleazy
hood on TV?" People were disgusted. Elvis Presley moved his hips,

and we couldn't watch because he was going to *morally corrupt* the whole nation. Have you been to a movie recently? They're moving lots more than hips in movies today! But there was Elvis and the other rock stars that followed. New heroes for the young, and the young began to imitate. By the 1960s young males in this country had discovered the most *amazing thing*. They discovered that long hair irritated the HELL out of the traditional generations! It drove them crazy. All their lives they had been programmed to *believe* that if you have long hair you're a bad guy. Good guys had short hair. Then their own son had it half way down his back. Parents moaned in anguish, "My God, my God, where have I gone wrong?" The answer was, "Nowhere." Hair, language, behavior, everything related to the gut-level value responses that had been programmed. Hair became a symbolic weapon in the growing clash between generational values.

Challengers blossomed forth in a variety of colors, ethnic clothing, and informal styles. By the 1970s, informality had intruded into the most austere institutions—blue jeans were commonplace among California bank tellers and the White House staff. Braless young ladies (ladies?) were commonplace. The future President of the United States carried his own luggage on the 1976 campaign trail. At the first "informal" management meeting (1978) of one of the world's largest banks, the traditional executives shed only their ties from their three-piece suit uniforms (although ties were probably tucked in a side pocket just in case the president had his on). Younger managers lounged around in cutoffs, T-shirts, and sandals— on the *other* side of the room!

Does clothing make a difference? The answer is emphatically yes, not only clothing but *all* aspects of appearance. In a totally objective analysis, dress and grooming may not have any effect on one's ability to perform a job. However, the reality is that we make value judgments based on appearances. When a fifty-five-year-old purchasing agent comes in contact with a twenty-two-year-old salesperson who is a little too hip, a shade too mod, that fifty-five-year-old is going to be turned off. The twenty-two-year-old may not like it, but he can't do his own thing and expect to be accepted by the fifty-five-year-old. Of course, many of the challengers have finally, sometimes painfully, learned this lesson and now play games. They dress and groom appropriately on the job, but their life style off the job may be totally different. One should not view this as a compromise; it is simply a pragamatic solution to the reality of the world as it exists.

Informality reigned in nearly every situation. Thank-you notes gave way to phone calls (with encouragement from the telephone company). At home the formal dining room gave way to the informal family room where entertainment revolved around the buffet with paper plates and plastic forks. Away from home, fast food restaurants were jammed and patrons willingly functioned as their own waiters. In the area of worship, some churches offered drive-in services and more traditional churches even allowed sun dresses and leisure suits without ties. All their lives the traditionalists purchased underwear that held everything in place. The challangers, if they wore it, selected styles that let it all hang out. At home, at work, at play, at worship, and in defense and direction of the country, informality in the late 1970s became more acceptable.

Military institutions yielded slowly but surely to the encroaching new value systems. More informality was allowed when people were off duty: in their living quarters, in the way they entertained themselves, and in how they were able to transport themselves (motorcycles on bases). While there was a general loosening, there was still a great deal of resistance, particularly from those entrenched traditionalists. The military establishment was stunned by the reality of "fragging" (lobbing hand grenades or other materials at officers). Those officers soon came to the realization that the enlisted men under them were not going to kowtow to dictatorial regimentation.

Formality at the highest level (Nixon was caricatured by political cartoonists saying "I am the President") gave way to "Hi, I'm Jimmy. Just call me one of the folks." The way we addressed one another not only eroded authority but illustrated the new informality.

Birth, death, and the major events in between have become more humanized, less structured, and more relaxed. Contemporary fathers are not content to sit in the waiting room and anticipate the birth of their children. They join their wives in Lamaze classes and actually assist in the delivery room. Cameras and tape recorders frequently capture the sounds and sights for future enjoyment. Even invited friends and relatives may watch. The use of midwives and delivery at home have returned. Nursing in public is becoming a common and accepted event. Death, from which children were once shielded and insulated, is now discussed openly in the media, covered in special sections of school courses, and displayed in special exhibits of children's museums. Funerals have become less ritualistic. The standard floral arrangements have given way to donations to charitable organizations, and services feature folksy testimonials from friends instead of a formal recap of the deceased's life. The deceased may well have opted on their driver's licenses for organ donations. Some parts live on to help others.

Major events such as graduation, bar mitzvahs, debutante balls, promotions, and retirement have all been influenced by trends toward informality. Weddings (if they got married) of the challenge generation extend across the land, sky, and sea. Many challenger weddings are held in the great outdoors. Their traditionalist parents cower among the bushes, respendent in white gloves and tie. Wedding parties look like early Salvation Army. None of the clothing matches. The official is not a recognizable priest, rabbi, or minister, but might be someone wearing an Aztec robe and following a script written by the bride and groom. After a rock group blasts the tranquil mountain air, someone whips out a jug of wine, passes it around, everyone takes a gulp, and they then toss the bottle over a cliff. Some traditional parents still won't discuss such events; they're not certain their children are actually married.

When traditionalists got married, they might have had a simple but formal religious ceremony. Gladiolas crawled across the alter, candles burned; people cried on cue, and a real authority figure performed the rites. The couple promised to love, cherish, and honor, and one of them agreed to obey. In the challenger weddings described above, they often do not promise to love, cherish, honor, and obey. Instead, they sign a five-year renewable contract with options. Traditionalists feel that non-traditional wedding ceremonies are tasteless, irreverent, sacrilegious, and frequently illegal. The way we are born, the way we get married, the way we die, what is important to us, and what is not important to us—all these things are rooted in our gut-level value systems.

Like all value differences, the conflicts between formal and informal behavior cannot be resolved with one person's being more right or correct than another. Rather, we need to accept the reality of the other's point of view.

PURITANISM VS. SENSUALITY

The rising informality of the challengers went hand-in-hand with an increase in the value of sensuality. The challengers' indulgence signaled a new openness in contrast to the rather closed, controlled, puritanical manner of the traditionalists. It was not that the traditionalists didn't believe in and have a little fun. They just didn't talk about things openly and they allowed themselves only controlled satisfaction of their senses. This restrained and regimented approach to life was reinforced by religious dogma, societal taboos, the lack of sex education, and an austere work ethic. Their real world demanded hard work. They believed that achievement for future payoffs was the best direction, and they generally expected that their true rewards would come later (perhaps in heaven) and their sacrifices would make life better for their children. Value programmed through a world that was in fact often harsh and demanding, the traditionalists automatically absorbed conservative and reserved attitudes. This was necessary if they were to *be in control* of their own lives and *accomplish* what they thought was important.

Challengers value programmed in an abundant world that appeared relatively secure. There was no need for them to be dedicated to hard work to guarantee their future. Instead, they had the luxury of being able to enjoy themselves in the here and now. Their programming was set in a world that was sanitized, homogenized, automated, prefabricated, and insulated—the good life that had been created by their traditional parents. But remember, what we grow up *without* is likely to become important to us, and what we grow up *with* we can accept or reject. Challengers rejected their sanitized world and sought instead diverse experiences in tastes, feelings, sounds, smells, and sights. They discovered that drugs could accentuate and accelerate their feelings. Technology opened up new doors to personal freedom. Their own cars provided mobility and privacy, and the pill insured safety in sexual gratification. Challengers enjoyed options totally unavailable to the traditionalists. As the young exercised their options, traditionalists recoiled in disgust and anger. Explicit media coverage of the sensual turn-ons of challengers added to the erosion of puritannical values.

Although a great deal of emphasis has been placed on the so-called sexual revolution, there were many other dimensions of the new sensuality. The abundance and acceptance of new foods, particularly ethnic and foreign dishes, signaled an increased awareness of taste. New forms and expressions of art and music offered new ranges of experiences. Perfumes, incense, soaps, and spices expanded sensory horizons. Massages, rolfing, and hot tubs beckoned with new sensations. Language offered direct and perhaps more honest means of expression. All of these and more were part of the major contrast between an orientation toward feelings (challengers) and an orientation toward goals, hard work, morality, self-discipline, and righteousness (traditionalists).

Challengers labeled traditionalists uptight. They were correct if one defines uptight as exercising restraint over deep feelings, inhibiting passions, and fearing ecstasy. Although the traditionalists built an economic system, a lifestyle, and a society unsurpassed in material wealth, the price was paid in frustration, inhibition, self-denial, hypocrisy, and guilt. The traditionalists' frustration was symbolized by the character Mrs. Robinson in the movie "The Graduate." She was materialistically obsessed and sexually frustrated, having grown up without excess and freedom in these areas. As she moved through middle age, she desperately sought to get as much mileage as she could before it was too late. Her behavior, although heavily criticized by the young, was absolutely normal. She was simply symbolically reflecting the values rooted back in her programming period.

Sexual behavior reflects the trend from puritan to sensual values. Early signals of change in the 1950s were in movies such as "Sadie Thompson" and "The Moon Is Blue." They explored intimacies previously never mentioned. In 1958, *Lady Chatterly's Lover* and *Peyton Place* topped best-seller lists and brought an explicitness to millions that had previously been available only to the select few who had been able to sneak copies of *Ulysses* back from Europe. By 1968, "Hair" was a smash hit New York musical that used *all* the four letter words and featured a climactic first act ending with total nudity. Studies for the United States Commission on Obscenity and Pornography in 1969 and 1970 revealed that the traditionalists not only had pornography, but they hid it; the challengers found it and did it; and the in-betweeners (confused as always) bought stacks of it. They continued to be primary consumers. It also seemed rather hypocritical when the Commission studies revealed that many National Guard units featured "illegal" stag movies at summer camps and numerous police departments boasted of having the best collections of porno in town—all confiscated from devious citizens.

For traditionalists, sex was mainly for procreation—a duty for wives. By the 1960s and 1970s, millions of women were discovering in analytical reports by such experts as Masters and Johnson that perhaps they had never truly experienced orgasm. Suddenly it became a right, not a duty. From puberty, challengers had assumed that sexual pleasure was their right. Contraceptives were readily available, and both parents working left homes open as the number one place for teenage sex. New sex symbols, especially stars like Marilyn Monroe, brought a rising awareness of sexuality to millions. Through the sixties and seventies, *Playboy* continued to promote its liberated life style for both men and women. Challengers expressed the new sensuality in wide-open hedonism. "If it feels good, do it," proclaimed their bumper stickers. By the late 1970s, narcissistic exhibitionism dominated the disco scene. It was a long way from waltzing along wtih Fred Astaire and Ginger Rogers.

New dimensions of feeling were extended not only to sex, food, music, and art, but to broader spheres. The affluent young (growing up without wanting) began experimenting with what it felt like to be poor. Secure in the knowledge that there was a well-provisioned home to bail them out if necessary, they took to the road and to communes by the hundreds of thousands. Life became a feast, a banquet of experiences. Language became a graphic expression of the new openness. Suddenly a lot of people, even "nice girls," were using those short Anglo-Saxon words that so directly expressed their emotions and moods. It was a weapon that effectively sent shock waves through the traditionalists. It was also a step toward eliminating one double standard that had so long separated the sexes.

In the early 1970s, a major chemical company produced a film that was to be used in affirmative action orientation programs. The purpose of the film was to jolt viewers. It used graphic language common to the real world. However, when the film was presented for final approval to one of the vice-presidents, he emphatically rejected it. "We don't talk like that at X Chemical Company, and furthermore our female employees will be completely turned off by such filthy language." Although the words he referred to were then commonly appearing on news broadcasts, the pages of the *New York Times, Time, Newsweek,* and other mass media, his traditionalist perspective (from the lofty sixth floor of the executive tower) obscured his view of reality. The production staff had time and money invested in the film, and they felt it would be effective, so they arranged a series of preview screenings. After each showing they asked for comments. One of the questions was: "It has been suggested that this film uses language that is offensive to many employees, especially women. What is your reaction?" Seventy-five percent of the women who viewed the film wrote "Bullshit!" Confronted with *that data,* the executive gave approval. The film went on to become the most widely discussed, critically acclaimed presentation in the history of the company. The executive apparently still believed that women "sit around on the veranda drinking mint juleps while waiting for the gentlemen callers."

Our present situation is a clash between the extremes of "don't do it, don't even think about it" *versus* "do it and don't even think about it." Mental health counselors agree that neither extreme is healthy. People need to express their emotions, but they should also consider the consequences and accept the responsibility for their behavior. The opportunity for such a blend is present. Willingness to accept feelings in oneself and in others will determine whether we can achieve that healthy mix. In dealing with any highly sensitive value difference, one key is the willingness to discuss and explore issues openly. The ostrich-like approach to young people's sensuality will not work, nor can they be isolated from exposure to sensual pressures in today's world. If traditionalists are willing to accept the challenge of frank and open discussion or seek help from qualified professionals, then it will not be necessary to continue drawing battle lines between the generations.

SOCIAL ORDER VS. EQUALITY

Americans have long prided themselves on living in a land of opportunity. Certainly we eliminated many of the rigid and archaic restrictions so characteristic of many other societies. It was possible for a poor farm boy to grow up and become President (Abraham Lincoln). Horatio Alger stories were real. However, definite "classes" did exist in the United States and controlled many social interactions. The social class system was dominated and controlled by white male Americans. Discrimination was common throughout all areas of our society. Doors opened or closed according to the dictates, whims, and values of those who headed the power systems. Distinctions were made on the basis of sex, race, ethnic background, and age. People knew their places and generally stayed in those places.

Traditionalists were programmed with a series of expectations about people: on which side of the tracks they could live; what the right religions were; where to sit in buses; etc. Society's major institutions reinforced and supported the biases that existed. The historical rules of social order faced major attacks during and after the 1950s. First came the civil rights movement, followed by other signals of old order erosion, such as the election of J.F.K. There was a furor raised over the fact that he was a Catholic, but that did not seem in the end to make any real difference in the voting.

The landmark 1954 Supreme Court decision in Brown vs. the Board of Education of Topeka signaled disruption in the traditional academic order. That decision started tremors that will reverberate through the values of our society for the next one hundred years. The court said states could not deny equal protection of the law and extended this concept into broad areas of society such as education and the work environment. The United States was facing increasing political criticism compounded by rising world protests and the end of European colonialism. To continue our position of blatant discrimination was to seriously jeopardize our leadership position in the world. Psychological studies in the early 1950s indicated that the separation of children in schools created real damage, both in self-concept and mental development. The media emerged with new capabilities for disseminating information and emotionally arousing large numbers of people. The combination of *all* these factors was volatile. The inevitable collapse of the long-standing social order which began in earnest in the 1950s swept on through the 1960s and 1970s. Our nation moved toward a goal of equality of opportunity, a major value strongly held and endorsed by in-betweeners, challengers, and those younger.

Those who were value programmed during and after the 1950s rejected the inconsistencies and prejudices that existed in the traditional treatment of people. Since Americans had long *professed* the right of equal opportunity, it now seemed only logical that equal opportunity should be provided to everyone. As in any such major social upheaval, there were overreactions on both sides. Some who had been long suppressed demanded compensation for past injustices. Certainly what one's grandfather or great-grandfather might have done should have no bearing on the way contemporary people interrelated. However, long-held hates die slowly. Many reacted in an entrenched manner and tried to forcibly maintain the social order. Others, such as judges and ministers, who had long straddled the fence on equality issues, suddenly found the fence was burning. They had to move to one side or the other. Many idealists leapt into the fray, joining the protesters and demonstrations. Some retreated and gathered with political constituents or flocks who were extremely supportive.

The collapse of the social order moved beyond black *vs.* white, old *vs.* young, or Catholic *vs.* Protestant to the broader concern for human rights. Millions of young Americans were intensely oriented toward their individual rights and also believed in the rights of other human beings. They did not understand (because they did not have the bias of historical patterns) why there should be so much conflict and concern over issues that seemed to them so logical and moral.

In the early 1960s a young college student was working in the reservations department of a major Las Vegas hotel. Having made reservations for a Dr. X, the student became disturbed when she overhead Dr. X attempting to check in and being denied a room. Coming out of her office, she saw that Dr. X was a Negro (black wasn't a common term just yet). The doctor was being put off by the clerk who insisted that an error must have been made, as the hotel was completely full. The clerk explained that the hotel kept "back-up" rooms down the street where they would be glad to accommodate the doctor's party. The student protested. She remembered making the reservation and saw that in fact it was recorded on the proper form. The student was told by her supervisor to "shut up and mind your own business."

"But that's not fair," was her response.

The supervisor exploded. "You don't know what you're talking about. You're fired. Get the hell out of here." So she lost her job for having done her job. Her only problem was she didn't know who she was doing her job for—at that time many hotels still did not accept blacks in their main buildings.

A lot of people who had not seriously thought about becoming involved with demonstrations or protests began to take action on their own. In 1971 a young white graduate student sat in the coffee shop in Chicago's O'Hare Airport and observed a middle-aged white waitress ignoring a young black who sat down at the counter. When she served five other businessmen who sat down after the black, he asked her if he could have a sandwich. She snapped, "You'll just have to wait your turn like everyone else." The incensed white student protested to the management. He was just one person who was concerned enough to say out loud that they had damn well better clean up the way they treated people. We may reserve the right to refuse service, but when one gets right down to it, what is that right? Who gave it to us? Where did it come from? These real questions were being asked more frequently. The white student's protest was but one note in a rising chorus of pleas for equality. The last two examples were concerned with race. However, the same situations could have been triggered by discrimination on virtually any basis. While traditionalists often looked the other way, the younger generations confronted issues directly.

There was a tremendous resistance to change, especially in the social orders so long favored by the traditionalists. The Supreme Court decision of 1954 was met with a volley of legislative actions by states trying to maintain segregated school systems. The 1964 Civil Rights legislation spearheaded by President Lyndon Johnson probably caused millions to wonder how such a real southerner could grant true equality to everyone. Somehow it just didn't seem right. At the opposite end of the age spectrum, many in-betweeners and chal-lengers also overreacted. There was a rush to right a lot of wrongs from the past. Inter-racial dating became popular on campuses. A lot of people suddenly had a lot of token friends. Although the value of equality and acceptance of equal opportunity for everyone was relatively real, there was a lot of superficial activity. The 1967 movie "Guess Who's Coming To Dinner?" typified a good way to shock one's parents.

With legislation, the extensive media coverage, and the actual reality of having to come in contact with others who were "different," a lot of people gradually began to accept, at least on the surface, those others. Quota systems were developed in business and education. Designed primarily by traditionalists, those systems sought to bring equalization of opportunity. They were successful to the extent that they opened some long closed doors. However, by the late 1970s the in-betweeners and the rejectionists were beginning to question whether the quota systems (systematic problem-solving devices of the traditionalists) were not in fact creating reverse discrimination. In a landmark case the 1978 Bakke decision upheld the legality of equal opportunity but challenged the way quota systems were being administered. Other cases on court dockets threatened opportunities on the job and in public education.

By the 1970s, the concern with equality had expanded from a primary emphasis on race to include a variety of biases. Some very obvious and some more subtle forms of past discrimination were challenged. Gay rights and women's liberation brought all sorts of skeletons out of thousands of closets. The blatant prejudice against women was easy to spot in jobs: they were paid less than men; they were stalled on promotional ladders and limited in access to many jobs; and even female Ph.D.s were asked if they could type and take shorthand. Awareness grew about distorted views of women in advertising stereotypes, as heroines in movies and on television shows, and as presented in educational materials.

As women moved up the management ladders of various organizations, it became obvious that social order restrictions still existed. After a major California bank successfully promoted women into high management, they were suddenly faced with a real problem. A lot of bank business was conducted over those famous business lunches. The women executives should now be included in these luncheon groups. However, the top management had always favored an exclusive private club in San Francisco where women and minorities were excluded. Problem: How does one hold a business lunch where someone who should can't attend because she is not allowed in? The answer to challengers seems relatively reasonable and logical: eat somewhere else. For the old guard, the answer wasn't so easy. Acceptance of women in their ranks was difficult enough; invasion of their bastions of male supremacy was intolerable.

The push for women's rights was an irritant to many traditionalists. But when gays demanded recognition and acceptance of their "alternative life style," millions reacted as if they were threatened directly. Long-held stereotypes of homosexuals were shattered: a macho professional football player wrote a book about being a gay athlete; some rock stars championed the advantages of bisexuality; lesbian couples won court battles for custody of their children; some public officials openly admitted their preference for the same sex; and across the nation gays and their supporters demonstrated for their human rights in housing, employment, and life style. Many older people recoiled in horror, while younger people tended to accept the gays' rights to freedom of choice. Some groups tooks on the fervor of witch hunts. Across the nation, communities struggled with gay rights, but the emotional conflicts were not easily resolved at the ballot boxes. In the gays' bids for equality, their rights became part of the larger issue of human rights.

In another sector of society the traditional social order carefully confined the handicapped to limited roles of participation. We dealt with our uneasiness about the handicapped through such conscience-soothing activities as charity balls, donations, Christmas turkeys, volunteer work, specialized agencies, separate institutions, etc. All of these insured that the handicapped stayed in their place. Until recently there were relatively few efforts to honestly allow the handicapped access to the mainstream, much less welcome them.

In retrospect, it seems strange that we built a world that effectively excluded the handicapped. However, since they couldn't successfully (normally) participate in pursuing the values of the traditional mainstream, the logical approach was to institutionalize them or confine them in homes. With recent concerns for human rights and the push for equality of opportunity, new doors (literally, financially, and figuratively) are opening for the handicapped. Buildings are being remodeled to accommodate those physically disabled. Transportation equipment has been altered and parking spaces reserved. New designs are available for private homes (the all-American split-level is a nightmare in a wheelchair). Financial assistance and job training have changed to lessen dependency. In general, greater acceptance of and adaptations for the handicapped have moved them out of society's shadows.

The falling social order barriers brought a whole series of new problems to the society. The solutions are not as easy in many cases as simply selecting another place for lunch. As traditional roles and rules blur, increasing responsibility is placed on each person to deal with other people on an individual basis. We must accept them for what they are: their capabilities, their shortcomings, their potentials.

Our emphasis should not be on some arbitrary designation, but rather on those things which will make a real difference in whether others can do an effective job or contribute in meaningful ways.

WORK FOR WORK'S SAKE VS. WORK FOR SELF-FULFILLMENT

Although every society has the same general range of activities, societies differ tremendously in the importance they attach to these activities. In the United States the most important activity for millions of people is making a living. Working is exalted for its own sake and for the surrounding cluster of values which increase its symbolic significance. Although work supplies many rewards (salary, social contacts, status, identification), millions of traditionalist Americans have been programmed to work for the sake of work. For many of them, actually accomplishing something is not necessarily critical. They are just there, on the job doing what they are supposed to be doing, taking coffee breaks, attending committee meeings, and contributing to some vague higher goal beyond their own personal concern.

It was inevitable that an obsession with work would develop in the United States. The Protestant ethic bestowed a saintly aura on those who worked hard. Steady work provided economic security and a sense of stability that was important if you grew up worrying about some future "rainy day." Until recent times most people had to work to survive. They weren't taken care of by the government's social welfare agencies. However, in a highly advanced economic state, welfare is accepted as a means to take care of those who *might* be in trouble. Further, for millions of young adults, parental support realistically continues to get them whatever they want. "You're bored with that toy? We'll buy you another. You broke your tricycle? We'll get it fixed."

Work also gave people something to do with their time. In fact, one of the biggest problems in recent years is retired people who don't know what to do when suddenly they are not expected to show up at work. Many of them drift back to haunt the old work site, hoping to be able to pitch in and feel useful.

America was founded on the concept of building something better, a better life for all. Although a large portion of the population had to wait a long time to achieve their opportunity for the good life, most people did anticipate a better tomorrow. With this orientation, it was inevitable that the process of work itself would take on significant value. People worked for their children, for the future, to win the wars, and to get out of the Depression. If one accepts the importance of work, then it follows that the elements of work are important as well. For traditionalists that includes groups and teams who are all working together; committees that meet to create a solution to a problem that confronts the work group; and the acceptance of authority figures (bosses are necessary in large complex organizations dedicated to achieving defined goals). If work itself is the most important aspect of one's life, then the institutions that are connected with perpetuating it are also accepted and not seriously questioned. As the single largest dominator of a person's time each week, the job influences every other aspect of life: how much time we spend with our family and how we feel like relating to them when we are there; how much we contribute to our church; how much we can depend on for retirement; where we live; what kind of car we drive; where our kids go to school; and who our friends are. Everything ultimately ties back into the job for millions of people. Traditionalists have been dominated by work for decades.

The challenger generation doesn't really relate to work very well. In fact they don't like to work, and many of them have never actually had to work. As children some had token jobs such as delivering the newspaper and doing a few chores around the house. But basically, the challengers, and to a large extent the in-betweeners prior to them, grew up in an affluent world with an atmosphere of permissiveness that supported them whether or not they worked to contribute to the family or any other institution. Their present commitment and responsibility is not to a benevolent employer but rather to themselves as individuals (their critical value-view). Challengers are not concerned with building and creating, but aim at revamping, restructuring, and reshaping institutions as they currently exist. They see many errors and faults that need to be corrected. They seriously question the historical goals of more, bigger, and better.

Their educational systems helped create a new orientation toward work. They were not exposed to repetitious recitation of basic information. Instead, they were fed information in a series of units. If they got it, fine; if they didn't they weren't flunked but granted a "social pass." Consequently, they weren't held *responsible* for accomplishing very much. When they became bored with one project they were encouraged to switch to another (they now lack "stick-to-it-niveness"). And bored they did become. Saturated by overindulgence, they search for new ways to get "turned-on" to something that is of interest to them. Television took them mentally into space, around the world to interesting spots, and to all of the major sporting events. Wherever they wanted to go became possible because their minds could go there. Problems on television programs were always solved quickly. There was no drudgery involved with performing one's job. If anyone was actually seen at a job, the duties of the job frequently were very vague. Characters simply finished a task and then took a break. Unlike real work, many jobs shown were glamorous, exciting, and stimulating (detectives, fantasy heroes, astronauts, explorers, etc.). So, looking for excitement and interested in personal satisfaction, seeing all problems solved in an hour (with several commercial breaks for the good life thrown in), they began to assume that when they got a job it would be interesting, exciting, challenging, and personally rewarding, and they would be able to stop and start at their whim or according to their individual needs. When these generations joined typical American production line situations, they predictably rejected monotony.

The traditionalist stands on a production line (perhaps not liking it, but not challenging his boss about how to do the job) and performs repetitious motions. If he is standing on an automotive production line, the doors pass by the traditionalist worker: bam–bam–bam–bam. The rivets jump into place. When the challenger is placed on the auto production line and doors start flowing past, for a while the rivets slam into place. Then, instead of bam–bam–bam–bam, the sequence changes: bam–bam–bam–bam–bam, or bam–bam, or a door goes by and there are no bams, or a door goes by and he drops in an empty beer bottle (knowing that whoever buys the car will go crazy when the bottle rattles). The young challenger is just trying to amuse himself on the job! Desperately seeking variety, self-fulfillment, and a sense of accomplishment, he brings on the wrath of traditional management.

Challengers also reject the connection between who they are and what they do. In their view, they are more than what they do. They are not a chemist, a bricklayer, or a pilot. They are John Jones, individual, who coincidently happens at this time to be working for X company doing Y things. Off the job, the challengers' social contacts are based on their interests and activities, while the traditionalists still use social contact and manipulation for job security or advancement. In the challenger view, a person's worth is measured *qualitatively*. For the traditionalist, a man's worth is measured *quantitatively* by output. There is no greater accolade for the traditionalist worker than to label him as a hard worker.

Millions of traditionalists subjugate themselves to their jobs never questioning or rocking the boat, for to do so would endanger job security. The challenger is interested, not so much in the economic security of his job (they can always pick up unemployment), rather in emotional security (reassurance that he's okay). The attitude of traditional managers is likely to be: "Hell yes you're okay. Now get out there and do the job you're supposed to do." Further, as more families have both spouses working, many challengers now have built-in economic security. If one spouse loses a job or decides to stop working, the other can support the family at least for a period of time. If one partner in a marriage wants to change jobs it's not the traumatic situation that once existed when there was typically only a single breadwinner.

It's not nearly as hard to survive in this country as it was just a few years ago. Workers were once so preoccupied with making enough money to provide for the basic needs of life and keep a roof over their heads that they never had time to even wonder whether there was anything more. Today's affluence has changed all that.

Since the challengers reject the job as being the dominant part of their lives (and in fact it isn't with shortened work weeks), their stress is on how to utilize their leisure time. They seek to learn new things and experience new thrills. They value their own personal time, and jobs are often intrusions. Their behavior is viewed by traditionalists as disloyalty. Many organizations now cry out for "loyal" employees. What they really want is a worker who will not question and who will submit slavishly to job conditions, even if they are unfair or demeaning, as was often the case in the past. The basic problem in today's work world is how do we get people to work. Management needs to learn what *now* motivates people and will keep them happy. Then management has to do something about it, rather than simply applying the old tried and supposedly true techniques. Even worse, some managers make glowing statements about "the importance of our people" and then manage as they always did.

Get a group of managers together today and very quickly you'll find them discussing the differences between the way people *used to* work and the way they *now* work. There are thousands of stories that underline the clash in values between working for the sake of work and working for self-fulfillment. A major chemical company for years had a policy of reprimanding people by forcing them to take time off without pay. Their approach was "We've had it with you. You keep fouling up. You take three days off next week without pay." Such statements strike fear in the economic hearts of traditionalists. They want the money. It is important to them. However, this chemical company has found for several years that the same statement to younger employees is likely to bring a response of "Hell, we'll take five. We'll take the whole week." Not needing the money and valuing their own time more, younger workers often react in ways extremely frustrating for traditional managers. This particular company changed its policies. It now allows supervisors to deal with individual employees on the basis of what seems important to those people as *individuals*. Management still typically tells a traditional employee to take three days off without pay, but for their younger employees the threat is not time without pay, but overtime (with pay and a half), and they *hate* it. They don't *want* overtime. That's their time, not the company's. It's an infringement on something that is important to them and as such it can be a strong motivator. Remember: what's important to us and what's not important to us are all tied up in values that govern our behavior.

One of the world's major banks attempted to motivate its own management group by offering them what top management saw as a sure-fire incentive. For the best ideas contributed on how to improve operations, managers would be eligible for a cash prize of $100 (in today's world that just might get a young couple through a full evening's entertainment), *plus* (and this was the real kicker) the opportunity to have dinner with the president and his wife at an exclusive club. When the plan was announced a voice from the back of the auditorium proclaimed, "One man's reward is another man's punishment." The response rate for this ingenious motivational scheme was 24 percent. Only 24 percent of the bank's own management *team* bothered to contribute an idea. Contributions came mainly from the traditionalists. Most of the younger managers ignored the whole proposition, as they feared dinner with the president would be devastatingly boring, and the $100 was relatively unimportant. When traditionalists were in equivalent positions as young managers several years ago, the opportunity for a little extra cash and to have dinner with the president was an extremely desirable carrot, but not in today's world.

Another bank recognized that most employees in their computer section were from the challenger generation. They allowed those employees to select their own working times, to structure work in batches (projects), and to select from a variety of rewards for meeting quotas and deadlines (extra time off, paid vacations to a resort with guaranteed babysitters, etc.). This bank experienced a tremendous response and has one of the best, most efficient computer sections in the country. This bank's management was tuning in and responding to the gut-level values of its employees.

Challenger attitudes often frustrate management. A major soft drink company recently conducted surveys in its bottling operations and found an increasing problem with scheduling route deliveries. Each morning drivers found their loaded trucks ready to go on their assigned delivery route. Those routes had been carefully structured to take an entire day. Aggressive younger employees were often able to cover their routes by twelve or one o'clock. Then they took time off, went home, took a nap, went to a movie, shot pool, or had a few beers, returning to the bottling plant dock at four-thirty or five— when they were *supposed to* be through. Management was irate. When they discovered this they said, "We'll re-do all the routes so that you work from eight to five." Response of the younger employees was "Why should we drag it out? We accomplished what we were supposed to. We delivered all the products. What's the hassle?" Management had no response except that "You're supposed to work all day."

The *way* we work, *when* we work, *how* we work, *whether* we work—all aspects of work are keyed into the value systems of employees. Likewise, management decisions are structured by *their* value systems. A major church hospital was faced with serious morale problems in its laboratory. Errors, accidents, and people taking extra time off contributed to low efficiency in operations. The hospital management decided to shift the time structuring, *when* people worked. They went to a seven-day-a-week, ten-hours-a-day schedule. Employees in the lab worked seventy hours for a week; then they were off for one week. Then they worked another full seven days. They were paid exactly the same as when they had worked fifty weeks a year with two weeks for vacation plus the other appropriate holidays. After initiation of the program, the hospital found that productivity (as measured by fewer accidents, less breakage, and less absenteeism) increased and stayed up nearly 40 percent. That's not bad for exactly the same cost in salaries. Virtually all of the younger employees loved the new plan. They had twenty-six full weeks a year to do their own thing. Nearly all of the employees over forty years of age went out and got a second job. Some of them seemed to fear that "God might get 'em" for sitting around!

Although massive efforts and expense are aimed at reinforcing the traditional work ethic, these attempts are doomed to failure against the onslaught of the new values related to work. No matter how much power-of-positive-thinking rhetoric may be aimed at workers, non-traditionalist employees respond to the reality of a work world where equality of opportunity does not exist. Bosses have been dictatorial too long. Institutions' goals have overshadowed more human needs. Group demands have subordinated individuals' freedoms, and puritan Protestant ethics have smothered feelings.

Today's work force still includes a large number of traditional workers who are motivated by money and benefits. These time-honored rewards are also important to challengers and in-betweeners, but they want *more* than work for the sake of work and what that has meant. They insist on psychological satisfactions and more opportunities to learn and grow and to exercise their talents and skills. They fight being a cog in a giant machine, and they yearn for a sense of accomplishment and involvement.

The basic approach to workers with "different" values is as simple as asking them what they want and then responding appropriately. Of course, management must maintain some prerogatives in decisions, but worker participation is very reasonable in many decisions (schedules, benefit packages, safety, salaries, etc.). Rather than *telling* workers, mangement can let them help uncover solutions. One company faced with demands for salary increases encouraged workers to form committees and study the competitive influences on their operations. The workers discovered information (that would typically have been distributed by management and probably immediately rejected as biased) that led them to recommend a salary *cut* to mangement. The situation was handled in such a way that management's problem was solved by the workers!

In the area of psychological counseling, management and supervisors often retreat because they feel inadequate. Realistically, unless a supervisor is trained in counseling, it probably should be handled by professionals. One Pennsylvania foundry solved the problem by hiring on a part-time basis a local minister with a degree in counseling. He was not viewed as a "resident shrink," but rather was generally accepted by the employees. Morale and productivity improved because he was able to help people with off-the-job problems that were influencing their on-the-job behavior. Problems such as alcoholism, divorce, and family turmoil cannot be "left at home." In this case, management responded to individual needs and *both* company and employees benefited. While traditional workers might never consider mixing their personal lives with the job, younger employees accept (and need) this new wholistic approach by management.

The most recent additions to the work force, those in their early twenties, are the lead edge of the synthesis generation. They are more "traditional" in their approach and commitment to the importance of work. But it would be naive to conclude that they represent a *return* to traditional feelings about job values. The pendulum has swung, *but* the reasons, needs, and values that guide today's youngest employees are very different from those that guided traditional workers. We must avoid being lulled into a sense of returning to old ways. Further, the very large cluster of in-betweeners and challengers must be dealt with (in different ways) for decades to come. Historically, management, institutions, and bureaucracies could operate effectively with standard policies that applied to everyone. We can no longer expect a single motivation scheme, punishment system, or communication style to produce the same result for all employees. We must develop customized approaches in tune with the value systems of each subgroup of employees.

PROBLEMS VS. CAUSES

Inherent in the traditional work ethic is an orientation toward problem solving. Traditionalists have faced a lot of direct and definable problems that could only be solved through organized action and applied technology. Once they define a problem, they throw all available resources into its solution.

A good example occurred in 1957 when Sputnik went "beep-beep" around the world. In the United States we said, "The Russians got into space first, but, by damn, we'll be the first on the moon!" We were first on the moon because the problem was defined and the ways to solve that problem were systematically laid out. Neil Armstrong's "giant step for mankind" depended on the problem-solving abilities of the traditional generations. However, the problem orientation of traditionalists sometimes causes tunnel vision: they can't see the broader picture. For example, an individual plant on the shores of Lake Michigan may be dumping pollutants into the lake. The traditional problem is the production of the plant, and the lake itself is ignored. As long as the bottom line (profits) guides decision makers, there is a tendency to downplay less tangible environmental factors.

Problems of production, speed, size, and time lend themselves to solutions using recipes. In the past, there seemed to be few, if any, recipes for focusing on human needs, dignity, and fulfillment. The key concern was quantitative: how much could we grow? New age questions ask about purposes, growth for whom, and growth for what. Until the 1960s our national direction had been toward increasing production and bettering ourselves and the world. Now we are moving toward a new perspective defined by generations with different values. The resources of Spaceship Earth are limited. When our problems were primarily centered on long-term physical survival and creating long-range security, those problems were relatively easier to solve. Our efforts focused on solutions gained through scientific discoveries, technological inventions, industrial innovations, business entrepreneurship, free enterprise economics, and tested knowledge about the management of large complex systems.

Part of the trouble with our traditional institutions is that they are badly designed for the *kinds* of problems we now face. These institutions are limited by the artificial boundaries that survived from historical rational disciplines (physics, biology, economics, and anthropology), from government activity in simpler times (mining, merchant marine, forestry, and regulation of commerce), and from the historic professions (law, education, medicine, and engineering). The *real* world now breeds mostly interdisciplinary, interdepartmental, and interprofessional problems. The scope of these complex problems helps elevate them to the level of causes. It is easier to create a machine that produces more product than it is to create a system that will provide social satisfaction, a sense of identity and self-esteem, and a feeling of self-fulfillment. With an economic base seemingly secure (although inflation may yet knock its props out), new generations are demanding more scientific responsibility and ecological awareness.

Challengers were value programmed with the luxury of both time and money, which allowed them to concentrate on broader issues. The media supported and championed these issues and brought a new awareness of past injustices. The injustices spotlighted were not only human, such as ethnic discrimination ("Roots" and "Holocaust"), but included other living things (baby seals in Canada, snail darters in Tennessee, and the hasn't-been-seen-for-five-years-but-we-think-it-might-still-be-around-and-it's-important Houston toad), and the broader environment. Who is polluting the Great Lakes? Why is the Cuyahoga River burning in Cleveland? Has the Brown Cloud smothered Denver? Can a malfunctioning reactor burn through to China?

An increased social consciousness and awareness of causes is the inevitable result of an economically secure base from which to operate, time to concern oneself with vague issues, and greatly improved education of the total population. Blame is directed toward big industrial concerns, the military-industrial complex, and a ballooning government bureaucracy. No longer able to ignore the new causes, the traditional systems respond with their typical problem-solving approaches, which are sadly ineffective given the dimensions of the "new" problems.

Tokenism became fashionable. Much as "concerned" students of the late 1960s spent a summer in the deep South to help the cause, businesses try quickie solutions. They plop black receptionists behind glass-paneled vestibules, add one female to the Board of Directors, and instruct production engineers to vent noxious fumes after dark when no one can see the sky darkening. Superficial changes could go a long way because they could be an opening for change in a lot of areas of concern to many people. However, the way they are often handled negates the effects. Well-meaning managers and administrators soon find that the backlash which follows is even more hostile than the original complaint. Tokenism is a storefront display that belies the chaos behind it: the old values, prejudices, biases, and ways of doing things go underground. No real opportunities are created, no real changes occur.

A lot of sincere, but naive people lost perspective in their concern with large-scale causes. The challengers lost sight of their own forest. Governor Dixie Lee Ray of Washington pointed out misdirected efforts when she related how a few oil-covered ducks washed up from Puget Sound, obviously caught in a leak from a passing tanker. Those few dead ducks became the object of a demonstration at the State Capitol. Each year, she noted, hunters shoot about fourteen million ducks in the United States. Essentially, no one gives a damn about those fourteen million dead ducks, but let four ducks die from an oil spill by a tanker and everyone gets up in arms. Some of the protestors had probably spilled as much oil and pollutant from their own power boats during the previous weekend's water skiing. Many who are so vehemently concerned about cleaning up the Great Lakes (and they are polluted and it is a problem) probably have fungus growing up their own shower stalls at home. Priorities are easily distorted. Perhaps if we really want to "clean up" the world, we should start with our own closets, attics, back yards, neighborhoods, desks, and relationships.

The resolution of this value conflict is difficult. Contemporary problems are more complex and the old solutions and techniques won't work. Causes are real, but one can lose perspective of the total picture very quickly. This is an area that has frequently seen more rhetoric than progress. The answer lies not in simplistic problem-solving approaches such as "The system is the solution." Millions firmly believe that the system *is the problem* since it helped create the current situation. We should synthesize: use the best of the old techniques, cut out dead wood, and then use the best of the new technology, and apply them *all* to the demands of today's world.

STABILITY VS. CHANGE/EXPERIMENT

Traditionalists have a deep-seated longing for stability. Perhaps it's an optimistic dream, but it seems to them that a stable system is possible, if only we can find it. Realistically, traditionalists were jolted during their value programming periods by a series of major disruptions: unsettling events such as the Depression, wars, and major social upheavals. Growing up without stability during at least part of their lives, the desire for stability became very real.

Most major institutions were not created to be flexible. Federal government checks and balances insure that no major change can be instituted without consulting and checking all of the ramifications. There is a general reluctance to alter the status quo. "This is the way we do things, this is the way we have always done things, and this is the way we will continue to do those things" is the general response to the questions that are raised.

Some have compared the current status of pressures for change in our society to the situation that existed during the middle 1800s. Underlying the Civil War was an inevitable clash between economic values; an agrarian society *vs.* an industrial society. Those who bemoaned the passing of the agrarian society predicted great disaster because of the shift. Yet the improved standard of living which industrialization brought was obviously an improvement for the entire society. The current American dilemma involves not only a shift in the economic base of our society—from production orientation to a service-information-recreation orientation—but it is accompanied by a dramatic broadening of the value spectrum within the society. This combination of forces creates even more stressful situations than existed when our nation shifted from an agrarian to an industrial orientation.

Our major institutions have been created and perpetuated to produce more *things*: from butter to guns to cars to planes to toys. As the production philosophy comes into more serious question, institutions find themselves unable to shift gears. An excellent example of this is the military. America now possesses the equivalent bombing force of 2,000 pounds of TNT for every man, woman, and child on the face of the earth. Why do we continue to produce more kill power? The answers provided by the military-industrial complex "do not compute" for millions of in-betweeners, challengers, and thoughtful traditionalists. The American automotive industry, until government mandated change, was geared towards producing bigger and better "blimps": comfortable behemoths that proclaim one's status, offer implied sexual connotations, and provide a playground for fantasies. To suggest that the industry should alter its production orientation and convert to something more realistic because of declining resources was heresy to the management of America's auto giants.

Blind to the realities of a changing world, our institutions plunge on in short-sighted but stable patterns. The social system (with its ordered structure of where people belong and how things should be done and what should be said) contributed to the general acceptance of stability. It was perhaps our nation's volatile birth, or perhaps our initial lack of *American* traditions and standards that led us to an obsession with creating, as fast as feasible, the best possible system and then maintaining it. For whatever reasons, stability is a real concern for millions of traditionalists.

In contrast, challengers grew up with, and therefore accepted, change and experimentation as a normal part of their lives. Their families fluctuated in their composition and life styles. Toys, music television programs, homes, schools, friends—virtually everything—came to be viewed as a "disposable product." There was little sense of permanency in the world of the in-betweeners and challengers. They were swept along in technological outdating that made ways of doing things obsolete: color television replaced black-and-white, stereo replaced hi-fi, stereophonic sound and full-dimension wide-screen color replaced black and white small screen movies, the hydrogen bomb we've never used replaced the atomic bomb, and now our premium on things *vs.* humans is reflected in the concern for the neutron bomb which will destroy humans but leave the things ready for someone else (if there's anyone left).

In education, majors did flip-flops. After Sputnik everyone wanted to be an engineer; soon we were oversupplied with engineers. Next everyone was to become a teacher to handle the baby boom; then we were oversupplied with teachers. Then everyone wanted to become a doctor, and we became oversupplied with doctors, and so it went. Laws changed, whimsically some thought, in virtually every area and those once stable benchmarks became flexible. Social relationships were transitory at best. As families moved from neighborhood to neighborhood, or state to state, friends became as disposable as paper plates—used for the convenience of the moment and then put aside until the next event, which would probably demand someone new anyway. Planned obsolescence in products, especially in the

1950s and 1960s, saw even once stable household items become fashionably in, then quickly out. If design wasn't the primary concern, then physical maintenance was, as the products frequently self-destructed when warranties expired.

The challengers especially were taught to question and were shown that new alternatives and options were available if one only explored. The old "black and white" stability disappeared, replaced by shifting grays. The result for the challengers is reflected in all aspects of their behavior. Their loyalty to brands and products has disappeared in the marketplace. They accept generic brands. They don't care about the label as long as they know it is: toilet tissue, bourbon, or tomato sauce. Fads that had occurred only occasionally are a permanent cycle: something is in, then out, then something else in, then out, then something else in, and on and on. Fashions in clothing change rapidly, moving through extreme variations in a relatively short period of time. Of course, some traditionalists still cling to a white shirt stability.

Life styles and belief systems have undergone rapid change. The frequent greeting between challengers is "What are you into?" The answer could be anything from jogging to health foods to skiing, racketball, est, meditation, Wayne Dyer, or astrology. (People used to introduce themselves by saying, "Hello, I'm John Jones Vice President of State University." Now the more likely introduction is "Hello, I'm Sam Smith. I'm a Libra. What are you?") While their parents still use their jobs and where they come from as identifying labels, the challenger children seek direction from the sun, moon, and stars, or tarot cards and tea leaves.

A natural outgrowth of the acceptance and perpetuation of continuing change is that many individuals become disoriented. They don't know who they are, where they are going, or what they should do. Questions such as Who am I? Where am I? What am I? What is the meaning of life? become very important. The identity crisis of the 1960s and 1970s was a real sociological/psychological phenomenon. Such a crisis did not exist back in the 1920s. In 1922, probably few people, if any, wandered around saying "Hey man, where's it at? What's happening? What's going on?" They knew they had damn well better get their butts in gear and get jobs if they were going to survive. Why should today's young people work? We've given them everything. Bored with that toy? Tired of that? Try something new. What do you want? How about an education? Want a vacation? Give, give. Take, take. And they've learned their lessons very, very well.

The traditionalists dug in, trying to protect those stable institutions they had fought so long and hard to establish. Bureaucracies multiplied. There is perhaps nothing so stable as a bureaucracy, nothing in which so little change is possible. The names on the doors may change, but the bureaucracy goes on. It seems impregnable to attack. A bureaucracy is like a giant science fiction amoeba that can absorb foreign matter and dissolve it. In businesses, universities, and communities, traditionalists form committees that meet religiously to formulate reports designed to foster continuity and stability.

Some traditionalists simply refuse to accept the new technology. They actually delay the introduction of computer-assisted techniques that will speed up new, desperately needed mass processing. Underlying all of this reluctance to accept innovative change is the threat to their economic security. When one week's work can be processed in an hour, *that* is a serious threat! At home, many traditionalist consumers reject instant foods, frozen foods, microwave cooking, and oil changes every 12,000 miles. It has taken years of very persuasive advertising messages to get them to even try many of the new products and services that entered the marketplace in the 1960s and 1970s. Some engineers, long "married" to their slide rules, actually expressed feelings of guilt about the new micro-computer hand-held calculators which perform tasks that used to take several minutes or even hours.

An excellent example of the resistance to change was demonstrated with the introduction of bank credit cards in 1967. The mass introduction of Master Charge and BankAmericards (now VISA) showed that values dictate how people relate to virtually everything in the world. For the introduction, banks automatically mailed cards to all approved credit customers. Upon receipt of the cards, the customers reacted according to their values. For the challengers, the new cards were a miracle: the ticket to fly now, pay later; if it feels good, do it; you only go around once in life, so live it with all the gusto you can. They used the cards enthusiastically. But millions of people in the traditionalist generation cut them up, sent them back, or threw them away. At a gut-level, at a value level, they knew: (1) credit was bad and (2) if you bought something you used money, not that silly card. Those traditionalist Americans who instinctively knew that "the eagle 'flew' on Friday night" were not about to replace money with that slippery plastic.

While acceptance of change seems a natural orientation for the challengers, resistance to change continues as a basic reaction of the traditionalists. If you want to create chaos in a community, bring up the concept of year-around school. The year-around school concept is extremely logical and rational from the point of view of economics and human resources. No longer do we have to use our school facilities only during the nine months from fall through late spring. Technology has changed. Now we have air conditioning to make the buildings comfortable. Knowledge of learning processes has changed. Now we know more about how people react in educational environments. Most critically, the economy has changed.

The nine-month school system in the United States was developed primarily because of economic pressures. Children were needed during the summers to help gather crops. Very few children have been out in the fields in the past few decades. Although recently a few of them have been out gathering some "crops" of their own during the summers, virtually none of them have been contributing to the economy. The reasons for the nine-month school year have disappeared. When the concept of year-around education is brought up, many communities divide across value lines, with traditionalists generally opposed to the idea. Recently, one member of a committee called The Concerned Citizens for Quality Education was heard in a radio interview proclaiming, "We're going to fight it. We're going to fight the year-around school system. The *normal* American way to go to school is nine months." There is no *normal* American way to go to school, do a job, make love, or anything else. There are *appropriate* ways that are based on the conditions that exist at a given point in time. There are no *absolute* standards for doing anything. Once conditions change, then behavior and values should follow. But we cling to the old established ways.

Many traditionalists worry about what other people will think if they violate customs that have been long enshrined. As an example, a major metropolitan school district built a new office building in the heart of the downtown area. This new nerve center for school administration drew 660 employees to the congested and polluted city core each day for work. After a few months the administration surveyed employees and asked them what they liked and disliked about the new work environment. One specific complaint concerned the lunch hour. (A traditional stable trap: You have a lunch hour. One hour, that's it. You get out there and you eat for one hour and then you come back and you work again until the end of the day.) Nearly 80 percent of the employees said that they didn't want a lunch hour. The cafeteria was very efficient and a lot of people were dieting or jogging or meditating. Therefore, what they really wanted was a thirty minute lunch break, staggered so that some of the employees could come to work thirty minutes later or leave thirty minutes earlier. They could avoid at least once a day, the congestion in the downtown area. When the results were presented to a vice-superintendent his emphatic reaction was, "Absolutely not! What will the people of this community think if they see us coming to work late or leaving early?" A challenger response to that, and probably an appropriate one, would be, "Who gives a flip what the people of the community think!" If the people of that community are really *thinking*, what they should be concerned about is whether the employees in that building are motivated, productive, and happy with their work. Further, they would contribute less to the pollution and the congestion in the downtown area. If *that's* what they would think about, then the proposed solution would be appropriate. But since it violates the way we've always gone to work, the way we've always done things, it was shot down by the traditional administration.

Within schools there are a lot of traditional administrators and teachers clashing with the young who are being programmed with new values. In the late 1960s a major experiment allowed children to start using computer terminals as early as the first grade. In the real world of today, a six-year-old can often sit comfortably at a computer terminal: "two times four . . . beep . . . equals eight; two times five . . . beep . . . equals   ten . . . beep . . . beep." Kids are growing up thinking a computer is as normal as a light or a telephone. For millions that didn't happen, and therefore they don't understand the technology. Computers wink, blink, and do funny things. Those people don't like computers, and they don't like people who work with computers either. Deep down they think, "It's not normal to screw around like that." For the children, it's normal.

Today's children are acutely aware of so many things. They know so much, sense so much, see so much, and experience so much. They have a sophisticated understanding that surpasses that of many adults. Certainly, at the same relative age, most adults didn't even know about, much less talk about, concerns of their parents' world. When many adults were in school they labored with "exciting" projects such as making fire prevention posters and feeding lizards that lived in jars. Many of today's school-age children can talk intelligently about resources, ecology, transportation for the future, inflation, ZPG, contraception, and abortion. If we'd only ask them, they'd explain those things to us. But that's not the way the world works. Most older people have never thought of learning from the young. Many traditionalists still ignore reality. Only in recent times have youth been uniquely accelerated in their "learning," so that they actually surpass many adults in knowledge and experiences. Perhaps if we stop automatically rejecting and *listen* to the young, they can help us restructure our long-held absolutes.

One public school teacher sums up the situation by relating this story. He was out on the playground supervising kindergarten children when one of the kids started watching a jet contrail cross the sky. "There goes a Boeing 747," the kid said. "It's powered by Pratt & Whitney engines. They each develop 65,000 pounds thrust, etc. etc. etc." He rattled more technical specifications. Another kid interrupted, "That's not a 747, stupid. It's a DC 10. Anyone knows that. It's not powered by Pratt & Whitney. It's powered by G.E., and they only develop 42,000 pounds thrust." The bell rang; recess was over. One little kid looked at the other and said, "Well, let's go back to stringing the damn beads now."

And that's about where we are in American education . . . and in business . . . and in government . . . and in religion . . . and in all our major institutions. Millions of people are still trying to string the damn beads: do it the way they've always done it because that's the way they know how to do it and, by God, that's the way they're going to continue to do it. So there! But it won't work any more. It's all changed. Everything's changed and the insistence on maintaining a stable system in the catalysmic world of the 1980s is a blindfolded approach to the reality that screams all around us. Still some won't give in; some won't accept the now world. They keep trying to do the same things the same ways, and they don't know why they don't work.

At a recent convention of florists a college professor (an in-betweener) presented some new approaches and thoughts for marketing floral products. He urged his audience to move away from the "funeral wreath" styles of the past. After the presentation, which included some innovative suggestions, a traditionalist in his late fifties approached the speaker. He sneered, "I've been in business thirty-five years, have been mayor of my town for two terms, and I bet I make more money and drive a better car than any smart aleck young college professor." He's "right," of course, given *his* value system. He's not going to let anyone tell him about his business. After all, his car and income *prove* he's successful!

MATERIALISM VS. EXPERIENCES

Material "things" tend to be important to many traditionalists because (1) they didn't always have the money to purchase those things and (2) a lot of the things that are taken for granted today simply weren't available when they were being value programmed. Until the good life arrived, millions of Americans didn't really possess the primary yardstick for measuring success in the United States:

money. Americans have been especially obsessed with accumulation of money as a measure of their own success and as a way of comparing themselves with one another and with other countries. From the traditionalist point of view, money makes the world go around. Money *potentially* buys happiness, and money certainly motivates people.

As traditionalists moved up the scale in standard of living and acquired more money, large numbers of them began to express their success through purchases. They bought not only for themselves, but especially for their children. Once the traditionalists acquire things they tend not to let go of them. They love to accumulate. They fill their attics, their basements, their garages, and some buy portable sheds to put in their backyards to store still more things. Their basic attitude toward things seems to be "You never know when you might need the June 1938 issue of the *National Geographic*." That 1938 issue, along with all of the others, is kept. Some traditionalists who programmed through the lean years of the Depression go to extremes. Someone recently found in a deceased aunt's attic a large box neatly labelled "String Too Short to Save." The box, of course, was full of little pieces of string. Hoarding and saving for those future inevitable rainy days is a gut-level value reaction of most traditionalists. The importance that they place on economic security and the accumulation of money is also reinforced by the various religions which emphasize that it's okay to make money as long as one contributes part of it to God to further His work.

The obsession with things has led to filled attics and garages and to a partial enslavement to technological advances. With each new technological adult "toy" that appears on the market, it becomes important to *acquire* those things. Gadgets fill kitchens, bathrooms, and all available space not taken up by old issues of the *National Geographic*. All those things accumulated by the traditionalists not only get in the way, they also tend to break and malfunction, thus creating high frustration levels. When the automatic icemaker starts spewing cubes across the kitchen, or the garage door opener jams halfway up and refuses to move in either direction, and the television antenna rotor sticks and channel 4 won't come in because the TV set's circuitry is malfunctioning, and the washing machine sticks on the spin cycle, and the car is mysteriously steering itself in undesired directions, and the disposal ate three pieces of stainless ware, and the snowblower is jammed with a newspaper, and the plumber can't come until next week, and a squirrel has built a nest in your chimney—life does become a bit frustrating. However, all of those things demonstrate the ability to spend money, and in America the ability to spend money proclaims that you are successful. Consequently, the ends seem to justify the means, however frustrating the means become.

The challenger generation was value programmed surrounded by all those things that their materialistic, traditionalist parents stockpiled. The young take the things for granted. What they grew up without was a great deal of direct experience with the world. After sitting for thousands of hours passively in front of television sets, when they did venture forth, or were taken out, they found themselves facing predictable "Disneyland" adventures and staying in sterile motels which offered no diversity. In fact, a late 1970s hotel chain advertising campaign suggested "The best surprise is no surprise." They were selling *boredom*. Younger people don't want to be bored. They want something exciting. They want to experience and to feel.

Another dimension of the challengers' experience orientation is found in an attitude of "Do it now." The in-betweeners and challengers were programmed in the shadows of the atomic bomb. While that was not a direct threat, there were enough concerns in the world around them that it seemed that one should try to get as much as possible out of life as quickly as one could. Why wait for some dim distant future? Why save for a future that might never arrive? Why not seek enjoyment in the here and now?

Television and movies provided an awareness of the opportunities for expanding horizons. As in-betweeners and challengers reached young adulthood, they left their sheltered, non-risk world provided by the institutions of family and schools. They suddenly scattered in all directions seeking new types of kicks, highs, and experiences. But by the time these clusters of people reached adulthood, inflation had clouded the view. One economist compares money to ice: it just keeps melting away. Inflation actually seemed to validate a "get it now because we won't be able to afford it in the future" approach to spending and living.

The challengers want things not just for display or to accumulate, but rather for what those things can provide for them in experiences. Although many challengers don't want to actually eliminate material things from their lives (they can always store them in extra space in their parents' attics), they tend to purchase products that provide direct rewards rather than sit around in some symbolic fashion to reflect their success. Their needs for financial and material security are minor compared to their needs for emotional security, feeling good about themselves, and pleasure in what they are doing. They even demand enjoyment on the job (if they have one).

Many in-betweeners and challengers simply aren't doing what they are supposed to be doing from the perspective of the traditionalists—they aren't collecting and acquiring. Rebelling against being tied down, many of them do not get married, buy homes, start having children, and collect things. They are not concerned with the building of estates (an obsession with many traditionalists and some of their institutions like the insurance companies). Their motto is: "Live now and let the future take care of itself."

Challengers were value programmed to accept experiences as important dimensions of life. For example, look at recreation and sports. The favorite sports for the challenger are individually structured: one person against the mountain, or against the course or against the slope, or against one other person. There's no real team orientation when the challenge is to the individual. Hang gliding, sky diving, motorcycles, jeeps, kayaking, tennis, racketball, and weightlifting are all directed toward individual participation. The traditionalists prefer to be spectators, or perhaps engage in a little symbolic recreational golf on weekends (more business may be conducted during play on the golf course than during any other activity). Recreational activities for many challengers are distinctive because there is little competition with other people or against other groups, and because there is often a high level of personal risk which provides kicks and excitement to the participants. The kicks are an escape from their boredom with the sterile, predictable, computerized, dehumanized, sanitized, Muzak-sounded, orthodontically-wired life from which they emerged.

Travel offers a kaleidoscope of experiences for the challengers. As children they were carted around by their parents to all the appropriate amusement parks and national monuments, but media tantalized them with views of a wider world which they became eager to explore. They took off in earnest. In foreign countries they actually live with the natives, hitchhike, and use local transportation. In the late 1960s and early 1970s there was a massive migration within the United States. It looked like the lemmings had returned as hundreds of thousands of hitchhikers roamed across that nation. Hitchhiking is an inexpensive mode of transportation, and it offers a lot of exciting experiences. New people, new places, and new adventures are just over the next hill or around the next curve.

When traditionalists travel, they prefer their own "home on the range." Motorized campers have all the comforts of home, including a television set just to keep them in contact. They line up row upon row in the national parks. It's a mini suburbia transplanted into the wilderness. When they venture into foreign lands, traditionalists prefer organized tour groups ("If it's Tuesday, it must be Belgium"). They expect hotels to provide ice, room service, and all the conveniences of their local inn. If the foreign lands don't have the same crisp postcard views seen in all those travel brochures, traditional travelers become upset. They want to see the real people and the way they live, but only in a cool tour bus from which they can retreat to clean beds, air conditioning, mixed drinks, and bacon and eggs for breakfast. A lot of foreign smells, sights, sounds, and tastes are repulsive to them. The ugly American goes on tour. "Why aren't these foreigners like us?" was a massive reality thrust upon an unsuspecting world during the 1960s and 1970s.

While the challengers try to *increase* risks, opportunities, and sensations in their lives, traditionalists prefer to isolate and insulate themselves from strangers and unknown experiences. Their definition of the good life includes protection at home and on the job. Government bureaucracies have evolved to guarantee such protection, even if it doesn't seem to make sense, as in many of OSHA's rules.

As a result of their values, traditionalists accumulate their estates and surround themselves with things. Then, instead of being able to enjoy their hard-earned leisure, they have to deal with heart attacks, intense competition, and ulcers. They turn to psychiatrists, sleeping pills, tranquilizers, and alcohol. Challengers use drugs and alcohol to heighten their experiences or to escape from the boredom and banality of the world as they perceive it. Many of them have become nature-oriented. Clomping around in their hiking boots (frequently having trouble getting over the curbs), they express a strong desire to return to the "good old days." They are probably correct in their assignment that modern life has become too complicated, but the good old days weren't so great either if viewed objectively. Things didn't work, people got sick more often, and there was less opportunity for leisure since one's primary concern was to make a living and survive. The variety of food, places, entertainment, recreation, and other experiences were certainly more severely limited. The same technology that now seems to enslave didn't even exist in the good old days, and the millions of challengers now enjoying and feasting on that good life would not have had the opportunity to do so just a few decades ago.

Perhaps nowhere are values more readily expressed than in the marketplace. An excellent example of differing values is evident in stereo equipment. Typical traditionalists have a large wood-finished console. *Better Homes And Gardens* and *Family Circle* said it would look terrific in the rec room. It has a lot of lights on it (because they paid a lot of money—$500 to $800—and they want to make sure the thing is working). It sits there and plays Muzak-type background entertainment. The challengers have stereos too, but they're not beautiful wood-grained pieces of furniture. A lot of equipment hangs around on the walls with wires running everywhere. They pay a lot of money too—$1500 to $1800—and then after the get it, they "wire" themselves into it because they want to *feel* the music. The traditionalists don't want to *feel* the music. If they feel too much of *that* music they have to take an Alka-Seltzer or Pepto Bismol.

The in-betweeners as usual are caught and don't know what to do. They like the idea of the quality of component systems, but they don't like the mess and don't want to antagonize traditionalist visitors. The typical in-betweener consumer has a component stereo system, but hides it in a closet or a cabinet specially purchased to conceal it. As in most of their behavior, they balance precariously between the extremes.

Another excellent example of values influencing products is evident in the American automotive industry. Run by people at the top of the traditionalist spectrum, these companies have produced giant, cosmetically beautiful monsters that cruise down the road with all the creature comforts. Why has the automotive industry insisted until recent times (when government and public pressure forced them to change) on producing these blimps? Simple: The people who head these companies were value programmed when cars were uncomfortable and undependable and roads were extremely rough. They set out to change all that—to create something better, bigger, and more comfortable. We've seen the resulting products on highways for the past few decades.

The in-betweeners and the challengers were value programmed in those blimps, and they don't relate to them. They accept them, but they prefer something else. Generally, in-betweeners were the first generation to accept automobiles as basic transportation, not as symbols of status or sexual prowess. (Get me from point A to point B). The lead edge of the in-betweeners was the first generation to widely accept the Volkswagen-scale car in the United States. Those cars were about as basic as one could get. The reaction of most traditionalists was that those weren't cars—they're toys! If you had a *car* you had to have a big blimp that went "gowong-gowong" down the road. But the in-betweeners love their "wheels." However, if money is no object and if given a choice, the in-betweeners and challengers place at the top of their preferred list as their favorite car the Porsche. With a Porsche, you can *feel* the road. Traditionalists *felt* the road, *felt* the road, *felt* the road. They don't want to feel the road any more. They want pleasure, enjoyment, comfort, isolation, and insulation from the confusion swirling around them. The way we spend our money, the way we raise our children, the way we do our jobs, the way we worship, the way we do *everything* is directly related to our gut-level values.

There are many other value differences that exist between the traditionalists and the challengers. However, after looking at some of the basic patterns of values for these two major clusters, we should now be able to deal more effectively with these people. For those in the clusters, we have gone beyond the surface, the superficial, to the gut-level, the value level that governs their behavior. Understanding people in this way, many of us should be able to deal with other people in a more productive manner: communicate with them more effectively, produce products and services that are more appropriate for their needs and values, motivate them better on the job, and manage them more efficiently.

Remember: all those other people out there who are "different" have value systems that they cherish and protect just as you do your own. You and all of them are each right, normal, and correct. What you are now is directly related to where you were when—when you were value programmed. If you will accept this general model, then you can improve your relationships with others. Understand and accept your own value-views; then do the same with others.

Part V

SOLVING YOUR OWN PEOPLE PUZZLES

Now we have the basic pieces of the people puzzle, but putting it together is really up to you. From the psycho-historical insights into ourselves and others, we can sense the very real challenge of dealing effectively with others who hold diverse values. Realistically, there are no simple solutions for understanding *how* to solve the inevitable conflicts between ourselves and those who are "different." Knowledge, acceptance of our own "normality" and that of others, and an open-minded willingness to try to relate and communicate are the first critical steps.

The Ever-Changing Puzzle

A final solution to the people puzzle can never be reached because the pieces (the world and its people) are constantly changing. What works today in a particular situation at home, at school, or on the job may not work tomorrow. In the past, things were simpler. Less change meant less diversity and more predictability. Now we must accept a continual process of reinterpreting our locked-in, gut-level values and expressing them effectively in our behavior under whatever conditions we may live. If we cloak ourselves in self-righteousness, we cannot hope to find solutions for coping with others in today's world.

Directions: Acceptance, Commitment, and Responsibility

There is a strong urge to seek checklist recipes to solve our dilemmas or to grab for "golden ring" solutions. Recent "pop-psychology" philosophies promise formulas for instant success and happiness. No such pat "answers" are offered in this book. No *single* recipe (child care book, teaching technique, management style, motivational scheme, communication pattern, or popular self-help prescription) can possibly solve all of the problems for all of the people all of the time. In fact, any solution that does not start with a basic acceptance of self and others can be counterproductive and can lead to unrealistic expectations about how people *should* feel and what life *should* be all about. Many popular "recipe" books today emphasize manipulation and/or self-centeredness. We contend that happiness and meaningful, productive relationships grow out of *commitment* and *responsibility*. We will be much happier and more effective in all dimensions of our lives if we are willing to accept who (and why) we are and grant this same acceptance to others.

The application of value programming analysis to the solution of the people puzzle must be dynamic, as is life itself. Open-mindedness, acceptance of other people, and understanding, examination, and re-evaluation of our values cannot be static processes. There are no people skills to memorize by rote and then apply consistently to everyone in all situations.

You are what you are because of where you came from, and the same is true for others, but this does not mean that you can escape the *responsibility for your behavior* now and in the future. Unfortunately, millions do try to ignore their responsibility for their own lives. It's so convenient to blame someone else when your life isn't working. "*My parents* don't (didn't) understand me." "The *teacher* gave me an F." "*They* don't like me." "The kids don't appreciate how we've sacrificed." "The computer screwed me up." "No one works the way they used to." "When is he/she ever going to grow up?" "But you didn't tell me I couldn't do it!" "Oh, I thought *he* was going to take care of that!" Such statements, and thousands like them, are copouts from responsibility.

Tuning In

We are responsible not only for our own lives but also for our dealings with others. Underlying our puzzles about people's behavior, especially during the past few years, has been our own lack of effort to tune in to what has happened. Too often we *isolate* ourselves from conflicting views, threatening ideologies, divergent life styles, varying religious philosophies, and foreign experiences. When we limit ourselves to our own value-views, it is impossible to be sensitive and aware of alternatives that are available and "correct" in their own right.

Many opportunities to expand our value horizons are within easy reach. If we look beyond the obvious—entertainment, news, information—"different" value-views cascade all around us. Consider the following:

1. Movies and theater are graphic reflections of our changing society. Anyone who saw and *thought about* the following sample of films and plays could see some interpretations of how values and behavior have changed through the years: *Rebel Without a Cause, The Last Picture Show, The Graduate, Z, Midnight Cowboy, Five Easy Pieces, The Godfather, American Graffiti, The Sting, Clockwork Orange, Patton, M.A.S.H., Lenny, The Turning Point, Guess Who's Coming to Dinner?, An Unmarried Woman, Taxi Driver, Easy Rider, The Deer Hunter, Butch Cassidy and the Sundance Kid, Billy Jack, Last Tango in Paris, Hair, Who's Afraid of Virginia Woolf?, Oh, Calcutta, A Chorus Line, Godspell, Tommy, In the Heat of the Night, One Flew Over the Cuckoo's Nest, Bob and Carol and Ted and Alice, Saturday Night Fever, Hud, Jesus Christ Superstar,* and *Coming Home.* Have you been to the movies or the theater recently?

2. Books range across the contemporary value spectrum. *The People's Almanacs* (both the original and #2) contain almost an excess of valuable information, especially in their coverage of the United States from 1770 to 1978. Time-Life's *This Fabulous Century* and William Manchester's *The Glory and the Dream* are living texts of history and how it has shaped values. Insights into past, present, and future behavior abound in *Roots, The Adjusted American, I'm OK— You're OK!, Passages, Shifting Gears, The Final Days, The Plug-In Drug, Future Shock, Families,* and *A Time for Truth. To Love Is To Be Happy With* offers a clear and effective process for examining your own values. Have you read any good books lately?

3. Television doesn't have to be a mental wasteland if you catch programs like "60 Minutes," "Holocaust," "Roots," "Scared Straight," "Reading, Writing, and Reefers," the national news, "Today," "Good Morning, America," documentaries, and thought-provoking talk shows with hosts like Phil Donahue, Tom Snyder, and Dick Cavett. Even popular and entertaining programs like "All in the Family," "One Day at a Time," "Family," "Lou Grant," and "The Waltons" are loaded with value messages. Try to inject some thoughtful analysis into your typical passive viewing. What's your TV diet each week?

4. Print media also open up new value-views. One of the best ways to tune in to change is to regularly read a newspaper such as the *New York Times,* the *Wall Street Journal,* the *Washington Post,* the

San Francisco Chronicle, or the *Chicago Tribune,* that covers "national" news. We need to read *beyond* the headlines, sports pages, comics, and "Dear Abby"—although even those are loaded with value information—and *think* about what we're reading. Magazines, such as *Time, Newsweek, The New Yorker, Harper's, Esquire, People, Atlantic Monthly, Psychology Today, U.S. News and World Report, Playboy,* and *Fortune,* can assist us in monitoring our dynamic world.

Open Your Mind and Say "Ah"!

These media are representative samples of means that we could all use to find out about ourselves and others. Certainly, we expand our value-views when we add other, more direct exposures to reality by breaking out of our standard patterns. Attend a variety of church services. Join a discussion group. Take part in community action forums. Go to a rock concert. Break off the "tourist" path on vacation. *Listen* to your children—let them introduce you to *their* world. Try a new sport. Sample ethnic foods. Open a new "window" and try a new "door"; travel down a "road" that you've never traveled before. Try it, you may like it. Even if you don't, you'll have enriched your knowledge and expanded your awareness. Education shouldn't stop with a diploma.

Many people avoid anything new. The idea that something *they* don't relate to can be just as normal as their own patterns is extremely threatening. To be open-minded requires a great deal of security about who we are. Many people refuse to accept (or even look at) the validity of their own past value programming. Consequently, they don't understand the basis of their *present* behavior. They erect mental walls of defense around their values for self-protection. An intriguing case of such value rigidity was seen when the movie "Oh, God" was released. Several groups mounted vocal protests against what they saw as a sacrilegious portrayal of the Deity. In reality, "Oh, God" had an extremely religious message. When questioned by reporters, many protestors admitted that they had not seen the movie. "Don't confuse me with the facts. I've already made up my mind." Strong value biases often come from a lack of information.

An open mind does not mean dumping old values for new ones on a daily basis. An open mind is not a sieve or a revolving door where nothing of permanence remains. It is a mind that makes room for new data, that can expand to take in new points of view. It is a mind that can accommodate the paradoxes, complexities, and ironies of life without feeling threatened.

Open-mindedness does not mean an "anything goes" world where anarchy reigns and all behavior becomes acceptable. Even extreme behavior may be "normal" for some (Hitler, Charles Manson, Jim Jones) in light of their value programming, but they still function in a social context where their behavior is not acceptable. Two hundred and twenty million people can't "do their own thing" without total collapse and chaos. In our relationships, each of us has the right to behave according to his or her own values and convictions. But the other people in the relationships have the same right and may react in turn to us. We each have the right and the obligation to respond to others when their behavior affects us, especially if it's negative. It's the old adage, "You have freedom to swing your arm as long as it doesn't hit me."

Compatibility Through Synthesis

When our values clash with someone else's, we can try to ignore the situation, get out of the relationship, or accept the responsibility for initiating change in ourselves, the situation, and/or the other person. A frequent response is the first—refusing to accept responsibility. It is typical among traditionalists. They complain behind people's backs but never confront them directly and honestly. They repress their feelings and suffer inside for it. The second response is currently popular, especially among the challenger group, who walk away from a job or out of a marriage, emotionally abandon their children or parents, and otherwise dump the whole mess and retreat into their own egocentric world. The third pattern offers the greatest challenge to us, but it has the greatest potential for solving our personal people puzzles. It is accomplished through synthesis.

Let's look at an example of how this approach can work effectively in a business setting. A manager's first responsibility should be to select productive employees. If he's not directly involved, then he is still responsible for making sure those people hired have values that are compatible with the job requirements. In today's world, this may mean that we have to ask more value-loaded questions. Interviewing should include dialogue about work values. ("How do you view work as it relates to your life?") Employers should spend more time on their recruiting sources and recommendations.

Realistically, problem employees are and will continue to be hired, and managers are and will be confronted with them. In dealing with a problem employee, a manager may accept his responsibility by (1) adapting the elements of the work environment to accomplish the company's desired end results (while still accommodating the employee's needs), (2) changing the employee's behavior, or (3) firing

236 Solving Your Own People Puzzles

the employee. The third choice may be restricted because of factors like unions or the fear of being accused of discrimination. The most responsible action (unless the third is unavoidable) is a combination of the first and second alternatives.

Many businesses (and individual managers) are moving toward such synthesis solutions to their current people problems. Introduction of flextime, career pathing, job enrichment, participative decision making, and a "cafeteria" offering of benefits are all variations from traditional work settings. We see increasing customization and personalization of jobs because it's demanded by the values of today's younger employees. Training programs and consumer research also signal an increased awareness of business's need to understand people. There are already many viable alternatives to the "way we've always done it," and as the people pressures grow, even more options will be developed.

Each of us is responsible for creating new solutions for our people puzzles, not only in business but also in our schools, homes, churches, and communities. Before we point an accusing finger at others, we must meet our responsibility for looking objectively at our *own* values and behavior and then practice finding new synthesis solutions.

Creating Change in Others

Even if we modify the situation and alter our own behavior, we may still be incompatible with someone else (boss, co-worker, neighbor, children, spouse, parent, etc.). We now face the responsibility for changing something about them. Change can occur on two levels: underlying values and resultant behavior.

Behavior will change if the consequences are *important* to us at the time. However, our values only slip into a holding pattern until the threatening conditions change. Our behavior is a response to the importance and make-up of each "carrot stick" that is dangled in front of us.

Most behavior changes are really very limited because they relate to only one segment of our lives. For example, if we force a worker to change job-related behavior, such as attendance or productivity, he will still retain his old behavior patterns with his spouse, his children, his friends, and within his community. All of these non-job-related areas continue to reinforce the old behavior and its value base, so change occurs only at work. There is certainly nothing wrong with the limited change in behavior, but the limitation should be recognized. We shouldn't naively assume that any gut-level value change has taken place. A pussycat at work may be a tiger at home, and an angel at church may be a devil at school.

Occasionally, a Significant Emotional Event (SEE), or a series of them, may actually *force* change in both behavior *and* gut-level values. An external, uncontrolled SEE may be of such high intensity (economic collapse, natural disasters, social and political upheavals, legal or religious mandates, or a technological revolution) that it changes the personal values of large numbers of people. Other SEEs slam into an individual on a direct and private basis (divorce, winning a sweepstakes, being fired, the death of a loved one, participation in a war, a brush with death, or overnight success). Wilbur Mills' splash with Fanny Foxxe in the Tidewater Basin is an example of a personal life-changing SEE. Sometimes SEEs may come from several sources. If you're fired, your wife leaves you, your kid runs away, and your best friend cheats you, it's virtually impossible to avoid examining your gut-level values.

An SEE occurs when your values and behavior are challenged, especially when you're confronted from multiple sources. One of the most moving stories of an SEE for a public figure was Betty Ford's disclosure of her battle with alcohol and drugs. Challenged by her husband, children, doctors, and friends, she could not avoid the reality of what had happened to her values and behavior. Certainly, the confrontation was not pleasant or easy for those who loved her, yet they were willing to take the responsibility for changing another person's behavior. If more people had the courage to accept such responsibility, our families, our jobs, and our world would be significantly improved.

Making the Choice to Try

If you are willing to take the initiative for changing another person's behavior, for forcing them to confront their actions, then you can create Significant Emotional Events. Such action should not be considered lightly, as you are challenging someone at his or her most basic emotional level. You may be held accountable for your actions. Furthermore, there are often real risks: you might lose your job; you might alienate the other person; you might destroy a relationship; or you might "burn bridges." However, if the situation is intolerable as it exists, the risk is necessary, and the payoff potential is enormously rewarding. If no change takes place, you'll remain trapped in a destructive bind that ultimately chokes your own happiness and effectiveness.

Some Who Succeeded

Significant Emotional Events come in many forms, from numerous sources, and with varying degrees of intensity. Recently, a major international manufacturing company faced a deteriorating situation in one of its plants located in a small midwestern community. Absenteeism was increasing, productivity was decreasing, and over 50 percent of the final products were defective. Since the company had extra capacity in a west coast facility, it informed the town that it was closing down. The townspeople panicked, since they were economically dependent on the company's presence. The schools, city council, churches, service clubs, youth groups, unions, and citizens all rallied and asked for another chance. Company executives were reasonable and flexible enough to postpone the final decision for three months. Using agreed-upon guidelines for improving the situation, the workforce did a complete turnaround. For that community, the company created an economic SEE. The company stayed.

A father who co-signed a note with his nineteen-year-old son on a $6,000 speedboat grew frustrated over the boat's care. Although he built a new dock, his son refused to tie the boat securely to prevent it from crashing into the pilings. The father threatened to let the boat sink if it continued to happen. The son's response was, "Sure, Dad, you owe for it, too. Go ahead, let it." And three days later, he did. As the boat sank, the son frantically dove after it. His father said, "I told you, and I meant it." For five weeks the son didn't speak to the father, but he got a job and repaired the boat. Finally, one day he walked up to his father, threw his arms around him, and said, "Dad, thank you for forcing me to think. Thank you for making me responsible." Both father and son cried. For both, it was an emotional SEE. Behavior and values had changed.

The award-winning documentary "Scared Straight" illustrated a unique SEE format that does what juvenile authorities can't seem to do—it changes the behavior of hardened juvenile delinquents. The kids are placed in isolation with convicted lifers (murderers, rapists, thieves, etc.). The criminals verbally blast the cocky kids. The no-holds-barred language, threats, and such degrading actions as making them take off their shoes and then throwing the shoes out of the cell shatter the delinquents' arrogant facade. The youths face the reality that they could be killed by the convicts—after all, a lifer has nothing to lose. The 80 to 90 percent successful conversion rate of these kids is better than any of our costly do-gooder social programs. The convicts created the program to try to help stop the self-destructive direction of the juveniles. The screaming, shouting, swearing, threats of violence and whatever else it takes are intended to scare the kids into really *listening* and *thinking* about the consequences of their delinquency. For the delinquents who experience it, the program is a personal SEE. Television's courageous airing of the documentary during prime time created a media SEE for many of those who watched.

Change: New Values and New Behavior

In all of the above examples a belief or value was impacted, enabling the target of the SEE to create change within himself. The company did not change the work values of the community. The workers "believed" that sloppiness would not endanger their jobs. When it *did,* the "belief" of the workers about sloppiness changed, and their behavior on the job was subsequently their *own choice.* The sinking of the son's boat challenged his belief about irresponsibility, and he then had to behave based on new information. This new behavior made him happier than the old, which is often the case. The delinquents' behavior came from beliefs or attitudes such as "I'm tough, nobody can hurt me!" When the lifers challenged this belief in the kids ("I could *really* get hurt here"), the youths chose to change their behavior based on new information. We can never change another person's values; only he can do that. What we *can* accomplish through an SEE is a breakthrough in awareness that *allows* the other person to change. To change or not to change is his own choice.

Significant Emotional Events have two critical requirements: *personal impact* and *clarity.* Personal impact occurs only when we internalize and think about the consequences (both positive and negative) for us. Clarity is present when an individual makes the connection between what is happening to him and how his value-based behavior triggered it. This means that we cannot expect to communicate on an SEE impact level with another person unless we reach him as an individual on a direct and personal basis. Toys won't do it. Memos won't do it. Signs won't do it. Generalizations slide past the gut level. Effective rewards and punishments must have meanings that are personally important.

Clearing Up Our Agreements

We tend not to be very clear with one another. We often neglect to agree or even to discuss our expectations and the consequences of unacceptable behavior. We would avoid many misunderstandings and confrontations if we made agreements that were direct and specific. The agreements may be the result of negotiation and/or compromise. They could be directives. Whatever their basis, our agreements should be clear, fair, and reasonable; have attainable expectations; and be understood and accepted by all parties. When agreements are broken, we must reckon with the consequences. A lot of people try to get off the hook. If we let them, we are not necessarily being compassionate or humane; rather, we're stupidly reinforcing their irresponsible behavior. They made an *agreement* (to do an assignment, to be somewhere on time, to take out the garbage, etc.). They violated the agreement, and the piper must be paid (they get an F, they have to redo it; they're locked out; they lose TV privileges; etc.). Threats ("If you do that again . . ."), nagging ("If I've told you once, I've told you . . ."), or warnings ("This is the last time . . .") are all unnecessary, ineffective, and counter-productive. There should be *only* predictable consequences.

With the Predictability of Gravity

Consequences should be established when agreements are made. They should be fair, reasonable, non-negotiable, clearly understood, and applied swiftly with the predictability of the law of gravity. The best lesson we can learn from gravity is that it *always works!* Children learn this simple fact early in life. It is how they learn to walk. When they get off balance, gravity "gets" them. Gravity never says, "Well, you screwed up, but we'll let you off this time." If you get off balance, gravity just busts your ass every time. This type of predictability could work miracles if it were applied in homes, schools, courts, and on jobs. We are not advocating an unthinking, insensitive, and arbitrary system of punishments and rewards for undesired behavior. Consequences need not be brutal nor devastating; they need only be *undesirable.* Rewards can be as simple as a "thank you." Consequences (both positive and negative) are essential reactions to behavior. Otherwise, we have no guidelines to follow, pitfalls to avoid, or goals to achieve.

Effective managers—like loving parents, compassionate clergymen, successful teachers, productive employees, developing children— all need to be flexible, adaptable, and sensitive in their relationships and agreements. We need to discover where the other person is "coming from" before we attempt to interact with him. Getting angry at someone says nothing about the other person; it only tells us about *our* values. We should not be afraid to re-evaluate ourselves, others, and the ways we interrelate.

To Care Is the Key

No one can really guarantee that solving people puzzles is going to be easy. It's not simple to incorporate acceptance and understanding of others into our own daily interactions. It's far easier to believe that we are right and others are wrong and to try to shape others in our image. Our ability to be effective human beings ultimately hinges on a four-letter word: CARE. As simplistic as this sounds, caring is far from simple.

What we care about and what we don't care about are direct reflections of our own gut-level values. A lot of people don't really care about anyone except themselves. If people really cared about others, we would not have nonsupportive families, ineffective schools, management/labor strife, lip-service religious commitments, superficial friends, biased media sensationalism, profiteering, dangerous and/or shoddy products and services, wasted resources and energy, discrimination, and arbitrary regulations. Obviously, we can't all agree on everything, but we can exercise enough concern to show that we really *care* about others.

Parents who substitute toys for hugs and time really don't care about their children. Recently, bumper stickers appeared with the question "Have You Hugged Your Kid Today?" Millions would have to say, "No, I gave them $5, but I didn't have time to talk to them." We can easily recoil at physical abuse. There are an estimated two million cases of child abuse each year in our country and countless other cases of neglect. But what of the more subtle ways of not caring? What of the millions of parents who now think it's unfashionable to discipline their children? That's not caring enough to set guidelines they so desperately need. How much commitment do we really have to being parents? How much do we respect our children as people?

The other side of the coin in family relationships is equally important. As a son or daughter, how do we show our love for our parents? How many of us have ever really bothered to say thank you to our parents? How many of us have ever sincerely apologized for the inevitable frustrations we created? How many of us cared enough to take the time and make the effort to see things through our parents' eyes and understand their perspective? As adults, have we reduced our relationships with our parents to telegraphed flowers and cards on appropriate occasions? Did we care enough when we became adults to be friends with our own parents?

Management cares when it makes certain that employees are adequately trained and know what is expected of them and when it considers the self-esteem and individuality of each worker. One of the most repeated indictments against management by workers is the lack of proper training. It seems so obvious, so why are we so negligent? Do we really not care? Can we be more honest, direct, and complete in our communications? Why not? Do we try to force employees into preconceived molds, or do we allow for individual differences? Employees care when they do what they have agreed to do—work. The world isn't working because a lot of people aren't working. They're not fulfilling their commitments. They don't give a damn or take pride in the products they produce or the services they provide. Wearing buttons that proclaim "I care" is not enough—their behavior so often contradicts the slogan.

When 11:00 A.M. Sunday continues to be the most fragmenting hour across the land, how much do we really care about religious tenets extolling compassion, love, concern, and empathy? How deep are our convictions and commitments? Do we "do unto others" differently on the job, in our neighborhoods, or within our families?

Do you contact your friends in times of need—*your* needs? What about *their* hopes, dreams, needs, sorrows, and successes? Are they pieces in your games to be manipulated and then discarded when they're no longer beneficial to you?

Do you accept sensationalized media reports? Or do you take the responsibility to get both sides of the story? Do you care enough to allow yourself to be confused by facts?

If you're in business, what are your real objectives? Is the "bottom line" more important than your employees and customers? Do you balance the need for profit with considerations for the human dimensions of safety, dependability, service, satisfaction, and quality? Do you operate on a philosophy of *caveat emptor* (let the buyer beware)? As a consumer, do you exercise your right to give feedback, both good and bad, about products and services?

How committed are you to conserving precious resources and energy? Have you seriously considered car pooling, turning out lights, setting thermostats lower, conserving water, driving a smaller car, taking the bus, recycling paper and aluminum, etc.? Are you reevaluating and changing your life style, or are you engaging in trendy tokenism?

Are you really not discriminating against others because of their sex, race, appearance, religion, sexual preference, nationality, beliefs, or values? Do you hate "them" as a group but love "them" as individuals? Or vice versa? How would you honestly fill in the blank:"Some of my best friends are _____"?

Do you impose arbitrary rules on others? As a parent, employer, bureaucrat, teacher, or "judge," do you care enough to continuously evaluate the appropriateness of your requirements of others and yourself?

If you don't like what's happening to you, what can you do about it? Many people just complain, grumble, and backstab. The shockingly low (and declining) voting rate clearly shows that the majority of us don't care enough about what our government does. We really don't try to change it. Do you communicate your frustrations to those who matter—those who are causing the problem, or those who can take action?

Caring works. It's the key to unraveling our people puzzles. If we care, we can understand and accept others for what they are. We accept a commitment for being open to those who are different. When we care about others, we create the time necessary to include them and their needs as priorities in our lives. In doing these things, we also show that we care about ourselves and our own happiness. Our own happiness and fulfillment are not found in an ego-centered vacuum of isolation, but rather in dynamic and productive relationships with others.

In these increasingly conflict-laden times, can we really afford not to try to solve our people puzzles? You owe this commitment to yourself and to all our futures. We will all be happier for it.

TRACKING VALUES

The material in this last section is not an appendix. It's a guide to help you begin exploring your own values and their sources. You can also "track" values in others. First, there's a timeline that lets you review chronologically some value-forming events. Then, you can see who else was "around 10" when you were. Finally, a sampling of value clarification exercises will bring you in touch with your specific beliefs and attitudes. This enjoyable and enlightening process can help us understand, relate, and begin to SEE.

TIMELINE:
A SWEEP THROUGH EVENTS (1920–1979)

The following telegraphic look at the years from 1920 to 1979 does not list all events of importance, but it does highlight some critical value-forming occurrences. In order for you to derive maximum benefit from the list, mark the happenings that you remember as particularly meaningful in your life, paying special attention to the years around your tenth birthday (eight through twelve years old). Customize this list by adding personal events that influenced your value programming.

Take the influences from your critical years one step further and try to assess how they are reflected in your behavior today. How did those events affect the development of the world around you and your value perceptions of it? The first challenge is to take an *objective* look at your own values and behavior.

Now use the list to look at the value sources for your children, your spouse, your friends, your employer, and others when *they* were around ten years old. Use this list as a stimulator for conversations involving comparisons of likes, dislikes, similarities, and differences among people. You'll increase your understanding of these people, their behavior, and their value systems. Such insights are a beginning for meaningful and improved interactions with others.

1920—Prohibition is enacted (18th Amendment)
Women's Suffrage Amendment (19th) is ratified
Black Sox scandal in baseball
Warren Harding is elected President of the U.S.
First municipal airport in U.S. opens in Tucson, Arizona
Mary Pickford and Douglas Fairbanks are married
"Jazz" age begins

1921—First Miss America is crowned in Atlantic City, New Jersey
D. H. Lawrence writes *Women In Love*
Cigarettes are legalized in Iowa
First live radio broadcast of a World Series baseball game

1922—King Tutankhamen's tomb is discovered
Ed Wynn becomes the first major star to go into radio
Gandhi is sentenced to prison in India for nonviolent protests
against British government
Mussolini and his Fascist party march to Rome and form a new
government
The Lincoln Memorial is dedicated in Washington, D.C.

1923—German inflation reaches levels requiring wheelbarrows of
money to buy bread
Time magazine is founded
First birth control clinic opens in New York City
"Yes, We Have No Bananas" is the #1 hit in America
"Teapot Dome" scandal rocks the Harding administration
Carnegie Steel institutes the eight-hour work day
Pancho Villa is gunned down in Mexico
A patent is issued to Jacob Schick for the first electric shaver

1924—Gershwin's "Rhapsody in Blue" is performed for the first time
U.S. citizenship is conferred on all American Indians
J. Edgar Hoover is appointed director of Justice Department's
Bureau of Investigations
Immigration laws are severely restricted to exclude Japanese

1925—The Charleston becomes the popular new dance
The Scopes "monkey trial" in Tennessee tests the legality of teaching Darwin's theory of evolution
Will Rogers replaces W. C. Fields in the Ziegfeld Follies
General William "Billy" Mitchell is found guilty of insubordination
Adolf Hitler writes first volume of *Mein Kampf*
First motel opens in San Luis Obispo, California
Charlie Chaplin stars in *The Gold Rush*

1926—Ford Motor Company announces cars in colors other than black
The Sun Also Rises, by Ernest Hemingway, is published
Actor Rudolph Valentino dies in New York. Outpouring of grief is overwhelming
Hirohito becomes emperor of Japan
Winnie the Pooh is written by A. A. Milne
The National Broadcasting Company becomes the first nationwide radio network
Rear Admiral Richard Byrd flies over the North Pole

1927—Charles Lindbergh becomes the first person to fly nonstop from New York to Paris in his plane, the "Spirit of St. Louis"
Babe Ruth hits 60 home runs
First talking movie, *The Jazz Singer,* starring Al Jolson, is released
Union organizers Nicola Sacco and Bartolomeo Vanzetti are accused of murder and executed
Leon Trotsky is expelled from the Communist Party in Russia
The first television picture is successfully transmitted
The "Long Count" fight between Jack Dempsey and Gene Tunney takes place
Show Boat opens in New York City

1928—Penicillin is discovered
First regularly scheduled television programming begins in Schenectady, New York
Mickey Mouse is born
First color motion pictures are demonstrated by George Eastman

1929—On Black Tuesday, October 29, the stock market crash precedes the Great Depression
First "Oscar" is presented for the film *Wings*
St. Valentine's Day Massacre occurs in Chicago
U.S. poverty line is set at $2,000 annually

1930—Later to be known as the "Lion of Judah," Haile Selassie I
   becomes emperor of Ethiopia
   The planet Pluto is discovered
   Ellen Church becomes the first airline stewardess for United
   Airlines
   Albert Einstein comes to the United States
   Grocery stores receive the first packages of frozen foods, devel-
   oped by Clarence Birdseye

1931—The Empire State Building is completed in New York
   Wiley Post and Harold Gatly complete around-the-world flight
   in 8 days, 15 hours, and 51 minutes
   Al Capone is sentenced to prison for income tax evasion
   The right of Negroes to serve on juries is established in the
   case of the "Scottsboro Boys" in Alabama
   The U.S. Treasury announces that 827 banks have failed in
   one month
   Car speed record is established at 246.086 m.p.h.
   The "Star Spangled Banner" becomes the national anthem

1932—Charles Lindbergh, Jr. is kidnapped
   "Brother, Can You Spare A Dime?" sweeps the country as a
   popular song
   Amelia Earhart becomes the first woman to fly solo across the
   Atlantic Ocean
   World War I vets demanding promised but undelivered bon-
   uses are driven out of Washington by general Douglas Mac-
   Arthur and majors Dwight Eisenhower and George Patton
   Babe Ruth points to a spot in Wrigley Field to which he then
   hits a home run
   Franklin D. Roosevelt is elected President of the United States
   The Palace Theatre closes in New York and vaudeville dies
   with it
   Fifteen million people are jobless
   The Nevada legislature limits people to three divorces in one
   lifetime
   The "New Deal" is proposed by Franklin D. Roosevelt

1933—The Chicago World's Fair opens
   Adolf Hitler is appointed chancellor of Germany
   FDR utters his famous statement, "The only thing we have to
   fear is fear itself"
   Prohibition ends
   Nation's banks collapse

Fan dancer Sally Rand makes people momentarily forget the Depression

FDR has his "One Hundred Days"

Walt Disney wins an Oscar for *The Three Little Pigs*

The Tennessee Valley Authority is formed as the first publicly owned utility in America

1934–The "dust bowl era" arrives with great storms in Oklahoma, Texas, and Colorado

The Dionne quintuplets are born

John Dillinger is shot and killed in Chicago

Shirley Temple debuts in *Stand Up and Cheer*

Dr. Townsend, Huey Long, and Father Coughlin challenge FDR

1935–The Social Security Act is passed

Will Rogers and Wiley Post are killed in a plane crash

John L. Lewis emerges as the voice of organized labor

Huey Long is assassinated in Louisiana

Joe Louis becomes heavyweight champion of the boxing world when he knocks out Max Baer

Parker Brothers introduces the game of Monopoly

Porgy and Bess opens in New York

1936–*Gone With the Wind* is published

Jesse Owens wins four gold medals at the Berlin Olympics. Hitler refuses to present the medals to this black American

Franco attempts to overthrow the Spanish government

FDR "buries" Alf Landon in 1936 Presidential election

1937–FDR unsuccessfully attempts to reorganize the Supreme Court

Hindenburg zeppelin explodes in New Jersey

First jet engine is developed

Golden Gate Bridge is dedicated in San Francisco

A patent is issued for nylon

The Memorial Day Massacre of striking steel workers occurs in Chicago

Japanese planes sink a U.S. gunboat, *The Panay*, in China

1938–Chamberlain returns from the signing of the Munich Pact and announces "peace in our time"

Orson Welles delivers his "War of the Worlds" broadcast

Thirty-two thousand people die in traffic accidents

Jitterbug is born in New York with Count Basie and Benny Goodman

Snow White and the Seven Dwarfs is the top movie of the year

1939—*The Grapes of Wrath,* by John Steinbeck, is published
New York World's Fair predicts the future
World War II begins—Germany invades Poland
FDR becomes the first President to appear on television
Gone With the Wind hits the silver screen
Nobel Prize is awarded to Ernest O. Lawrence for development of the cyclotron or "atom smasher," a major step in the production of nuclear reaction
Ten million people are unemployed
Kate Smith sings "God Bless America" for the first time
The Wizard of Oz catapults Judy Garland into the hearts of Americans

1940—U.S. population is 131,669,275
Hattie McDaniel becomes the first Negro to win an Oscar for her role in *Gone With the Wind*
Nylon stockings go on sale in the U.S.
Germany captures most of northern Europe
Battle of Dunkirk occurs
Battle of Britain occurs
France falls
FDR is elected to an unprecedented third term
Grandma Moses has her first art show

1941—The Atlantic Charter is drawn up by Churchill and FDR
Germany invades Russia
Japanese planes attack Pearl Harbor on December 7
Under pressure from religious groups, City College of New York dismisses Bertrand Russell for his ideas on sexual behavior
Marian Anderson, a Negro, is denied permission to sing in Constitution Hall by the D.A.R. Civil Rights movement gains momentum.

1942—"White Christmas" is written by Irving Berlin
Bataan Death March occurs
Battle of Guadalcanal occurs
U.S. experiences heavy losses in the Pacific
A fire in the Coconut Grove nightclub kills 491
One hundred twelve thousand Japanese-Americans are detained in camps until the end of World War II
Douglas MacArthur vows "I shall return"

1943—German troops surrender in Africa
Race riots erupt in Los Angeles and Detroit

The Withholding Tax Act is signed
Battle of Anzio is fought
Hitler orders the destruction of the Jewish ghetto in Warsaw, Poland
Italy ousts Mussolini
Hot dogs are replaced by "Victory Sausages" made of meat mixed with soybean meal
U.S. bombers hit Germany for the first time

1944—Russians begin to expel Nazi invaders
Forever Amber by Kathleen Winsor is published and condemned as obscene and indecent
Germany launches V1 and V2 rockets to destroy London
GI Bill of Rights, providing educational and vocational benefits for veterans, is signed
An assassination attempt on Hitler fails
Battles of Saipan and Leyte are fought
Battle of the Ardennes Forest in Luxembourg—"Battle of the Bulge"—is fought
"Mairzy Doats" is a popular song
D-Day occurs
DeGaulle triumphantly returns to Paris

1945—Grand Rapids, Michigan, adds fluoride to its water supply to help prevent tooth decay
Kamikaze pilots die in droves
Germany surrenders
Atomic bombs are dropped on Hiroshima and Nagasaki
Japan surrenders
Mussolini is killed
Hitler commits suicide
Tito establishes the republic of Yugoslavia
John M. Birch is killed in China; John Birch Society springs from his death
FDR dies
German annihilation of six million Jews is discovered
Nuremburg trials of war criminals begin in Germany
John D. Rockefeller, Jr., donates money for the purchase of land where the United Nations building is to be constructed
United Nations is chartered

1946—First computer is used (Pennsylvania)
First U.N. session is held in London
Winston Churchill coins the phrase "Iron Curtain"

Negroes vote for the first time in Mississippi
The Atomic Energy Commission is created
"Electronic blankets" go on sale
A bank in Chicago offers the first "auto-bank" service

1947—The Truman Doctrine is enacted
Jackie Robinson becomes the first Negro baseball player in the
major leagues
Voyage of the Kon-Tiki verifies migration routes to Polynesia
The Marshall Plan is announced
Babe Ruth retires
The tubeless tire is introduced by B.F. Goodrich
The sound barrier is broken when Charles Yeager flies faster
than the speed of sound

1948—U.S. recognizes the republic of Israel
Berlin airlift is inaugurated
Columbia Records introduces the "long-playing" 33⅓ rpm
record
The *Kinsey Report* on human male sexual behavior is released
Gandhi is assassinated in India
The Alger Hiss case is pursued by Richard Nixon
Truman upsets Dewey in the Presidential election
The first solar home heating system is installed

1949—"Tokyo Rose" is convicted of treason
Mao Tse-tung leads Communists to victory in China
U.S.S.R. explodes an atomic bomb
The NATO pact is signed
Death of a Salesman by Arthur Miller opens
Herbert A. Philbrick testifies in a trial of eleven Communists.
His life is later popularized in a TV show called "I Led Three
Lives"
Levittown opens, beginning the suburban era
"Rudolph the Red-Nosed Reindeer" is sung by Gene Autry
First mass reports of flying saucers
Cortisone is discovered

1950—Joe McCarthy creates the "Red Menace" scare
Korean War begins
The Hollywood Ten are accused of being Communist sympa-
thizers
U.S. population is now 150,697,000
George Jorgenson returns from Copenhagen as a woman, Chris-
tine Jorgenson

1951—Color TV is introduced
Julius and Ethel Rosenberg are sentenced to death as spies
Douglas MacArthur is relieved of his duties
Paul Robeson, a Negro singer-entertainer, presents a petition
accusing the United States of pursuing a policy of genocide
against his race
The twenty-second amendment is passed, limiting presidents
to two terms
Television replaces radio as America's Number One entertain-
ment medium

1952—Richard Nixon delivers his "Checkers" speech
U.S. detonates the first hydrogen bomb
Charlie Chaplin leaves the U.S. under harassment from the
FBI and the IRS
Dwight Eisenhower is elected President

1953—The Korean War ends
Stalin dies
Edmund Hillary and Tensing Norgay conquer Mt. Everest
Playboy begins publication
The Rosenbergs are executed
New York Yankees win their fifth straight World Series
Fidel Castro leads a futile attempt to overthrow Batista's gov-
ernment in Cuba
The Supreme Court rules that restaurants may not refuse service
because of race

1954—Jonas Salk's polio vaccine is distributed in the U.S.
French-held Dien Bien Phu falls to Ho Chi Minh; North and
South Vietnam are created
The Army–McCarthy hearings are televised, and Joseph Mc-
Carthy is one of the first to experience the power that TV
can wield
Brown v. The Board of Education is decided by the Supreme
Court, disallowing "separate but equal" education and re-
quiring equal, integrated education
Oral contraceptives are tested on women for the first time
Roger Bannister breaks the four-minute mile record

1955—U.S. population is 160,000,000
"Rock Around the Clock" by Bill Haley and the Comets begins
the rock and roll era
Davy Crockett is the object of a new craze, complete with coon-
skin caps

Secretary of State John Foster Dulles declares a new policy concerning nuclear power—"Massive Retaliation"

Rosa Parks, a young Negro woman, refuses to give up her bus seat to a white man and is arrested. Dr. Martin Luther King, Jr., organizes a year-long boycott. Bus segregation is declared "unconstitutional" by the Supreme Court

"Blacks" becomes the popular new name for Negroes

George Meany becomes president of the newly merged AFL-CIO

The Dodgers finally beat the Yankees in the World Series

1956—A new singing star, Elvis Presley, has two giant hits, "Hound Dog" and "Don't Be Cruel"

Grace Kelly marries Prince Rainier of Monaco

The *Andrea Doria* sinks off Long Island. There is live TV coverage

U.S.S.R. invades Hungary and crushes a revolt

Peyton Place becomes a best seller

The Suez Canal is closed by sunken ships in a Mideast battle involving Egypt, Israel, France, and Great Britain

1957—Senator John F. Kennedy is awarded a Pulitzer Prize for *Profiles in Courage*

Dr. Martin Luther King, Jr. organizes Southern Christian Leadership Conference

Edsel is a major failure for Ford Motor Company

U.S. troops are sent to Little Rock, Arkansas, to protect blacks entering a previously all-white school

U.S.S.R. launches Sputnik—first manmade satellite—and the space race begins

U.S. has a severe setback in the "space race" with rocket disaster at Cape Canaveral

Teamsters are expelled from AFL-CIO

1958—Common Market is formed in Europe

Sherman Adams resigns because he allegedly accepted gifts, including a vicuna coat

Lolita is a best seller

Explorer 1, the United States' first satellite, circles the globe

Dr. Zhivago wins a Pultizer Prize for Boris Pasternak

Hula hoops are the rage

Nixon's motorcade is attacked in Venezuela

1959—Fidel Castro's revolution takes control of Cuba

Charles Van Doren is exposed as a fraud

The first seven astronauts are chosen

Alaska and Hawaii become states

D. H. Lawrence's *Lady Chatterly's Lover* is published and is later banned from being sent via the U.S. mail

Nixon and Khrushchev engage in the "Kitchen Debate"

1960—U.S. population is 179,323,175

Sun City opens in Arizona

Francis Gary Powers is shot down over the U.S.S.R. while flying a U-2 spy plane

Bye Bye Birdie opens on Broadway

Caryl Chessman is executed at San Quentin for robbery, kidnapping, and rape, despite appeals from many respected people in the world

Kennedy defeats Nixon with a little help from Richard Daley in Chicago. First major use of television in covering debates betwen major candidates

Payola scandal involving over 200 disc jockeys is uncovered in New York

The "pill," Enovid, is approved by the FDA

1961—"Ask not what your country can do for you; ask what you can do for your country"———Inaugural speech of John F. Kennedy

The Peace Corps is founded

U.S.S.R. sends a cosmonaut into space

U.S. sends Alan Shepard into space one month later

Adolf Eichmann, a former Nazi officer, is executed in Israel for World War II crimes against the Jews

Freedom Riders test segregation laws

Bay of Pigs invasion fails in Cuba

First bricks of the Berlin Wall are laid

Roger Maris hits 61 home runs

First major "skyjacking" in the U.S.

First U.S. troops enter Vietnam

1962—John Glenn, U.S. astronaut, becomes the first American to orbit the earth

Supreme Court bans prayer in public schools

Students for a Democratic Society (SDS) is formed

Thalidomide babies, with severe deformities, are born in Europe and the U.S.

Pope John XXIII fosters ecumenism with the convening of the Second Vatican Council

James Meredith, by court order, is the first black student to attend the University of Mississippi

Marilyn Monroe dies of pill overdose in Los Angeles

The first "singles only" weekend in the Catskills
Cuban Missile Crisis makes the world tremble

1963—". . . Segregation now, segregation tomorrow, segregation for-
ever."———George Wallace
Beatles tour the U.S. for the first time. "Beatlemania" runs
rampant
"Blowin' in the Wind" by Bob Dylan is sung by Peter, Paul
and Mary
Bull Connor opposes Martin Luther King, Jr. with police dogs
and fire hoses in Birmingham, Alabama
A hot-line is established by phone between Washington and
Moscow
Call girl Christine Keeler ends the political career of British
War Secretary John Profumo
"I have a dream. . . ." ——Martin Luther King, Jr., in Wash-
ington, D.C.
First woman in space—a Russian cosmonaut
Bomb blast kills four black girls in a church in Birmingham,
Alabama
President Diem assassinated in Vietnam
President John F. Kennedy assassinated November 22. Lyndon
B. Johnson becomes President

1964—Gulf of Tonkin incident in Vietnam and resulting resolution
gives LBJ the power to wage war
Beatles appear on Ed Sullivan's TV show and earn eight gold
records during the year
President Johnson signs the Civil Rights Act and the "long hot
summer" begins across the U.S.
Dr. Martin Luther King, Jr. wins the Nobel Peace Prize
Campus protests begin in Berkeley, California, with the Free
Speech movement
China develops its own atomic bomb
The WarrenReport is issued to explain the death of JFK
Dr. Strangelove, a movie about nuclear holocaust, is extremely
popular
LBJ swamps Barry Goldwater in the presidential election

1965—Malcolm X is assassinated in New York
Marches for civil rights are held in Selma, Alabama, and riots
occur in the Watts district of Los Angeles
Dr. Zhivago entertains millions of moviegoers
One hundred and twenty-five thousand U.S. troops are in
Vietnam

U.S. troops are sent to quell a rebellion in the Dominican Re-
public
First teach-in on a college campus opposes the Vietnam war
A great power blackout darkens the Northeast
Frisbees are introduced

1966—U.S. troop strength reaches 300,000 in Vietnam, and U.S.
spends $1.2 billion a month there
John Lennon says the Beatles are more popular than Jesus
U.S.S.R. lands an unmanned spacecraft on the moon
Stokely Carmichael and others proclaim "Black Power"
Richard Speck kills eight student nurses in Chicago
Charles Whitman shoots 44, kills fourteen from the top of a
tower on the University of Texas campus
Timothy Leary leads LSD cultists to "turn on" and "drop out"
Ralph Nader leads a fight for safety regulations against auto-
makers and begins the modern consumerism movement
"Is God Dead?" asks *Time* magazine's cover story
The Georgia legislature refuses to seat black legislator Julian
Bond
Bill Russell becomes the first black coach of an NBA team
Quotations from the Works of Chairman Mao Tse-tung is pub-
lished at the height of the Cultural Revolution in China
First sex change operation in the U.S.

1967—Hundreds of thousands protest Vietnam war across the U.S.
Reis Tijerina leads a group of Chicanos in New Mexico to
claim land that they assert is theirs because of their Spanish
ancestry
"Flower children" flock to Haight-Ashbury district of San Fran-
cisco—"hippies" are born
Riots plague the nation's cities, most notably in Newark and
Detroit
Expo '67 is staged in Montreal
The Six Day War in the Mideast leaves Israel the victor
China detonates an H-bomb
Che Guevara, a revolutionary, is executed in Bolivia
First human heart transplant is performed in South Africa by
Dr. Christiaan Barnard
U.S. population is 200 million

1968—*U.S.S. Pueblo* is captured by North Koreans
Troop strength in Vietnam reaches 550,000 and there are
30,000 dead
North Vietnamese troops launch a powerful drive, called the
Tet Offensive

My Lai incident exposes death of innocent civilians in Vietnam
Dr. Martin Luther King, Jr. is assassinated
George Wallace runs for President of the U.S.
LBJ announces that he will not seek re-election
Robert F. Kennedy is assassinated
Chicago Democratic Convention turns into a bloody riot
Jackie Kennedy marries Aristotle Onassis
Paris peace talks begin to settle Vietnam issue
Student riots in France nearly topple DeGaulle
Soviet Union crushes liberal reforms in Czechoslovakia
Richard Nixon edges Hubert Humphrey for President
Hair opens in New York

1969—Chicago Seven trials for disruption of the Democratic convention begin
Chappaquiddick mars Edward Kennedy's career
Woodstock, a gigantic rock festival, is held outside a small town in New York
Neil Armstrong takes ". . . one giant leap for mankind" on the moon
Charles Manson and his "family" are tried for murder, and in the process, they terrify America
American Indians occupy Alcatraz Island

1970—U.S. population is 203,211,926
Nixon orders an "incursion" into Cambodia. Five days later, four students at Kent State are killed by Ohio National Guardsmen during a protest of the military action
Joseph Yablonski and members of his family are found murdered during his campaign for the presidency of the United Mine Workers of America. Four years later, Tony Boyle, the incumbent, will be convicted for their murder
Kissinger approves expenditure of millions for the CIA's attempt to overthrow the Communist government of Salvador Allende in Chile
"Hot pants" hit the streets
Angela Davis and George Jackson make headlines with murders in courtrooms and prisons. George is killed in prison; Angela is acquitted

1971—Daniel Ellsberg leaks the Pentagon Papers, classified documents chronicling U.S. involvement in the Vietnam war
Twenty-sixth Amendment gives eighteen-year-olds the right to vote

People's Republic of China displaces the Taiwanese delegation at the U.N.

Team of U.S. ping-pong players visits Red China

Twelve thousand are arrested in Washington, D.C., for anti-war demonstrations and herded into RFK stadium

White House "plumbers" break into Daniel Ellsberg's psychiatrist's office

Thirty-one prisoners and nine hostages are killed at Attica prison in New York during a riot protesting prison conditions

U.S.S.R. lands a spacecraft on Mars

1972—Nixon visits China, a major diplomatic breakthrough

Robert Vesco contributes $200,000 to Nixon's re-election fund, despite the fact that he is under investigation by the Securities and Exchange Commission

George Wallace is shot and paralyzed from the waist down while campaigning for the Presidency

Bobby Fischer beats Boris Spassky of the U.S.S.R. for the world chess championship in Iceland

Haiphong harbor is mined

Five "plumbers" are arrested for breaking into the Democratic National Committee's headquarters in the Watergate complex

Kissinger declares that ". . . peace is at hand" in Vietnam

Bernstein and Woodward break the Watergate story in the *Washington Post*

Nixon-Agnew win in a landslide over McGovern-(Eagleton) Shriver

1973—The Watergate saga unfolds as Nixon declares, "I'm not a crook"

U.S. and North Vietnam sign a peace treaty

American Indian Movement, led by Russell Means, occupies a trading post and a church at Wounded Knee, S.D.

Israel and Egypt go to war again

Spiro Agnew resigns as Vice President after being suspected of receiving kickbacks and being convicted for income tax evasion

Gerald Ford is named Vice President by Richard Nixon

Arabs initiate an oil embargo against the U.S., creating problems at U.S. gas stations

1974—Patty Hearst is kidnapped by the Symbionese Liberation Army in Berkeley, California

Henry Aaron hits home run number 715, breaking the lifetime record of Babe Ruth

Alexander Solzhenitsyn is expelled from the U.S.S.R. for being incompatible with the requisites of being a Soviet citizen

House Judiciary Committee recommends impeachment of Richard Nixon for criminal activity. On August 8, Nixon resigns in disgrace from the U.S. Presidency

One month later, President Gerald Ford pardons Nixon for any wrongdoing, despite the fact that the former president had not yet been formally charged

Muhammad Ali regains his heavyweight boxing championship when he KO's George Foreman in Africa

Northern Ireland continues to be wracked with terrorism

Rush Springs, Oklahoma, residents ban public dancing

1975—Nixon cohorts are sentenced to prison terms

Saigon is overrun by North Vietnamese

Smokey the Bear retires

Cambodians capture the U.S. merchant ship *Mayaguez.* President Ford responds with a successful rescue attempt

King Faisal of Saudi Arabia is assassinated by his American-educated nephew, who is then beheaded for his crime

Two unsuccessful attempts are made on President Ford's life

1976—U.S. celebrates its two hundredth birthday

Israel rescues 110 passengers and crew from Palestinian terrorists with a daring raid at Entebbe Airport in Uganda

U.S. lands Viking spacecraft on Mars

Jimmy Carter defeats Gerald Ford for the Presidency

SST is banned from landing in the U.S.

Karen Ann Quinlan's parents win in court the right to stop the life support systems which keep her alive

1977—Gary Gilmore is executed by firing squad in Utah

The U.S. experiences devastating winter weather

Spain holds first free election since 1930s

New York suffers a major blackout. Looting is widespread

President Anwar Sadat of Egypt makes an historic trip to Israel to seek peace

Smallpox "ceases to exist" in the world

U.S. farmers strike for higher prices, which they express as "parity"

Elvis Presley dies at 42, and the world mourns the loss of the "King of Rock and Roll"

1978—A baby conceived in a test tube and then gestated in the
mother's womb is born
California taxpayers shake the country with Proposition 13, an
expression of the "taxpayer revolt"
Allan Bakke wins a case of reverse discrimination in a decision
by the Supreme Court. The Court endorses the idea but not
the way in which it was handled in the Bakke case
John Paul II becomes the world's first Polish Pope
Nine hundred and eleven Americans take their lives in a mass
suicide in Jonestown, Guyana. The victims are followers of
the Reverend Jim Jones, a religious cult leader
United States breaks its ties with Taiwan and formally recognizes Red China
Star Wars becomes all-time movie moneymaker; spawns space
craze

1979—Gasoline prices reach $1/gallon in U.S.
President Carter helps to negotiate a peace settlement between
Egypt and Israel
China invades Vietnam. Russians react strongly, at least ver-
bally
Shah of Iran is overthrown and ultimately replaced by the
militant Islamic rule of Ayatullah Khomeini
U.S. tests its space shuttle, a reusable spacecraft
Disco dancing becomes the most popular form of the art in the
U.S.
A near disaster in Pennsylvania occurs at a nuclear power plant
Masters and Johnson's research explodes myths about hetero-
sexual and homosexual behavior
Rhodesia elects Black Prime Minister; Idi Amin "missing" in
Africa

WHERE THEY WERE WHEN

You may find it enlightening to review a list of individuals from
a number of fields—government, business, entertainment, sports, the
arts, education, etc.—and look at them as *groups* of people who were
ten years old at the same time. Since they have all achieved some
measure of fame, they embody a certain amount of hero status and
reflect certain values. We do not infer that all within each group have
the same set of values, but they have all, to a certain degree, experi-

enced some of the same events on the timeline. Some of these people are definitely "deviants" from the norm values of their generation; others are very typical.

The list is admittedly limited. Some names will be familiar to you; others won't. If we left out your favorites, we apologize. Most of these people are still alive; many are still in the position mentioned. Many were difficult to characterize. Their fame overlaps more than one area, and they far transcend the short phrase we used to identify them.

As you look from the early 1950s on (people who are now in their late thirties and younger), you'll note the sharp decline in chief executive officers (CEOs), chairmen of the board, presidents, etc., of major corporations and institutions. It appears that fame and hero status among the young have come chiefly to those who became "instant" stars of television, movies, recordings, or sports.

We should remember that our future leaders, the people who will be in key power positions by the end of the century, are *out there right now*—our young employees, college students, and children on playgrounds—future famous names. Many are still in their value programming years. What happens to them will affect how the future unfolds. Much is already determined as far as *directions* (given present trends); *when* and *how* are yet to unfold.

With this in mind we permitted ourselves to hypothesize and fantasize a bit. We decided to create a few hypothetical blanks in the last few years and try to plug in some real and potential future entries. You can probably think of more.

Enjoy yourself as you scan the list. Look at who your contemporaries were when you were ten. Remember, the year above the names is *not* a birth year, it is when these people were ten. We start with some people who were ten *before* 1920 because their influence on our society continues.

They'd Already Been There When . . .

Norman Rockwell (artist) 1904
George Meany (labor leader) 1904
George Burns (entertainer) 1905
Bishop Fulton J. Sheen (clergyman) 1905
Norman Vincent Peale (clergyman) 1908
Charles Richter (seismologist) 1910
James Beard (chef) 1913
J. Robert Oppenheimer (physicist) 1914
Leon Jaworski (lawyer) 1915

Philip Johnson (architect) 1916
Warren Burger (Chief Justice, U.S. Supreme Court) 1917
Lewis Powell (Supreme Court Justice) 1917
John Wayne (actor) 1917
Harry Blackmun (Supreme Court Justice) 1918
Thurgood Marshall (Supreme Court Justice) 1918
Arthur Burns (economist) 1918
Michael DeBakey (surgeon) 1918
Lyndon B. Johnson (U.S. President) 1918
Nelson Rockefeller (philanthropist) 1918
Edwin Land (inventor) 1919
Peter Drucker (management consultant) 1919 (Austria)

Where Were They When?

1920—Abe Burrows (playwright)
    Robert Cummings (actor)
    E. G. Marshall (actor)
    Harold Geneen (Chief Executive Officer [CEO], ITT)
    Joan Bennett (actress)
    Eero Saarinen (architect) (Finland)

1921—Clark Kerr (educator)
    Ronald Reagan (actor/politician)
    Maureen O'Sullivan (actress)
    Hubert Humphrey (U.S. Senator)
    Vincent Price (actor)
    Broderick Crawford (actor)
    Tennessee Williams (playwright)
    Leonard Woodcock (labor leader/ambassador to China)
    Lucille Ball (actress)
    Chet Huntley (TV journalist)
    Ginger Rogers (actress/dancer)

1922—John Cheever (author)
    Studs Terkel (author)
    Pat Nixon (former First Lady)
    Gene Kelly (entertainer)
    Sam Snead (golfer)
    Charles Addams (cartoonist)
    Julia Child (chef)
    Lady Bird Johnson (former First Lady)
    Woody Guthrie (singer)
    Minnie Pearl (singer)

Roy Rogers (actor)
Dale Evans (actress)
Milton Friedman (economist)
Eric Sevareid (TV journalist)
Art Linkletter (author/TV personality) (Canada)

1923—Richard Nixon (U.S. President)
Danny Kaye (entertainer)
Woody Hayes (football coach)
Gerald Ford (U.S. President)
Mel Allen (sportscaster)
Jimmy Hoffa (labor leader)
Richard Helms (CIA director)
James Pike (clergyman)
Frankie Lane (singer)
Sammy Cahn (songwriter)
Sylvia Porter (economist)
Paul "Bear" Bryant (football coach)
Eliot Janeway (economist)
Burt Lancaster (actor)
Vivien Leigh (actress)
Lew Wasserman (CEO, MCA)
John Mitchell (U.S. Attorney General)

1924—William Westmoreland (army officer)
Ernest Tubb (singer)
Al Ullman (U.S. Congressman)
Bill Veeck (baseball team owner)
William Hewitt (CEO, John Deere)
Loretta Young (actress)
Danny Thomas (entertainer)
W. S. Mitchell (CEO, Safeway)
Gypsy Rose Lee (entertainer)
Howard K. Smith (TV journalist)
Mary Martin (singer)
Frank J. Dunnigan (CEO, Prentice-Hall)
Joe Louis (boxer)
Dixie Lee Ray (Governor of Washington)
Jonas Salk (discoverer of polio vaccine)
Hank Snow (singer) (Canada)

1925—Orson Welles (actor/director)
Theodore White (author)
Lorne Green (actor) (Canada)

Maurice Granville (CEO, Texaco)
Stewart Potter (Supreme Court Justice)
John D. deButts (former CEO, ATT)
John Ireland (actor) (Canada)
Garry Moore (TV personality)
J. Paul Austin (Chairman of Board, Coca-Cola)
William Proxmire (U.S. Senator)
Norman Cousins (author)
David Rockefeller (CEO, Chase Manhattan Bank)
Thomas Murphy (CEO, General Motors)
William Masters (sex researcher)
Paul A. Samuelson (economist)

1926—Robert McNamara (President, World Bank)
Les Paul (singer)
Edgar Speer (Chairman of Board, U.S. Steel)
Jackie Gleason (entertainer)
E. Cardon Walker (CEO, Walt Disney)
Walter Cronkite (TV journalist)
Glenn Ford (actor) (Canada)
Irving Shapiro (CEO, DuPont)
William Coors (CEO, Adolph Coors)
Harold Robbins (author)
Kirk Douglas (actor)
Richard A. Riley (CEO, Firestone)
Bud Wilkinson (football coach)
Gregory Peck (actor)
Jerry McAfee (CEO, Gulf Oil)
Herbert Stein (economist)

1927—Eugene McCarthy (U.S. Senator)
W. F. Martin (CEO, Phillips Petroleum)
Dinah Shore (singer)
Elton Rule (CEO, ABC)
David Lewis (CEO, General Dynamics)
Raymond Burr (actor)
Dennis Day (actor)
Lena Horne (singer)
Buddy Rich (drummer)
Lou Boudreau (baseball player)
Phyllis Diller (comedienne)
James R. Shepley (President, Time Inc.)
Tom Bradley (Mayor of Los Angeles)
Katharine Graham (publisher, *Washington Post*)

Dean Martin (singer)
Robert Mitchum (actor)
John F. Kennedy (U.S. President)
Andrew Wyeth (artist)
I. M. Pei (architect) (China)
Alfred Kahn (economist)
Cyrus Vance (Secretary of State)
Larry O'Brien (NBA Commissioner)
Henry Ford II (CEO, Ford)
John Connally (politician)
Frank Sinatra (singer)

1928—Ann Landers (columnist)
Abigail Van Buren (columnist)
Mickey Spillane (author)
Griffin Bell (U.S. Attorney General)
Russell Long (U.S. Senator)
A. Dean Swift (President, Sears Roebuck)
Alan Jay Lerner (songwriter)
Ted Williams (baseball player)
Spiro Agnew (U.S. Vice President)
John Forsythe (actor)
George Lincoln Rockwell (American Nazi Party leader)
Charles O. Finley (baseball team owner)
Pearl Bailey (singer)
Billy Graham (evangelist)
Charles J. Pilliod Jr. (CEO, Goodyear)
Donald T. Regan (CEO, Merrill-Lynch)
Eddy Arnold (singer)
Betty Ford (former First Lady)
Leonard Bernstein (conductor)
Edward G. Harness (CEO, Proctor-Gamble)
Robert E. Kirby (Chairman of Board, Westinghouse)
Art Carney (actor/comedian)
Ella Fitzgerald (singer)
Walter A. Fallon (CEO, Eastman-Kodak)
Harold W. McGraw, Jr. (CEO, McGraw-Hill)
William Holden (actor)
Jack Paar (TV personality)
Robert Byrd (U.S. Senator)
Oral Roberts (evangelist)
Mike Wallace (TV journalist)

1929—Celeste Holm (actress)
Edward Brooke (U.S. Senator)

Malcolm Forbes (President, *Forbes*)
Ella Grasso (Governor of Connecticut)
Liberace (pianist)
Edwin Newman (TV journalist)
Curt Gowdy (TV sportscaster)
Pierre Trudeau (Prime Minister of Canada) (Canada)
Pete Seeger (singer)
George Wallace (Governor of Alabama)
Hugh Carey (Governor of New York)
Charles Percy (U.S. Senator)

1930—David Brinkley (TV journalist)
Timothy Leary (guru of drug culture)
William Colby (CIA director)
Mike Douglas (TV personality)
Albert V. Casey (CEO, American Airlines)
James Farmer (civil rights leader and founder of CORE)
Frank Carey (CEO, IBM)
George Gobel (comedian)
Walter Matthau (actor)
Harding Lawrence (CEO, Braniff)
Roy A. Anderson (CEO, Lockheed)
Mickey Rooney (actor)
John Paul Stevens (Supreme Court Justice)
Arthur Hailey (author) (England)
Frank Rizzo (Mayor of Philadelphia)
Bella Abzug (U.S. Congresswoman)
Edward Estlow (President, E. W. Scripps)
Howard Cosell (TV sportscaster)

1931—Rodney Dangerfield (comedian)
Rawleigh Warner, Jr. (CEO, Mobil Oil)
Hugh Downs (TV personality)
Jane Russell (actress)
Juanita Kreps (Secretary of Commerce)
Cary Middlecoff (golfer)
Gordon MacRae (singer)
Benjamin Bradlee (journalist/author)
C. C. Garvin, Jr. (CEO, Exxon)
John H. Perkins (President, Continental Bank Chicago)
John Glenn (U.S. Senator/astronaut)
Jim McKay (TV sportscaster)
Whitney Young (former Executive Director of Urban League)
Thornton Wilson (CEO, Boeing)
Daniel Berrigan (activist/priest)

Betty Friedan (feminist leader)
Steve Allen (entertainer)
Donald Kendall (CEO, Pepsico)
Chuck Connors (actor)

1932—Carl Reiner (actor)
Elmer Bernstein (composer)
Paul Laxalt (U.S. Senator)
John W. Hanley (CEO, Monsanto)
Melvin Laird (Secretary of Defense)
Madeline McWhinney (President of first womens bank)
Norman Lear (TV producer)
Norborne Berkeley, Jr. (President, Chemical Bank)
Sanford McDonnell (CEO, McDonnell-Douglas)
George Allen (football coach)
Jack Anderson (columnist)
Redd Foxx (comedian)
James Ling (business executive)
Kurt Vonnegut, Jr. (author)
J. F. Bookout (CEO, Shell Oil)
Bill Blass (fashion designer)
Rene Levesque (Premier of Quebec) (Canada)
Charles Bronson (actor)
George McGovern (U.S. Senator)
Jay Silverheels (actor)
Helen Gurley Brown (author/editor)
Sid Caesar (comedian)
Ava Gardner (actress)
Judy Garland (actress/singer)
Jack Klugman (actor)
Dick Martin (comedian)
Dan Rowan (comedian)
Charles Schultz (cartoonist)
William Manchester (author)

1933—Carol Channing (singer)
Norman Mailer (author)
John Ogden Merrill (architect)
Theodore Brophy (CEO, GTE)
Red Schoendienst (baseball player)
Phillip Berrigan (activist/priest)
L. E. Smart (CEO, TWA)
A. W. Clausen (CEO, Bank of America)
Paddy Chayefsky (playwright)

Arnold Miller (labor leader)
Richard Avedon (photographer)
Ed McMahon (TV personality)
Richard P. Cooley (CEO, Wells Fargo Bank)
Richard Lyman (President of Stanford University)
James Arness (actor)
Alan Shepard (astronaut/first American in space)
Mark Shepherd (CEO, Texas Instruments)
Robert L. Bernstein (CEO, Random House)
Wally Schirra (astronaut)
Harry Reasoner (TV journalist)
Joseph Heller (author)
Robert Dole (U.S. Senator)
Henry Kissinger (Secretary of State) (Germany)

1934—Marlon Brando (actor)
Doris Day (singer)
Patricia Harris (Secretary of HUD)
Frank Church (U.S. Senator)
Chet Atkins (entertainer)
Audie Murphy (war hero/actor)
James Baldwin (author)
David Roderick (President, U.S. Steel)
Carroll O'Connor (actor)
Jimmy Carter (U.S. President)
Shirley Chisholm (U.S. Congresswoman)
Allen H. Neuharth (CEO, Gannett Publishing)
Telly Savalas (actor)
Alexander Haig (army officer)
Edward Koch (Mayor of New York)
Lee A. Iacocca (President, Chrysler)
Lauren Bacall (actress)
George Bush (CIA director)
Charles Schultz (economist)
Truman Capote (author)
Lee Marvin (actor)
Buddy Hackett (comedian)
Charlton Heston (actor)
Henry Mancini (composer)
Phyllis Schafly (anti-ERA leader)
Tony Randall (actor)
Bess Myerson (consumer advocate/former Miss America)
Leon Uris (author)

1935—Medgar Evers (civil rights leader)
Eva Gabor (actress)
Yogi Berra (baseball player)
Robert Kennedy (U.S. Senator)
Carl Rowan (journalist)
Gwen Verdon (dancer)
Robert Altman (movie director)
Edward N. Ney (CEO, Young and Rubicam)
Howard Baker (U.S. Senator)
Clay Felker (publisher, *Esquire*)
Dennis Weaver (actor)
Johnny Carson (TV personality)
Virginia Johnson (sex researcher)
Billie Sol Estes (financier)
Russell Baker (journalist)
Robert Jastrow (scientist)
Sam Peckinpah (movie director)
Art Buchwald (columnist)
Dick Van Dkye (actor/comedian)
William F. Buckley (author)
Tony Curtis (actor)
Sammy Davis, Jr. (entertainer)
Merv Griffin (TV personality)
Monty Hall (TV personality)
Gore Vidal (author)
Jonathan Winters (comedian)
Robert A. Beck (President, Prudential Insurance)
Hal Holbrook (actor)
Benjamin Hooks (Executive Director, NAACP)
Rock Hudson (actor)
Malcolm X (activist)
Jack Lemmon (actor)
Paul Newman (actor)
Rod Steiger (actor)
John Ehrlichman (former presidential aide)

1936—Charles Van Doren (TV quiz contestant)
Andy Griffith (actor)
Marilyn Monroe (actress)
James L. Ferguson (CEO, General Foods)
Ralph Abernathy (civil rights leader)
Duke Snider (baseball player)
Patricia Neal (actress)

Joe Garagiola (baseball player/sportscaster)
Richard D. Wood (CEO, Eli Lilly)
George Weyerhaeuser (CEO, Weyerhaeuser)
Alan Greenspan (economist)
William S. Sneath (CEO, Union Carbide)
Mel Brooks (comedian/writer/director)
Chuck Berry (singer)
Paul Lynde (comedian)
Allen Ginsberg (poet)
Arthur Ochs Sulzberger (Chairman of Board, *New York Times*)
Bowie Kuhn (baseball commissioner)
Tony Bennett (singer)
Lenny Bruce (comedian)
Hugh Hefner (publisher, *Playboy*)
Leslie Nielsen (actor) (Canada)
Elizabeth II (Queen of England) (England)
Jerry Lewis (comedian)
Don Rickles (comedian)
Jacqueline Susann (author)
Pete Rozelle (NFL commissioner)
Christine Jorgenson (transsexual)
H. R. Haldeman (former presidential aide)

1937—Sidney Poitier (actor)
William Simon (author/ Secretary of Treasury)
Tom Wicker (journalist)
Peter Falk (actor)
George C. Scott (actor)
Brock Adams (Secretary of Transportation)
Harry Belafonte (singer)
Harold Brown (Secretary of Defense)
John Chancellor (TV journalist)
Mort Sahl (comedian) (Canada)
Cesar Chavez (labor leader)
Janet Leigh (actress)
George Plimpton (journalist)
Daniel Patrick Moynihan (U.S. Senator)
Leontyne Price (opera singer)
Coretta Scott King (civil rights leader)

1938—Eartha Kitt (singer)
Walter Mondale (U.S. Vice President)
Eddie Fisher (singer)
Bob Bergland (Secretary of Agriculture)

Billy Martin (baseball manager)
Maya Angelou (author)
Alvin Toffler (author)
F. Ray Marshall (Secretary of Labor)
Sarah Caldwell (conductor)
Birch Bayh (U.S. Senator)
John D. Macomber (CEO, Celanese)
Joyce Brothers (psychologist)
Shirley Temple Black (child star/ambassador)
James Garner (actor)
Robert P. Zabel (President, N. W. Ayers)
Frank Borman (astronaut/CEO, Eastern Airlines)
Mary Wells Lawrence (advertising executive)

1939—Dr. Martin Luther King, Jr. (civil rights leader)
Edgar Bronfman (CEO, Seagrams) (Canada)
Berry Gordy (music executive)
Grace Kelly (actress/princess)
Christopher Plummer (actor) (Canada)
William Safire (columnist)
James Schlesinger (energy expert)
Burt Bacharach (composer)
Edward Asner (actor)
Dick Clark (TV personality)
Arnold Palmer (golfer)
A. R. Abboud (CEO, First Chicago)
Jacqueline Kennedy Onassis (former First Lady)

1940—Frank Gifford (TV sportscaster)
Harold Pinter (playwright)
James L. Ketelsen (CEO, Tenneco)
David Kearns (President, Xerox)
Andy Williams (singer)
Don Shula (football coach)
Jimmy Breslin (journalist)
Polly Bergen (actress)
Derek Bok (President of Harvard University)
Jack Lord (actor)
Robert Evans (movie producer)
Steve McQueen (actor)
Robert Wagner (actor)
Andy Warhol (artist)
Adlai Stevenson III (U.S. Senator)
Neil Armstrong (astronaut/first man on moon)

1941—Daniel Ellsberg (activist)
    Roone Arledge (TV executive)
    Lowell Weicker (U.S. Senator)
    Gene Shalit (critic)
    Joseph Califano (Secretary of HEW)
    Bert Lance (banker)
    Leonard Nimoy (actor)
    Cecil Andrus (Secretary of Interior)
    Dan Rather (TV journalist)
    E. L. Doctorow (author)
    Clint Eastwood (actor)
    Barbara Walters (TV journalist)
    Tom Wolfe (journalist/author)
    Anne Bancroft (actress)
    James Earl Jones (actor)
    Willie Mays (baseball player)
    Mickey Mantle (baseball player)

1942—Edward Kennedy (U.S. Senator)
    Elizabeth Taylor (actress)
    Andrew Young (UN ambassador)
    Halston (fashion designer)
    Dick Ferris (CEO, United Airlines)
    Eydie Gorme (singer)
    Kenneth Gibson (Mayor of Newark)
    Richard Alpert (Ram Dass) (higher consciousness guru)
    Ray Charles (singer)
    Dick Gregory (comedian/activist)
    Dennis Banks (co-founder of American Indian Movement)
    Elaine May (actress)
    Debbie Reynolds (actress)
    John Updike (author)
    Yvonne Braithwaite Burke (U.S. Congresswoman/lawyer)

1943—Quincy Jones (composer)
    Dr. David Reuben (author)
    Rod McKuen (poet)
    John Unitas (football player)
    Philip Roth (author)
    F. Lee Bailey (lawyer)
    Robert Goulet (singer)
    Flip Wilson (comedian)

1944—Henry Aaron (baseball player)
    Van Cliburn (pianist)

Charles Manson (cult leader)
Jane Byrne (Mayor of Chicago)
Bill Moyers (journalist)
J. Carter Brown (director of National Gallery of Art)
Bill Russell (basketball player)
Sparky Anderson (baseball manager)
Leroi Jones (poet/activist)
Carl Sagan (astronomer)
Shirley Jones (singer)
Bobby Unser (automobile racer)
Shirley MacLaine (actress)
Ralph Nader (consumer advocate)
Bart Starr (football coach)

1945—Herb Alpert (musician)
Richard Chamberlain (actor)
Eldridge Cleaver (activist/author/preacher)
Daniel F. McKeithan, Jr. (CEO, Joseph Schlitz)
Rene Richards (transsexual tennis player)
Frank Robinson (baseball player/manager)
Woody Allen (actor/director/ comedian)
Lou Rawls (singer)
Lee Remick (actress)
Floyd Patterson (boxer)
Werner Erhard (human behaviorist)
Ken Kesey (author)
Vernon Jordan (civil rights leader)
Elvis Presley (singer)
Joan Rivers (comedienne)
Steve Lawrence (singer)
Loretta Lynn (singer)
Johnny Mathis (singer)
Ron Dellums (U.S. Congressman)

1946—Wilt Chamberlain (basketball player)
Jim Brown (football player/actor)
Kris Kristofferson (actor/singer)
Barbara Jordan (U.S. Congresswoman)
George Segal (actor)
Phil Donahue (TV personality)
James Thompson (Governor of Illinois)
Tom Snyder (TV personality)
Michael Landon (actor)
Preston Jones (playwright)

Jim Henson (Muppets creator)
Richard Bach (author)
Burt Reynolds (actor)
Gloria Steinem (journalist/feminist leader)
Dick Cavett (TV personality)
Carol Burnett (comedienne/singer)
James Darren (actor)
Rona Barrett (gossip columnist)

1947—Margaret O'Brien (actress)
Merle Haggard (singer)
Peter Duchin (bandleader)
Jack Nicholson (actor)
August A. Busch III (CEO, Anheuser-Busch)
Marilyn Van Derbur (top woman speaker/former
    Miss America)
Richard Petty (automobile racer)
Stewart Mott (philanthropist)
Peter Max (artist)
Mary Tyler Moore (actress)
Robert Redford (actor)
Erich Segal (professor/author)
Warren Beatty (actor/director)
Bill Cosby (comedian)
Jane Fonda (actress)
Dustin Hoffman (actor)
Marabel Morgan (femininity promoter)
Gary Hart (U.S. Senator)
Waylon Jennings (singer)
Alan Ladd, Jr. (President, Twentieth Century Fox)
Fred Silverman (President, NBC)
Gail Sheehy (author)
Janet Guthrie (automobile racer)

1948—Natalie Wood (actress)
A. B. Giamatti (President of Yale University)
Maynard Jackson (Mayor of Atlanta)
Charley Pride (singer)
Edmund "Jerry" Brown, Jr. (Governor of California)
George Carlin (comedian)
Jon Voight (actor)
Evel Knievel (stunt performer)
Elliot Gould (actor)
Barry Goldwater, Jr. (U.S. Congressman)

Rudolph Nureyev (dancer) (Soviet Union)
Mary Francis Berry (Assistant Secretary of Education)
Rich Little (impressionist) (Canada)
John Dean (former presidential aide)

1949—Francis Ford Coppola (movie director)
James Caan (actor)
Cicely Tyson (actress)
Russell Means (co-founder of American Indian Movement)
Cale Yarborough (automobile racer)
Lily Tomlin (actress)
Peter Bogdanovich (movie director)
Jim Bouton (baseball player/author)
Peter Fonda (actor)
Ali MacGraw (actress)
Al Unser (automobile racer)
Neil Sedaka (singer)

1950—Jack Nicklaus (golfer)
Allen Bakke (medical student)
Tom Hayden (activist)
Al Pacino (actor)
Anita Bryant (singer/activist)
John Lennon (Beatle) (England)
Ringo Starr (Beatle) (England)
Richard Pryor (comedian)
Tom Brokaw (TV journalist)
Roberta Flack (singer)
Rex Reed (critic)
Mario Andretti (automobile racer) (Italy)
Wayne Dyer (author)
Raquel Welch (actress)
Frankie Avalon (singer)
Julian Bond (state legislator)
Michael Sarrizan (actor) (Canada)
Fran Tarkenton (football player)

1951—Joan Baez (singer)
Ann-Margaret (entertainer)
Ryan O'Neal (actor)
Stokely Carmichael (activist)
Jesse Jackson (activist)
Neil Diamond (singer)
Faye Dunaway (actress)

Bob Dylan (singer)
Art Garfunkel (singer)
Leon Russell (singer)

1952—Wayne Newton (singer)
Karen Black (actress)
Madelyn Kahn (actress)
Pete Rose (baseball player)
Paul Simon (singer)
Jimi Hendrix (rock star)
Paul McCartney (Beatle) (England)
Erica Jong (author)
Michael Crichton (author)
Isaac Hayes (composer)
Huey Newton (activist)
Sandra Dee (actress)
Paul Anka (singer) (Canada)
Larry Flynt (porno crusader)
Aretha Franklin (singer)
Annette Funicello (mouseketeer)
Lee Majors (actor)
Barry Diller (CEO, Paramount)
Barbra Streisand (singer)
Muhammad Ali (Cassius Clay) (boxer)
Roger Staubach (football player)

1953—John Denver (singer)
Bill Bradley (basketball player/politician)
Bobby Fischer (chess champion)
Joni Mitchell (singer)
George Harrison (Beatle) (England)
Geraldo Rivera (TV journalist)
Billy Jean King (tennis player)
Bob Woodward (journalist)
Robert DeNiro (actor)
Janis Joplin (rock star)
Joe Namath (football player)

1954—Diana Ross (singer)
Marvin Hamlisch (composer)
Carl Bernstein (journalist)
Marjoe Gortner (Marjoe) (evangelist/actor)
Angela Davis (activist/professor)
Tom Seaver (baseball player)

Rita Coolidge (singer)
Lauren Hutton (model)
Tony Orlando (singer)
George Lucas (*Star Wars* producer)

1955—Carly Simon (singer)
Don McLean (singer)
Henry Winkler (actor)
Neil Young (singer) (Canada)
Steve Martin (comedian)
Bette Midler (singer)
Melba Moore (singer)
Goldie Hawn (comedienne/actress)
Gabe Kaplan (actor/comedian)

1956—Gilda Radner (comedienne)
Dennis Kucinich (Mayor of Cleveland)
Cher (singer)
Dolly Parton (singer)
Sylvester Stallone (actor)
Candice Bergen (actress)
Mia Farrow (actress)
Liza Minnelli (actress/singer)
Diane Keaton (actress)
Barry Manilow (singer)
Linda Ronstadt (singer)

1957—Johnny Miller (golfer)
Jim Ryun (runner)
Richard Dreyfuss (actor)
Thurman Munson (baseball player)
Johnny Bench (baseball player)
Frank Shorter (runner)
Gregg Allman (rock star)
Arlo Guthrie (singer)
Karen Valentine (actress)
Kareem Abdul-Jabbar (Lew Alcindor) (basketball player)
O. J. Simpson (football player)
Cheryl Tiegs (model)
Bill Rogers (runner)
Farrah Fawcett-Majors (actress)

1958—Sally Struthers (actress)
Garry Trudeau (cartoonist)
Alice Cooper (rock star)
Mikhail Baryshnikov (dancer) (Soviet Union)

1959—Bruce Jenner (Olympic champion)
      Vida Blue (baseball player)
      Kate Jackson (actress)
      Lindsay Wagner (actress)
      Donna Summer (disco singer)

1960—Stevie Wonder (composer/singer)
      Julius Erving (basketball player)
      Eugene Fodor (violinist)
      Jane Pauley (TV personality)
      Mark Spitz (Olympic champion)
      David Cassidy (singer)

1961—Richard Thomas (actor)
      David Duke (KKK leader)
      Lucie Arnaz (actress)
      Crystal Gayle (singer)
      Janis Ian (singer)
      Melissa Manchester (singer)

1962—Bill Walton (basketball player)
      Jimmy Connors (tennis player)
      Cathy Rigby (gymnast)
      Gelsey Kirkland (dancer)

1963—Desi Arnaz, Jr. (actor)
      _____ (future Mayor of New York)
      _____ (future Chairman of Board, General Motors)

1964—Ron Howard (actor)
      Chris Evert (tennis player)
      Freddie Prinze (comedian)
      John Travolta (actor)
      Vitas Gerulaitis (tennis player)
      David Thompson (basketball player)
      Patty Hearst (victim/heiress)

1965—Fernando Bujones (dancer)
      _____ (first man on Mars)
      _____ (future Masters golf champion)

1966—Kurt Thomas (gymnast)
      _____ (discoverer of cancer cure)

1967—Donny Osmond (singer)
      Nancy Lopez (golfer)
      _____ (first woman President of United States)

1968—Shaun Cassidy (actor/singer)
_____ (future founder of househusbands' union)

1969—Marie Osmond (singer)
_____ (future Pope)

1970—Steve Cauthen (jockey)
_____ (future Director, International Society of
Genetic Engineering)

1971—_____ (future Chairman of Board, Solar Generator
Corp. of America)
_____ (future CEO, Global Television Network)

1972—Jodie Foster (actress)
Tracy Austin (tennis player)
Kristy McNichol (actress)

1973—Tatum O'Neal (actress)
Tracy Caulkins (swimmer)
_____ (future winner of Nobel Peace Prize)

1974—_____ (future President of Harvard University)
_____ (future author, *Kitchen Computer Handbook*)
_____ (future Governor of Moon)

1975—Brooke Shields (actress)

CLARIFYING YOUR VALUES

What do *you* value? What is to be done with *your* life? What do *you* want? What makes *you* happy? These questions challenge all of us, although too often we do not attempt to answer them directly. More tragic is the fact that many of us do not even ask ourselves these questions.

One important movement in humanistic education today is called *value clarification*. The goal is to help us identify the values programmed into us and weigh them in view of our personal experiences in present day life. It helps us to make a conscious effort to determine where we stand, where we are going, and why.

The process of value clarification helps provide a road map for our lives. Those who learn to use this map are likely to be less bewildered, apathetic, and irrational and more positive, consistent, purposeful, concerned, and energetic.

Values clarification involves an intellectual model of choosing, prizing, and acting upon values. It sensitizes us to value issues. It gives us experience in thinking critically about our values and allows us to share these perceptions with others. It helps us learn cooperative problem-solving skills.

Clarifying methods, such as role playing, discussion of value dilemmas, and self-analysis, are often like games, but as such they become involving and thought-provoking. The following strategies can be used in schools, in churches, with the family, with friends, and even individually. They are easily adapted to any situation or group. The format for these exercises can be determined by the group or its leader. Their benefit rests in the creation of awareness of values in yourself and others. The only guidelines are that: (1) there are no right or wrong answers; (2) the right to pass and not participate in a particular question is guaranteed; and (3) any sharing of values that is done should emphasize sharing, not imposing, values.

What's In Your Wallet?

Choose three things from your billfold or purse that say something about three things you value. Verbalize what you've learned about yourself.

In a large group situation, you can use this activity to form smaller groups. Each person chooses only one item, and then one person selects someone he is interested in on the basis of what that person chose. The person chosen selects another person on the same basis. Other possible variations are to name three things in your home or three things in your town that reflect your values.

Baker's Dozen

List thirteen of your favorite home appliances that require electricity. To conserve electricity, eliminate three. Then, choose three that you value most and couldn't do without. Examine your decisions. Why did you pick those three items to do without? Why did you keep the other three? What values do you see expressed in your decision? What other possessions could you do without if you had to? Which do you prize the most or miss the most when you are without them?

The "Capsule" Game

Make the decision required in the following situation. The entire world is about to be subjected to a violent holocaust. Scientists have devised a special protective chamber that will keep its occupants alive through this experience, and it is supplied with materials to guarantee their happy survival in the future. The chamber has been designed to hold twelve persons. Those already selected are:

1. An accountant of Mexican-American descent
2. The accountant's pregnant wife, who is an ex-drug addict
3. A go-go girl who is a known marijuana user
4. A professional basketball player (American Indian)
5. An intelligent female movie star
6. A black militant medical student
7. A famous Jewish novelist
8. A pharmacologist
9. A seventy-year-old priest
10. An armed policeman
11. A student women's lib advocate of Chinese descent
12. A male chauvinist wheat farmer

At the last minute, the scientists announce that, contrary to their previous calculations, only seven persons can be safely kept in the capsule.

You decide which of the people listed above should be deleted from the list. Only seven can be the sole survivors of the human race. Your group must decide which five will not survive. List the five people you deleted and explain why. What assumptions did you make about age, sex, potential contribution, race, family, etc.?

Unfinished Sentences

This exercise can be adapted to various forms and clarification needs. The sentences provide windows to examine our values. These are only a sample. You can develop others about family, friends, work —whatever you choose to examine and understand. Make statements that will cause you to probe your value expectations, relationships, needs, wants, likes, dislikes, and objectives.

1. If I had twenty-four hours to live, I would . . .
2. If I had a million dollars, I would . . .
3 If I were boss (principal, supervisor, etc.), the first thing I would change is . . .
4. The hardest thing for me to do is . . .
5. The most rewarding thing I ever did was . . .
6. I admire people who . . .
7. I get angry when people . . .

8. One cause I'm willing to die for is . . .
9. The most fun I ever had in my life was when . . .
10. My children won't have to . . .
11. My most important goal is . . .
12. The way I show love is . . .
13. The five words which I hope people use to describe me are . . .
14. The important thing I learned in (and out of) school was . . .
15. When I was ⎯⎯ years old my heroes were . . .
16. The most important function of government is . . .
17. A teacher's obligation is . . .
18. It is appropriate to spank a child when . . .
19. Competition makes people more . . .
20. I want friends who . . .
21. Things I think are obscene are . . .
22. Sexual relationships should be . . .
23. The problem with most people is . . .
24. My biggest problem is . . .
25. Things that make me unhappy are . . .
26. I can take the responsibility for improving my life through the following changes . . .

The preceding are only a few samples of value clarification techniques. For further ideas and exploration, the following sources are highly recommended:

Leland W. Howe, Howard Kirschenbaum, and Sidney B. Simon, *Values Clarification: A Handbook of Practical Strategies for Teachers and Students* (New York: Hart Publishing Company, Inc., 1972).

Barry Neil Kaufman, *To Love Is To Be Happy With: The First Book of the Option Process* (New York: Fawcett Crest Books, 1978).

REFERENCE NOTES

Overview: Right/Wrong?

p. 3 OPERATIONALLY-BASED CONCEPTS: For in-depth coverage of Rokeach's study of values, see Milton Rokeach, *The Nature of Human Values* (New York: The Free Press, 1973).

Educators and researchers have become increasingly involved with values education in an effort to help others identify and develop their personal values. Among the leaders attempting to define values are Milton Rokeach, Jack Fraenkel, Sidney Simon, Merrill Harmin, Louis Raths, Harold Lasswell, Carl Rogers, Benjamin S. Bloom, and Lawrence Kohlberg. Although these individuals may differ in theory and emphasis, they have a common objective of helping other people recognize and understand their personal values and those of others. For further information, see: David Purpel and Kevin Ryan, eds., *Moral Education . . . It Comes With the Territory* (California: McCutchan Publishing Corporation for Phi Delta Kappa, 1976), hereafter referred to as Purpel and Ryan, *Moral Education;* Michael Silver, *Values Education* (Washington, D.C.: National Education Association, 1976); *Values Concepts and Techniques* (Washington, D.C.: National Education Association, 1976); and Douglas P. Superka *et al., Values Education Sourcebook: Conceptual Approaches, Materials Analyses, and an Annotated Bibliography,* No. 176 (Boulder, Colorado: Social Science Education Consortium, 1976).

Part I   The "Computer" Arrives: Your Programming Begins

p. 7 VALUE CREATION BEFORE BIRTH: Heredity versus environment has been debated for decades by philosophers, psychologists, biologists, educators, and representatives of other disciplines. Entertaining discussions of this issue may be found in Carl Sagan, *The Dragons of Eden* (New York: Ballantine Books, 1977); Desmond Morris, *The Naked Ape: A Zoologist's Study of the Human Animal* (New York: McGraw-Hill Book Company, 1968; Dell, 1969); and Eric Berne, *What Do You Say After You Say Hello?* (New York: Grove Press, 1972), p. 63 (hereafter referred to as Berne, *What Do You Say*).

Sociobiology, the controversial scientific discipline that focuses on the biological basis of behavior, adds to the debate in Edward O. Wilson's "Our Selfish Genes," *Newsweek*, October 16, 1978, pp. 118–23. This article indicates that everything from sex roles to religion is determined by genetics. In his book *On Human Nature* (Cambridge, Mass.: Harvard University Press, 1978), Wilson makes the provocative claim that religion, altruism, and morality have a physical base in biology and have evolved through generations.

IMPACT OF BIRTH ON BEHAVIOR: For a discussion of the implications of a traumatic birth event, read Berne, *What Do You Say*, pp. 76–77 and Frederick Leboyer, *Birth Without Violence* (New York: Alfred A. Knopf, 1976).

9 IMPRINTING: Fabun reinforces the critical importance of the imprinting period, the first seven years of a child's life. Don Fabun, ed., "The Children of Change," *Kaiser Aluminum News* 27 (May 1969), 17; hereafter referred to as Fabun, "Children of Change."

"GIVE ME A CHILD UNTIL HE IS SIX . . ." Eric Berne and Transactional Analysis reinforce the idea that a child's early parental programming determines the way he relates and reacts to others for the rest of his life. See *What Do You Say*, p. 97.

11–12 THE "PLASTIC" YEARS: Claude M. Steiner, *Scripts People Live* (New York: Grove Press, Bantam Books, 1974), is another Transactional Analyst. He further substantiates the concept of "script development," an early value/behavior lock-in that provides a basis for all future behavior

A further discussion of the critical nature of a child's first experiences may be found in Berne, "The Plastic Years," in *What Do You Say*, pp. 97–109. For an in-depth look at the first five years of a

1974); Richard C. Robertiello, *Hold Them Very Close, Then Let ing* (Englewood Cliffs, N.J.: Prentice-Hall, Spectrum Books, 1975), p. 3.

p. 15 SELECTION OF MODELS: The processes of identification and modeling have been observed and analyzed by many psychologists and sociologists. For a succinct coverage, refer to Robert M. Goldenson, s.v. "Identification," *The Encyclopedia of Human Behavior: Psychology, Psychiatry, and Mental Health,* 2 volumes (New York: Doubleday and Company, 1970), 1:590–91; hereafter referred to as Goldenson, *Encyclopedia.*

17 TEEN-AGE YEARS: See Goldenson, s.v. "Adolescence" and "Adolescence (Theories)," *Encyclopedia,* 1:24, 28, for further discussion.

"EARLY ADULT TRANSITION": The use of ages 17 to 22 as the transition period from childhood/adolescence to early adulthood is explored in Daniel J. Levinson, *The Seasons of a Man's Life* (New York: Alfred A. Knopf, 1978), pp. 49, 56–57; hereafter referred to as Levinson, *Seasons.*

18 A detailed discussion of the sequence of stages in an individual's life cycle and the processes involved in moving from stage to stage appears in Levinson, "Developmental Periods: The Evolution of the Individual Life Structure," in *Seasons.*

Part II   Value Inputs: A Kaleidoscope of Sources

25 THE PRIMARY CRITICAL INFLUENCE: The family's critical significance in programming and socializing children is examined in Chapter 18, "The Family as an Institution," of Peter Farb's *Humankind* (Boston: Houghton-Mifflin Company, 1978), p. 386. This is an enjoyable, provocative book that synthesizes many disciplines for the study of human behavior.

25–26 FAMILY AS BASIC SOURCE OF SOCIAL BEHAVIOR: The chapter on "Socialization" of Goldenson's *Encyclopedia* (2:1229) explores differing family structures and interrelationships as they affect the developing child. Goldenson's contention is that the most critical part of the socialization process is the early years. Since socialization begins with birth, the family has the most crucial influence on the child.

26–27 EFFECTIVE PARENTING: Among the many sources of information to help parents understand and deal with their children are: Henry Biller and Dennis Meredith, *Father Power* (Garden City, N.Y.: Doubleday and Company, 1975); Sydney Callahan, *Parenting: Principles and Politics of Parenthood* (New York: Penguin Books, child's life, see Laurie Braga and Joseph Braga, *Learning and Grow-Them Go: How to Be an Authentic Parent* (New York: Dial Press, 1975); James P. Corner and Alvin F. Poussaint, *Black Child Care* (New York: Simon and Schuster, Pocket Books, 1976); Lee Salk, *Preparing for Parenthood: Understanding Feelings about Pregnancy, Childbirth, and Your Baby* (New York: David McKay Company, Bantam Books, 1975); Thomas Gordon, *P.E.T.: Parent Effectiveness Training* (New York: Peter H. Wyden, 1970); Benjamin Spock, *Raising Children in a Difficult Time* (New York: Pocket Books, 1976); Joseph C. Pearce, *Magical Child: Rediscovering Nature's Plan for Our Children* (New York: E.P. Dutton, 1977).

p. 27–28 NUCLEAR FAMILY CONCEPT: There are numerous books and magazine and newspaper articles about the family. For a concise and interesting account of current social changes as they affect the family in the United States, see Israel Shenker, "American Family in Transition," *Denver Post*, December 4, 1977, Contemporary section, pp. 12, 46, 48.

28 SOCIAL JUSTICE: For an interesting discussion of the development of social behavior and moral concepts in children, see Goldenson, s.v. "Character Development" *Encyclopedia*, 1:196–97.

29–30 INCREASING PEER INFLUENCE: See Goldenson, "Adolescence," *Encyclopedia*, 1:23. See also Charles E. Bowerman and John W. Kinch, "Changes in Family and Peer Orientation of Children between Fourth and Tenth Grades, *Social Forces*, 37 (March 1959), cited by Harold W. Berkman and Christopher C. Gilson, *Consumer Behavior: Concepts and Strategies* (Encino, Cal.: Dickenson Publishing Company, 1978), p. 208 (hereafter referred to as Berkman and Gilson, *Consumer Behavior*). Both sources examine the peer group and parent influence on a child's values during adolescence.

Goldenson, in "Adolescence," *Encyclopedia*, 1:23, examines various adolescent roles within peer groups as they relate to roles in adulthood.

See also Elizabeth Dorvan and Joseph Adelson, *The Adolescent Experience* (New York: John Wiley and Sons, 1966), cited by Berkman and Gilson, *Consumer Behavior*, p. 209.

30 GROUP STANDARDS: For a discussion of implicit and explicit group standards, read Goldenson, "Social Norms (Group Norms)," *Encyclopedia*, 2:1231.

31–32 RELIGION: An interpretation of religion as it relates to social organization and values may be found in the following sources: Milton Yinger, "Religious Pluralism in America," in *Sociology Looks at Religion*, ed. J. M. Yinger (New York: The Macmillan Company,

1963); and Peter Berger, "Religious Institutions," in *Sociology: An Introduction*, ed. Neil J. Smelser (New York: John Wiley and Sons, 1967). Both works cited by Berkman and Gilson, *Consumer Behavior*, pp. 150–51.

For a discussion of research on youth where religion was included as a variable, see Merton P. Strommen, *Five Cries of Youth* (New York: Harper and Row, 1974), p. 2; and the book *Research on Religious Development*, edited by Merton P. Strommen (New York: Hawthorn Books, 1971); hereafter referred to as Strommen, *Research*.

Studies of religion are contradictory, inconclusive, or nonexistent. It is difficult to isolate variables and determine cause and effect among church, religion, and value development. The researchers seem to be in agreement that there is much disagreement among themselves.

Regarding cheating and Sunday school attendance, see Goldenson, "Character Development," *Encyclopedia*, 1:198.

An excellent compilation of religious research is Merton P. Strommen's *Research*.

p. 33 In *The Child and the Christian Faith* (Richmond, Virginia: Covenant Life Curriculum, 1964), p. 25, Dorothy Bertolet Fritz examines the factors involved in a child's religious education and development.

33–34 The developmental growth theory as outlined by Baker and Koppe is covered in Strommen, *Research*, p. 705. The interrelationship of religious commitment, church attendance, and a mastery of religious dogma (p. 709) varies greatly among individuals and must be studied carefully. Religious variables may or may not be related to the value development and ethical behavior of an individual.

For an in-depth collection of religious studies and theories, read H. Newman Malony, ed., *Current Perspectives in the Psychology of Religion* (Grand Rapids, Mich.: William B. Eerdman, 1977), p. 133.

35 "RELIGIOUSNESS WITHOUT RELIGION": This phrase is from Judith R. Porter, "Secularization, Differentiation, and the Function of Religious Value Orientation," *Sociological Inquiry* 43 (1973): 70, cited by James F. Engel, Roger D. Blackwell, and David T. Kollat, *Consumer Behavior*, 3d ed. (Hinsdale, Ill.: The Dryden Press, 1978), p. 184; hereafter referred to as Engel, *Consumer Behavior*. Engel's book offers statistics on church membership and attendance and an interesting interpretation of the changing impact of religion (pp. 182–84).

35–36 DISILLUSIONMENT WITH CHURCH ESTABLISHMENT: This topic is covered in Vernon Jones, "Attitudes Toward the Church," *Genetic*

Psychology Monographs (1970), p. 52, cited by Engel, *Consumer Behavior*, p. 184.

A cursory examination of religious training and religious affiliation as they affect values and consumer behavior may be found in Berkman and Gilson, *Consumer Behavior*, pp. 151–52.

Today's popular religious movements and an interpretation of their impact on future values may be found in Engel, *Consumer Behavior*, p. 185.

Purpel and Ryan, ed., *Moral Education*, p. 7, discusses today's decline of religious influence and our resulting value dilemma.

p. 37 THE FOUR RS—READING, 'RITING, 'RITHMETIC, AND RELIGION: For a brilliant, historical narrative that examines the philosophy of achievement and success in the United States, see Richard M. Huber, *The American Idea of Success* (New York: McGraw-Hill Book Company, 1971), p. 25; hereafter referred to as Huber, *Success*.

Historically, there have been many conflicting theories about the way children learn and the importance of early childhood. Child rearing and educational practices fluctuate with these conflicts. Braga and Braga, in *Learning and Growing*, p. 4, support the belief in the critical nature of early childhood and examine the important motor, language, cognitive, and socioemotional developments during this time.

38 "NEW" TEACHERS WITH DIFFERENT VALUES: See Berkman and Gilson, *Consumer Behavior*, p. 150; and Harvey C. Burke, "The University in Transition, *Business Horizons* 12 (August 1969): 5–17, cited by Engel, *Consumer Behavior*, p. 187.

38 NEW TEACHING TECHNIQUES: The belief in learning and growth of education in the post-Civil War days is entertainingly discussed in Time-Life Books, eds., *This Fabulous Century, Prelude: 1870–1900*, p. 145; 8 volumes (New York: Time-Life Books, 1969–70).

ARCHIBALD MACLEISH QUOTATION: This quotation is from Engel, *Consumer Behavior*, p. 187.

40 ARCHIE BUNKER: See Neil Bidmar and Milton Rokeach, "Archie Bunker's Bigotry: A Study in Selective Perception and Exposure," *Journal of Communication* 24 (Winter 1974): 36–47, cited by Engel, *Consumer Behavior*, p. 335. It is interesting to note that reactions to Archie Bunker, a leading character in CBS's popular sitcom, "All In the Family," have varied greatly. It was assumed that Archie and the series would be perceived as a satire on bigotry and prejudice— and for many that was true. However, others whose values, preconceptions, and prejudices were similar to Archie's reacted to him as a hero.

p. 41 EDUCATION AND VALUES: The relationship between values and degree of education is examined in Berkman and Gilson, *Consumer Behavior*, p. 150.

44 TELEVISION: For excellent coverage of the pros and cons of television and its impact on children, read Marie Winn, *The Plug-in Drug* (New York: The Viking Press, 1977; Bantam Books, 1978); hereafter referred to as Winn, *Plug-in Drug*.

46 U.S. FOCUSES LOCALLY: In "The Balkanization of America," *Harpers* 256 (May 1978), Kevin Phillips gives a startling new insight into how compartmentalized our nation has become by examining economic, geographic, and biological (sex, sexual preference, age, race, and ethnic group) fragmentation within the United States. (Hereafter referred to as Phillips, "Balkanization.")

47 VALUE APPROACHES: NORTH VERSUS SOUTH: See Huber, *Success*, pp. 31–32.

48 REGIONAL RIVALRIES: Phillips explores regional rivalries as one aspect of national fragmentation in "Balkanization," p. 41.

48–49 DECLINE IN MOBILITY: An analysis of the apparent slowdown in mobility within the United States is offered in "Americans Put Salve on the Moving Itch," *Detroit News*, May 24, 1978, p. 3F.

Part III   Putting It Together—
"Where Were You When You Were Ten?"

52 TEN YEARS OLD: The age of approximately ten might be thought of as an "age of awareness—the period of beginning to apply the materials that have already been programmed." According to Berne, "This is a time of rehearsal, a tryout before the show takes to the road" (*What Do You Say*, p. 166). In *Psychology of Adolescence* (cited in Goldenson, *Encyclopedia*, 1:28), Edward Spranger notes that this age begins a period of basic personality development where a "dominant value direction" is achieved. Others indicate that this period is a process of integrating the values, customs, and beliefs of a particular culture into one's personality (Goldenson, *Encyclopedia*, 1:30).

Arnold Gesell's "maturity profiles" illustrate the developmental patterns during the years from ten to sixteen years old. He notes that the ten-year-old is in a state of " 'developmental balance,' accepts life with ease and confidence, enjoys family activities, recognizes authority, denies any interest in the opposite sex, and engages in group activities with members of his own sex" (Goldenson, *Encyclopedia*, 1:31).

Some social researchers point to an earlier lock-in; others consider it to occur later. However, as noted, a great deal of literature indicates that this period of "around ten" is generally accepted as a critical, formative lock-in period.

p. 53–54 GENERATIONAL VALUE CHANGES: For an expansion of these ideas as they relate to marketing and consumer behavior, read Engel, *Consumer Behavior*, pp. 188–96.

58–59 "GENERALLY-HELD TRUTHS": For a concise look at the United States during different periods of history, see Fabun, "Children of Change," p. 18.

59 WORKING MOTHERS: One of the most definitive reports about women may be found in: U.S. Department of Commerce, Bureau of the Census, *A Statistical Portrait of Women in the U.S.*, Special Studies Series P-23, No. 58 (April 19, 1976).

60 $UCCE$$: Erich Fromm, quoted by Huber, offers an insightful analysis of the interrelationship of money, success, and religion in *Success*, p. 108.

61–75 1920s, 1930s, 1940s: This section draws from Time-Life Books' series, *This Fabulous Century*, which provides a concise and lively narrative of history. With the inclusion of songs, jokes, headlines, magazine covers, comics, advertisements, and pictures, each book gives a sense for a particular decade. This section is based on pages 23–36 of *1920–1930*. *1930–1940* captures the desperation of the Depression in pictures on pages 46–73. *1940–1950* (pages 21–25) gives an account of our domestic and foreign affairs as the United States began to gear up for World War II. Volume 5 (*1940–1950*), page 148, covers the tremendous influx of women into the work force during World War II, contributing to the tremendous production and also affecting those women directly as they gained more economic power.

75 SOCIAL CHANGES BROUGHT BY WAR: This description is drawn from William Manchester's *The Glory and the Dream: A Narrative History of America 1932–1972* (Boston: Little, Brown and Company, 1974), p. 290; hereafter referred to as Manchester, *Glory and the Dream*.

76 CHANGES IN EDUCATION: For further information, see Joseph H. Stevens, Jr. and Edith W. King, *Administering Early Childhood Education Programs* (Boston: Little, Brown and Company, 1976), p. 7.

76–77 A NEW BREED: TEEN-AGERS: The emerging teen-age cult is captured in pictures on pages 28–51 of Time-Life Books' *This Fabulous Cen-*

tury: 1940–1950. Page 142 of this volume covers the media. See pages 180–89 of the same volume for an entertaining look at songs, comics, motion pictures, and magazines as the media moved in to help the war effort.

p. 79 JACKIE ROBINSON QUOTATION: This quote is from Nala Lantrac, "America: 1945–1950," *Mainliner* 11 (September 1973): 39, 63.

82 THE GOOD LIFE: Covered in Manchester, *Glory and the Dream*, p. 773.

92–93 TELEVISION: Scenes and portions of scripts from popular TV shows may be found on pages 250–81 of Time-Life Books' *This Fabulous Century: 1950–1960*, 6:250–81.

94 TV MAKES TIME COLLAPSE, HORIZON DISAPPEAR: These concepts are discussed in detail by Fabun in "Children of Change," pp. 6–7.

97 GOOD GUYS/BAD GUYS—WHO'S ON TOP? Based on Manchester, *Glory and the Dream*, pp. 850–52.

98 ELVIS PRESLEY QUOTE: From Alan Cartnal, "America: 1955–1960," *Mainliner* 11 (November 1973): 26.

"SOUL" SOUND IN MUSIC: More discussion may be found in Sheldon Zalaznick, "The Youthquake in Pop Culture," *Fortune* (January 1969), cited by Fabun in "Children of Change," p. 25.

99 CLARK KERR QUOTATION: From Manchester, *Glory and the Dream*, p. 847.

102–103 JFK QUOTATION: This quote is from Time-Life Books, *This Fabulous Century: 1960–1970*, 7:26. Page 36 of the same volume presents a pictorial essay of Kennedy's years in the White House.

103 PEACE CORPS: "The symbolic dedicated Peace Corpsmen" are discussed in Manchester, *Glory and the Dream*, p. 906.

103–105 CIVIL RIGHTS, VIETNAM: For a look at the beginning expansion of the Civil Rights Movement and Vietnam involvement, read Time-Life Books, *This Fabulous Century: 1960–1970*, 7:26–29.

106 TIMOTHY LEARY QUOTATION: Leary's quote is found in Manchester, *Glory and the Dream*, p. 1115. There is an interpretive account of love children/hippies in Manchester's book on pp. 1113–18 and in Time-Life Books, *This Fabulous Century: 1960–1970*, 7:56–59 (illustrated in pictures pp. 62–89).

106–107 ARLO GUTHRIE QUOTATION: From Time-Life Books, *This Fabulous Century: 1960–1970*, 7:59. Beatlemania is covered on page 60.

108 TV AND DRUGS: The connection between these two phenomena is discussed by Marie Winn in *Plug-in Drug*, pp. 109–16.

108–109 CLAY-FOOTED GODS AND THE NEW MORALITY: In his Foreword to

Great Songs of the Sixties (ed. Milton Okun [Chicago: Quadrangle Books, 1970]), p. 12, Tom Wicker gives an entertaining and articulate account of the culture-shocked 1960s from the perspective of music and the popular songs of those times (hereafter referred to as Wicker, *Great Songs*).

p. 109 "VATICAN . . . OK FOR CATHOLICS . . ." See Lynda Rosen Obst, ed., *The Sixties: The Decade Remembered Now, by the People Who Lived It Then* (New York: Random House, Rolling Stone Press, 1977), p. 166.

110–111 "CONSERVATIVE HEDONIST'S" QUOTATION: Quotation is from Manchester, *Glory and the Dream*, p. 1035. In Part IV of his book, entitled "Reaping the Whirlwind," Manchester takes an in-depth look at the 1960s as they affected all areas within society. Information on Sun City is from Manchester, pp. 1034–35.

112–116 1960s: This discussion draws from Wicker, *Great Songs*, pp. 13–16.

117 "PAMPERED YOUTH": Drawn from Manchester, *Glory and the Dream*, pp. 1100–1103.

119 PAST VALUES ERODE: For an interpretation of what the changes of the 1960s mean for the future, read Wicker, *Great Songs*, pp. 16–17.

125 YOUTH'S SENSE OF HUMOR: Fabun offers another view for sorting out the pluses and minuses of the 1960s in "Children of Change," pp. 6, 38–39.

128 "THE ROARING CURRENT OF CHANGE": For a vivid description of the overwhelming change that families, individuals, businesses, communities, and institutions are experiencing in our technological revolution, read Alvin Toffler, *Future Shock* (New York: Random House, 1970; Bantam Books, 1971), p. 1.

128 SAUL PETT ARTICLE is "Snap!—The Plastic Life Cracks at the Seams," in *Denver Post*, February 15, 1970, p. 44E.

138 KENT STATE: From Manchester, *Glory and the Dream*, pp. 1195, 1224–25.

139 JAMES RESTON QUOTE: The last days of the Vietnam War and the peace talks are detailed in Manchester, *Glory and the Dream*, pp. 1292–97.

139 WATERGATE: Bob Woodward and Carl Bernstein, in *The Final Days* (New York: Simon and Schuster, 1976), provide a detailed backstage portrait of the events that led to Nixon's resignation. Both this book and their other best-seller, *All the President's Men*, offer extraordinary, dramatic accounts of the Watergate affair.

p. 139 Gallup poll statistics are from Manchester, *Glory and the Dream*, p. 1287.

141 GOHEEN QUOTE: From "How America Is Changing," *U.S. News & World Report*, February 25, 1974, pp. 30–31.

142 DRUGS AND CULTS: Manchester, in *Glory and the Dream*, pp. 1190–91, looks at America entering the 1970s.

143–144 GUYANA SUICIDES: Henry Allen, in "Smiling, Literate Adults Happy at Suicide Fate," *Denver Post*, November 26, 1978, pp. 25, 35B, gives an excellent history of cults and mass suicides as well as a discussion of current cults, mind control, and messianic leaders in the 1970s United States.

144–145 CHANGES IN MEDIA: Covered in Manchester, *Glory and the Dream*, pp. 1191–93.

144 PRESIDENTIAL COMMISSION ON PORNOGRAPHY: For an in-depth study of pornography, refer to *The Report of the Commission on Obscenity and Pornography* (Washington, D.C.: U.S. Government Printing Office, September 1970), p. 128.

145 SEX EDUCATION. Manchester, in *Glory and the Dream*, pp. 1193–94, discusses the new sexual awareness and the controversial development of sex education.

145–46 SATURDAY NIGHT FEVER: Discussed in "Sex Education is Back in the Spotlight: Educators Alarmed by Teen-age Pregnancies," *Phi Delta Kappan* 60:3 (September 1978).

Russell Baker's article, "The Good Life: Dead at 28, But Mourned by All Survivors," appears in *Denver Post*, March 26, 1974, p. 24B.

148–49 MCDONAGH QUOTE: From "How America Is Changing," *U.S. News & World Report*, February 25, 1974, pp. 30–31.

150 CENSUS FIGURES: From Department of Commerce, Bureau of the Census, *U.S. Statistical Abstract and Monthly Vital Statistics Reports, 1867–1900: Historical Statistics of the U.S.*

SINGLE-PARENT HOMES: Figures are from Howard, *Families*, p. 17.

SINGLES: Linda Bird Francke *et al.*, in "Going It Alone," *Newsweek*, September 4, 1978, explore the growing singles life—its freedom, problems, affluence, and psychological bases.

151 WORKING MOTHERS STATISTICS: Source is U.S. Department of Commerce, *A Statistical Portrait of Women in the U.S.*, p. 26.

151 ROLE REVERSAL AT HOME: "Saving the Family," *Newsweek*, May 15, 1978, p. 67, provides a detailed examination of the changes and variety in America's families (for blacks and whites); governmental

and legislative actions as they affect the family unit; family therapy; and an historical look at the family as seen on television.

p. 152 NON-NUCLEAR FAMILIES: Jane Howard celebrates the diversity, change, and survival of the family in her book *Families* (New York: Simon and Schuster, 1978), p. 15.

CHRISTOPHER LASCH ON "HELPING PROFESSIONS": Terry Kirkpatrick sees a shift in the family's responsibility for children in "Has Family Been Victim of 'Helping Professions'?" *Boulder* (Colorado) *Daily Camera*, August 2, 1978, p. 46.

156 EDUCATION OPPORTUNITIES FOR WOMEN: Statistics from U.S. Department of Commerce, *A Statistical Portrait of Women in the U.S.*, p. 21.

157 CHANGING VALUES OF WOMEN: Social Research, Inc., *Working-Class Women in a Changing World* (n.p.: Macfadden-Bartell Corporation, 1973).

159 "NEW ELITE": David Lebedoff, "The Dangerous Arrogance of the New Elite," *Esquire*, August 29, 1978, pp. 20–27. According to Lebedoff, an elite class that defines itself in terms of its inherited intelligence is emerging in America. He contends that this group does not believe in majority rule and is a threat to American democracy. Besides their political tendencies, he examines their heroes, recreation activities, professions, humor, life style, and purpose.

159 MOBILITY AND ECONOMIC CHANGE: Figures are from Manchester, *Glory and the Dream*, p. 732.

162 RIGHTS OF UNWED FATHERS: David Gelman *et al.*, in "How Men Are Changing," *Newsweek*, January 16, 1978, p. 54, uses pictures and text to explore role changes men are experiencing as a result of pressure from the women's movement and their own repressed feelings.

163–165 PARENTING AND EFFECTS ON CHILDREN: Kenneth L. Woodward and Phyllis Malamud, "The Parent Gap," *Newsweek*, September 22, 1975, p. 48. Today's parents are pressured by our quickly changing society; articles such as this one (pp. 48–56) offer parents support and guidance in parenting.

165–166 PARENTING: Joseph C. Pearce, *Magical Child: Rediscovering Nature's Plan for Our Children* (New York: E.P. Dutton, 1977).

166 NEGATIVE ASPECTS OF TELEVISION: From commercials to content to the process of viewing, TV is under careful examination and is receiving criticism from many. Read Harry F. Waters, "What TV Does to Kids," *Newsweek*, February 21, 1977, p. 63.

AMA ON TV VIOLENCE: "AMA Poll Links TV Violence, Illness," *Denver Post*, June 20, 1977, p. 5.

p. 169 NO SIGNIFICANT LEARNING GAINS FROM TV: See Winn, *Plug-In Drug*, pp. 37–42, where Winn discusses the effect "educational TV" has on the development of verbal and nonverbal thought. Also see Winn, "Unplugging TV May Turn on Children," *Denver Post*, September 11, 1978, p. 29D.

170 NEWSWEEK: Wally McNamee, "TV of Tomorrow," *Newsweek*, July 3, 1978, p. 62. The second generation of the television industry will find a variety of new video options. The tremendous technological change has the potential of revolutionizing broadcasting as well as the lives of American video customers.

SOURCES FOR TIMELINE

Manchester, William. *The Glory and the Dream: A Narrative History of America 1932–1972.* Boston: Little, Brown and Company, 1974.

Millgate, Linda. *Almanac of Dates.* New York: Harcourt, Brace, Jovanovich, 1977.

Mirkin, Stanford M. *When Did It Happen?* New York: Ives Washburn, Inc., 1957.

Wallace, Irving, and Wallechinsky, David. *The People's Almanac.* New York: Doubleday and Company, Inc., 1975.

———. *The People's Almanac #2.* New York: Bantam Books, 1978.

The World Almanac and Book of Facts. New York: Newspaper Enterprise Association, Inc., 1977.

BIBLIOGRAPHY FOR
WHERE THEY WERE WHEN

Delury, George E. *The World Almanac and the Book of Facts 1979.* New York: Newspaper Enterprise Association, Inc., 1979.

Dolmatch, Theodore B. *Information Please Almanac 1979.* New York: Information Please Publishing, Inc., 1979.

Louis, Rita Volmer. *Biography Index,* vols. 5–10. New York: The H. H. Wilson Company, 1961–1978.

Moritz, Charles. *Current Biography Yearbook,* 1940–1978. New York: The H. H. Wilson Company, 1940–1978.

Who's Who in America. 40th edition, vols. 1 and 2. Chicago: Marquis Who's Who, 1978–1979.

Who's Who in Finance and Industry. 20th edition. Chicago: Marquis Who's Who, 1977–1978.

Who's Who in Government. 3rd edition. Chicago: Marquis Who's Who, 1977–1978.